Beyond blame

Whenever there is news of another child abuse death, the public asks 'why?' And despite the time, expense and heartache expended on inquiries into child abuse, little of practical value seems to emerge. *Beyond Blame* is the first book to summarise all major inquiries since 1973, and to set them in their social context.

The authors, a psychiatrist, a psychologist and a social worker, draw on their experience in child protection work to make sense of the bewildering, inconsistent and tragic behaviour which these inquiries so graphically illustrate. They stress the need for those who work day to day in child protection to develop and apply a more sophisticated level of analysis to assessment and intervention. They identify common themes within abusing families, in the relationships between members of the professional networks, and in the interactions between the families and the professionals. In particular, they show that the psychological aspects of professional collaboration are as vital to working well together as the need for sound organisational structures.

Beyond Blame offers a way of looking at fatal child abuse cases from which it is possible to draw important lessons. The authors' insights will be of direct practical value to all professionals involved in child protection, including social workers, psychologists and child psychiatrists, as well as to policy makers such as managers and politicians.

Beyond blame

Child abuse tragedies revisited

Peter Reder, Sylvia Duncan
and Moira Gray

London and New York

First published in 1993
by Routledge
11 New Fetter Lane, London EC4P 4EE

Simultaneously published in the USA and Canada
by Routledge
29 West 35th Street, New York, NY 10001

© 1993 Peter Reder, Sylvia Duncan and Moira Gray

Typeset by LaserScript Limited, Mitcham, Surrey
Printed and bound in Great Britain by
Mackays of Chatham, PLC, Chatham, Kent

British Library Cataloguing in Publication Data

A catalogue record for this book is available from the British Library.

Library of Congress Cataloging in Publication Data also available

ISBN 0-415-06678-6
0-415-06679-4 (pbk)

To the children

Contents

Figures and tables

Figures

Tables

Foreword

Professor Olive Stevenson

This is a welcome and timely addition to the literature on child abuse, for two reasons. First, the review of the child abuse inquiries on which it is based was much needed. Previous work, including that of the DHSS (Department of Health and Social Security 1982; Department of Health 1991) and my own (Stevenson 1989), did not examine these cases systematically from a specific theoretical standpoint. As the authors demonstrate, the sad stories of these families and of the professionals who sought to work with them are a rich mine to quarry. Others will read their significance differently but this is in a sense unimportant. What has to be done – and this is an excellent start – is to seek to make sense of the bewildering, inconsistent, tragic behaviour which they so graphically illustrate.

The second reason for a warm welcome follows from these observations. It has seemed to me for some time that there is an urgent need for those who work day to day at field level in child protection to develop and apply a more sophisticated level of analysis to assessment and intervention. Much effort in the past twenty years has been put into the construction and adaption of procedures to protect children (and workers). On the whole, these have been valuable and should not, in my view, be denigrated. But they must be complemented by professional and inter-professional advances in understanding and skill. Some have been made in the field of assessment, the Department of Health (1988) guidelines making a useful contribution to this. Yet, both in assessment, as I have pointed out elsewhere (Stevenson 1989), and most particularly in the matter of intervention, conceptual frameworks for the understanding of phenomena have been little utilised. The authors represent a particular frame of reference. There are others which do not necessarily coincide and may be in conflict. This is a healthy part of a process of learning. The trouble is that, intense as these debates may be, they have taken place in very restricted circles and left the vast majority of social workers struggling on in a kind of intellectual fog; for example, alternative modes of intervention and their evaluation have been rarely examined in any depth on qualifying or even post-qualifying courses in social work. When a theoretical position emerges, sui generis, from social work itself, it may then be seized upon avidly and uncritically, as happened in the case of the work of Dale *et al.* (1985). I hope, therefore, that this book will be widely used as offering a way of looking at cases from which it is unquestionably possible to draw important lessons.

Many examples could be cited here. For me, however, there are two, one specific, one more general. Specifically, the authors write of 'closure' – by which they mean the process by which families withdraw from the professionals when under stress or in a crisis. The inquiries show, starkly and tragically, how important these phases are and how inadequately they have been dealt with. The insights brought to bear on this matter in their book should be of direct practical value to workers and their managers. More generally, the chapter on family–professional systems contributes valuably to a growing (but slowly) awareness of the interaction between workers and clients which profoundly affects case management and outcome. An excellent and neglected early work by Mattinson and Sinclair (1979) blazed a trail, following the work of Menzies (1970), cited by the authors. It is imperative that the concept of dynamic, systemic interplay between organisations and families is grasped and applied to these turbulent and dangerous situations.

A final reason for welcoming this book is its tone, reflected in the title. It is right to be shocked by these tragedies and outraged, on occasion, by the failure of the professionals adequately to protect children. To lose the capacity to be shocked and outraged is very dangerous. Yet, as the authors show, it is arid to stop there. Moral outrage as an end product is not constructive. This book takes the debate a stage further, for which we can be very grateful.

Olive Stevenson
Professor of Social Studies
University of Nottingham

Acknowledgements

This book could not have been written without the assistance of many people. The three of us who made up the project team were members of the Charing Cross Hospital Department of Child and Family Psychiatry (now called Wolverton Gardens, part of the Riverside Mental Health Trust) and the time required for research and writing had to be balanced with the everyday demands of the clinical service. Our colleagues supported this project by, at times, shouldering an extra burden of the Department's work. We are especially grateful to the Departmental secretaries who typed up the chronological accounts of the cases. They were aware of the nature of our project and knew that the case histories they were typing were harrowing and were leading up to the death of a child. They contributed to the project without reservation. We were encouraged by the enthusiastic response we received from colleagues when we discussed our work with them and their feedback was invaluable, helping us consolidate or revise our thinking. In particular, Glenda Fredman read a draft of this book and offered very helpful advice on the presentation of our ideas. We thank all the agencies who sent us copies of inquiry reports and gave us permission to use material from them. Librarians at the Charing Cross and Westminster Medical School helped obtain references for us and Anne Wadmore of the Charing Cross Hospital Medical Illustration Department prepared the figures and tables that appear in this book. Above all, our own families tolerated the many hours we spent absorbed in our task with considerable forbearance and their support sustained us and made this work possible.

Chapter 1

Introduction

Neither the outcries of public indignation, nor trial by newspaper, nor emotionally tinged accusations against individuals are conducive to the atmosphere necessary for a sober appraisal and step-by-step examination of such events.

(Goldstein *et al.* 1979: 143)

This book is an attempt to get beyond the blaming stance so often adopted when children known to statutory agencies die at the hands of their caretakers. An atmosphere of blame and criticism always surrounds the public inquiries set up to investigate the deaths and becomes encapsulated in the judgemental tones of the final reports. This book tries to make sense of events which culminated in the tragic deaths and to understand more about the behaviour of the families and the professional workers. We hope that it will make some contribution to future professional practice.

This is an emotive subject. No one can hear about the death of a child without being moved. When that child dies as a result of abuse, we inevitably feel a mixture of horror, anger, pity and sadness. If that child was already known to professional workers whose task was to help protect him or her, the question is inevitably asked: 'Shouldn't they have prevented it?' It is only a small step to identify with the helpless child and focus all our rage on the professionals, even blaming them for the child's death. Indeed, newspaper editors capitalise on this process through provocative and accusing headlines. Not only does the death of a child from abuse horrify us but front-line professionals, especially social workers, have become extremely sensitive to the critical and often mindless rage that is heaped upon them at the news that another child known to statutory agencies has died.

BACKGROUND

The authors of this book began working together in 1985 as members of the Child and Family Psychiatry Department of the Charing Cross Hospital (now known as Wolverton Gardens, part of the Riverside Mental Health Trust) in London. From our respective backgrounds in psychiatry, psychology and social work we had developed a common interest in applying systemic ideas to our clinical work together in the Department. That work included considerable involvement with problems of child abuse (Baker and Duncan 1985, 1986) and the emotional demands they make on professional workers. We had also given a great deal of thought to the psychology of inter-professional behaviour and the interaction between families and their networks of helping professionals (Reder and Kraemer 1980; Reder 1983, 1985, 1986; Reder and Duncan 1990). We were also informed by the work of colleagues who were applying systemic thinking to problems of child protection. These included teams at the Great Ormond Street Hospital for Sick Children (Bentovim *et al.* 1988), the Mater Misericordiae Hospital in Dublin (McCarthy and Byrne 1988), the Rochdale NSPCC Unit (Dale and Davies 1985; Dale *et al.* 1986), the Marlborough Family Service in London (Asen *et al.* 1989), the Tavistock Clinic (Furniss 1991) and in Leeds (Stratton *et al.* 1990).

In December 1985 we read the report into the death of **Jasmine Beckford**. Its conclusions began: 'On any conceivable version of events under inquiry the death of Jasmine Beckford was both a predictable and preventable homicide . . .' and continued: 'The blame must be shared . . . ' (**Jasmine Beckford** Inquiry Report 1985: 287). Statements such as this were contrary to our clinical approach and way of thinking and had more the tone of a judgement handed down by a court rather than an attempt to learn constructively from the tragedy. Although some professionals involved in the case had shown errors of judgement, such conclusions appeared ultimately unhelpful in understanding how the errors had come about. The inquiry seemed to have focussed on 'rightness' or 'wrongness' and degrees of blame-worthiness. We considered that an appreciation of the psychological aspects of these complex cases was missing and there was little awareness of emotional factors within families and professional networks which can dislodge workers from objectivity. As an example, the inquiry heavily criticised the key social worker's conduct but in studying the report we discovered that her senior had been absent from work on maternity leave during a crucial six months of the case. During that time the social worker had acted up for her senior as well as performing all her usual duties and, in a sense, she had become her own supervisor. Front-line workers know of the profound effects this can have on them but the inquiry panel accords it no significance, to the extent that we had to hunt around in different sections of the text to piece this information together.

Two years after the **Jasmine Beckford** report appeared, the inquiry panel into the death of **Kimberley Carlile** published its findings. We were struck even more forcibly by the apparent belief that blame must be apportioned and how this framework not only limited the usefulness of the report but also produced contradictory statements that undermined its credibility. Referring to the social work Team Leader, the panel concluded that: '[He] was the prime candidate for blameworthiness in failing to prevent Kimberley Carlile's death . . . [and] we recommend that he should not in the future perform any of the statutory functions in relation to child protection . . . '. However, on the same page it adds:

his written statement [to the inquiry] is an outstanding document of insight into the nature of a social worker's tasks . . . [and his] employing authority should make the document available as an educational tool for the training of social workers generally, and for those involved in child abuse particularly.

(**Kimberley Carlile** Inquiry Report 1987: 22)

We believed that the accusatory styles adopted in these two reports, grounded in the adversarial framework of the legal system, would have the drawback of increasing front-line workers' defensiveness rather than helping them to examine their roles in difficult cases. Furthermore, we thought that the reports would only go some way to improve professional practice because they told us little that was new about *how* things can go wrong. For example, as in many of the inquiries which had preceded them, the **Jasmine Beckford** and **Kimberley Carlile** reports indicated that procedures were not always properly followed and that communication between professionals was, at times, inadequate. Although the panels recommended structural refinements in procedures and organisation their reports did not further understanding about how inter-professional communication and co-operation can break down. Without such understanding, we thought that it would be unlikely that the structural changes could be enacted effectively.

We found ourselves in agreement with the conclusions of Minuchin after he had reviewed the **Maria Colwell** inquiry report:

It is difficult to take a positive view and impossible to sympathize with the murderers of a child. But unless we begin to see cases like Maria's not from the point of view of fixing the blame, but from the point of view of possible solutions, we will still be doomed only to the repetition of ineffective interventions.

(Minuchin 1984: 155)

We therefore decided to review all known reports into the deaths of children from non-accidental violence or neglect in order to apply our clinical approach to the cases at the centre of the inquiries. We hoped that a systemic analysis of each tragedy might suggest some of the psychological processes which had influenced events. We anticipated that common themes or patterns might then emerge from this review.

There have been many responses to particular inquiries and their aftermath in the professional literature (e.g. Mawby *et al.* 1979; Shearer 1979; Allen 1983; Dingwall 1986; Parton 1986). More detailed appraisals of individual cases have also been published, for example about **Maria Colwell** by Howells (1974), Goldstein *et al.* (1979) and Minuchin (1984), about **Malcolm Page** by Jay and Doganis (1987) and concerning **Jasmine Beckford** by Greenland (1987). However, we only know of a few previous attempts to use material from several reports for a more comprehensive study. Prompted by the widespread perception that the reports had much in common with each other, the Department of Health and Social Security (1982) collated their principal comments. Just before this present book went to press, the Department of Health (1991) published a follow-up review of more recent inquiries. Hallett (1989) discussed the process of the inquiries that followed the children's deaths, basing her review on comments made by the inquiry panels as well as involved professionals.

Greenland (1987) focussed more on the cases themselves as part of an international review of situations in which children died at the hands of their caretakers. In one study he obtained access to the Coroner's records and the Child Abuse Register in Ontario, Canada and was able to identify a cohort of 100 confirmed child abuse and neglect deaths over a ten-year period. These cases were compared to identify common characteristics and patterns and since the findings can be taken as a valid baseline for certain features of fatal child abuse in a defined population, we shall refer to them at appropriate points in later chapters. Greenland then added to his review a group of British cases, including many of those studied by us. He identified help-seeking behaviour by the caretakers and the children and warning signs of impending danger to the child and went on to formulate a 'high-risk checklist' as a guide to front-line professionals.

THE BOOK

We knew our project would be an arduous one which was bound to affect us deeply as we read more and more accounts about the abuse and deaths of children. We also expected that our report of the project, this book, would be likely to provoke strong emotions in the reader. We chose the title carefully to reflect our desire to get beyond the blaming stance of so many inquiry reports and newspaper headlines. The title *Beyond Blame* is not meant to suggest that professionals with child care and protection responsibilities should not be held accountable for their actions. On the contrary, we believe that responsibility must always remain a core feature of professional practice, together with clear lines of accountability when cases go wrong. However, we have placed less emphasis on this aspect of the cases because such issues are all too well covered by the inquiry reports themselves. Our concern has been that the reports tended to focus over-much on matters of professional responsibility and accountability at the expense of analysing the psychological aspects of the cases and the responsibilities of the caretakers. In our opinion, reviewing what did happen and what should have happened needed to be balanced with an attempt to understand how the errors had occurred.

We follow this introductory chapter with discussions of the historical and social context of child abuse and then how we applied our systemic thinking to the inquiry reports. We then go on to describe recurrent interactional patterns that we were able to identify within the abusing families, within the professional networks surrounding them and between the families and the professionals. Because problems of inter-professional communication occurred in the majority of cases, we have devoted three chapters to a discussion of various aspects of this issue. The **Doreen Aston** case is presented separately since it illustrates the inter-relationship of many of the common patterns over the course of one case. Finally, we consider some of the implications of our review for future practice and for responses to cases which end in tragedy. The Appendix contains summaries of each case we reviewed and the full reference to each inquiry report.

A brief comment is necessary about our use of the term 'case' throughout the book. To some this has a clinical and impersonal connotation, as though the people concerned are reduced to objects of study. This is not our intention, since we use the term in a much wider sense to describe all persons involved in the events that unfolded. We use 'case' as a shorthand to describe members of the family, members of the professional networks and their interaction together over time and in the present.

Chapter 2

The wider context

We have described the context within which this project was conceived and developed. In this chapter we shall consider the phenomenon of 'child abuse' and professional responses to it in their social, political and historical contexts. We shall discuss how the very concept of 'child abuse' is an evolving one and that professional practices are part of a complex social scenario. It is our view that the behaviour of families and professionals in these tragedies must be considered in relation to the contexts within which they lived and worked.

THE EVOLVING PHENOMENON OF 'CHILD ABUSE'

Gelles (1975) pointed out that there is no objective phenomenon which can automatically be recognised as child abuse and Freeman (1983a) observes that being 'at risk' is not an objective 'condition' but is a label, a social construction. Taylor, too, refers to the phenomenon of child abuse as: 'a social construction whose meaning arises from the value structure of a social group and the ways in which these values are interpreted and negotiated in real situations' (Taylor 1989: 46).

Figure 2.1 depicts how acknowledgement of child abuse as a problem and the need for society to respond to it changes over the years. The figure shows some of the factors which we believe are integral to the process and the continuous feedback between them, each factor modifying the others over time. As society progressively alters its attitudes to children and their welfare, expectations of parents are reviewed and refined. Unacceptable standards of care are defined, which warrant state intervention. Professional practice is itself sensitive to prevailing social beliefs and is guided by contemporary theories and knowledge, while new research is prompted by questions arising from professional work and social beliefs. From time to time, social attitudes become consolidated through political initiatives and legislation. At other times, social concern about state interventions lead to public inquiries, the results of which help to modify practice and may lay the groundwork for new legislation.

Therefore, the concept of 'child abuse' is an ever-changing one and is a construction arising out of a number of social and historical contexts. Because

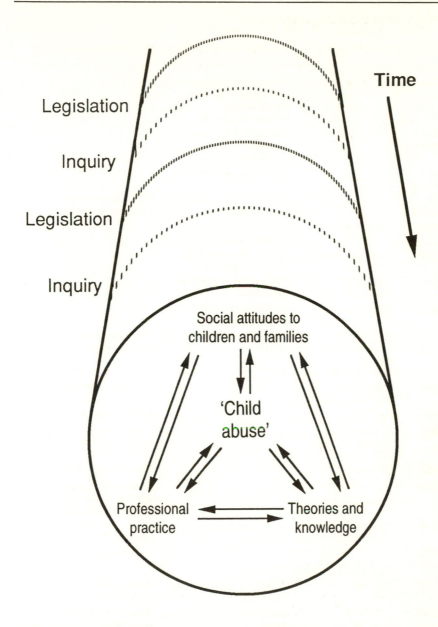

Figure 2.1 The social construction of 'child abuse'

these contexts are so relevant to the project reported in this book, we shall consider each of these themes in more detail. Their progressive inter-relationship is summarised in Table 2.1.

Table 2.1 The evolution of 'child abuse'

Year/s	Transitional event	Prevalent social attitude	Professional involvement
Medieval	Poor Law Act	Childhood denied; caring problems caused by moral failings; communality of life	
17th century		Children's inherent badness needed disciplining	
18th century		Family life more private	
19th century		Influence of private philanthropists	Child maltreatment observed but denied
1833	Factory Act	Children's need for protection recognised	
1834	Poor Law Reform Act	Family's moral failings needed correction	
1872	Infant Life Protection Act	Children recognised as individuals	
1880	Education Act	Children's developmental needs recognised	
1889	Prevention of Cruelty to and Protection of Children Act	Child cruelty considered a crime	Emphasis on prosecution of perpetrators
1889	Poor Law (Children) Act		Poor Law Guardians for children introduced
1890			NSPCC established
1904	Prevention of Cruelty to Children Act		Local authority empowered to remove child from their family
1908	Children Act		Special courts for juveniles
1920s			Child's emotional life acknowledged; child guidance clinics established
1933	Children and Young Persons Act	Welfare of the child emphasised	Care proceedings introduced
1940s			Child abuse 'rediscovered'
1945	Denis O'Neill inquiry		
1948	Children Act	Children's best interest paramount	Attempts to keep families intact
1950s		Sanctity of the biological family	Attachment theory elaborated
1963	Guardianship of Infants Act		Local authorities to undertake preventative work to keep families intact
1969	Children and Young Persons Act		Local authorities given clear powers to remove children from their families

Table 2.1 Continued

Year/s	Transitional event	Prevalent social attitude	Professional involvement
1970			At Risk Registers and Area Review Committees introduced
1974	Maria Colwell inquiry	Blood-tie re-evaluated; media interest in child abuse	
1975	Children Act		Permanency policy
1980s			Child sexual abuse 'rediscovered'
1985	Jasmine Beckford inquiry		
1987	Kimberley Carlile inquiry		
1988	Cleveland inquiry	Media interest in child sexual abuse	
1989	Children Act	Parental responsibility emphasised; ambivalence to family vs state	

PROFESSIONAL RECOGNITION

Kempe (1979) suggests that society's recognition of abuse to children progresses over time through a number of specific stages. In stage one there is a denial that either physical or sexual abuse exists to any significant extent and abuse that is acknowledged is believed to be perpetrated by psychotic, drunken or drugged parents or foreign visitors. During stage two the community pays attention to the more lurid forms of abuse or 'the battered child'. More effective ways begin to be found of coping with severe physical abuse and, through early recognition and intervention, with less severe abuse. Stage three occurs when physical abuse is better handled and attention is now paid to the infant who fails to thrive and is neglected physically. More subtle forms of abuse, such as poisoning, are also recognised. Stage four is reached when society recognises emotional abuse and neglect and patterns of severe rejection, scapegoating and emotional deprivation. In stage five the community pays attention for the first time to the plight of sexually abused children.

Although nineteenth-century physicians had considerable evidence that parents physically and sexually abused their children (Masson 1985), they appear to have largely denied its relevance. Initially, Freud believed his patients if they reported that their parents had sexually abused them during childhood. However, within a few years he was suggesting that their accounts were based in fantasy (Freud 1905). His change of heart may well have been influenced by his own personal conflicts (Reder 1989) as well as by the social attitudes and professional knowledge of the day.

The 'rediscovery' of child abuse by the medical profession was made in the United States by Caffey (1946), a paediatric radiologist, who described bone lesions and subdural haemotomata resulting from trauma. Woolley and Evans (1955) then proposed that some injuries were the result of parental assaults. In 1961 Kempe reported research into the physical abuse of children to the American Pediatric Association in a paper entitled 'The battered-child syndrome' (Kempe *et al.* 1962). In Britain, two orthopaedic surgeons, Griffiths and Moynihan (1963), alerted paediatricians and forensic pathologists to the problem. With the death of **Maria Colwell** in 1973, attention became focussed during the next few years on the extreme forms of physical abuse and it was only with the death of **Heidi Koseda** in 1984 that more subtle forms of abuse began to gain recognition. The 1980s was the decade of the rediscovery of sexual abuse with a plethora of research studies, massive media and political interest and the Cleveland Inquiry (1988).

With the acknowledgement that child abuse is a social problem, there have been increasing demands for information about its prevalence. However, as we have noted, the definition of child abuse is a social construction and therefore statistical data are bound to be elusive and contradictory. For example, in 1977 the Select Committee on Violence in the Family quoted 300 children under the age of 4 years dying every year in England and Wales as a result of child abuse, whereas in 1985 the Registrar General recorded only ten deaths from 'child battering and other maltreatment' (Office of Population Censuses and Surveys 1987). This discrepancy may well arise because the Registrar General only records deaths as homicides when criminal proceedings have found someone guilty of the offence. When a child's death is suspicious, but parents deny causing the injury and there is insufficient supporting evidence, a coroner will record an open verdict. The NSPCC have estimated from their records that 136 child deaths per year in England and Wales are caused by parents or caregivers (Creighton and Gallagher 1988). When deaths from natural causes where violence has played a part are added and allowances made for deaths which are misdiagnosed, this estimate increases to 198 child deaths per annum either caused or contributed to by abuse or neglect. Among these 198 deaths it is estimated that 154 would have been caused by parents or caregivers.

SOCIAL ATTITUDES

Social attitudes to children's need for care and protection

In order to recognise that child abuse occurs and is a social problem, there must exist a notion of the child as an individual in his/her own right, who is immature and dependent and has special needs for care and protection. Such concepts have not always existed through history. For example, Ariès (1962) suggests that medieval society showed a benign indifference to infancy since the child was regarded as a small adult. When the concept of childhood did emerge in the seventeenth century it was based on a belief in childish innocence and weakness but also innate badness that required eradication through discipline and punishment.

Such attitudes inevitably resulted in what we would now consider to be severe maltreatment of children. They were put to work from a very young age, were violently punished and were used by adults as their sexual playthings. De Mause (1976) catalogues the terrible maltreatment of children throughout history, including murder, abandonment, severe physical and sexual abuse and neglect of their immature needs. Only gradually did a view emerge that children have a need for care and protection. Freeman (1983b) suggests that the emergence of the capitalist economy demanded greater attention to education and training and hence a closer focus on children's special needs. But it was only from the nineteenth century that the raising of children was considered a process of socialising and helping rather than domination and control by adults (de Mause 1976).

This gradually increasing awareness of children's needs can be traced through relevant legislation, from the first state interventions guaranteeing basic survival for children and families, to the most recent Acts providing for child care and protection (see also Dingwall *et al.* 1984; Parton 1985).

The Poor Law Act of 1601, whereby parishes intervened on behalf of the helpless, needy and poor, was the first formal recognition that some families needed help even to survive. However, this Act and the 1834 Poor Law Reform Act reflected prevalent attitudes that child care problems were due to parents' moral failings. The state therefore adopted a harshly punitive attitude, believing this would encourage parents to overcome their inadequacies. Deprived and abandoned children were set to work as part of their care by the state in order that they could rise above the weakness of their parents.

During the Industrial Revolution, many children suffered extreme cruelty at work and only the minimum of protection was offered the orphaned and those from poor families through a number of Factory Acts, beginning in 1833. Legislation recognising the need to protect all children from exploitation by adults at work came only towards the end of that century. In 1875 children were prevented from being employed as chimney sweeps and in 1887 boys under 13 years of age were prohibited from working underground in mines.

At that time, violence towards and neglect of children at home was dealt with under criminal legislation without an accompanying regard for the child's welfare. For example, the 1889 Prevention of Cruelty to and Protection of Children Act made it a criminal offence for any adult (over 16 years of age) with custody, control or charge of a boy under 14 years or a girl under 16 years to have: 'wilfully ill-treated, neglected or abandoned the child in a manner likely to cause unnecessary suffering or injury to health'. However, the beginnings of change can be seen in the Poor Law (Children) Act of 1889 which gave authority for the state to assume parental rights over children already in the care of Poor Law Guardians if they were satisfied that the parents were irresponsible.

The first legal step recognising children as individuals in their own right was the Infant Life Protection Act of 1872. Then, in 1874, came the compulsory registration of births and deaths following the 'baby farming' scandals in which many babies died at the hands of paid caretakers. Until the 1908 Children Act, children had been treated as little adults in the criminal courts. This Act set up juvenile courts for children under the age of 14 years and from this time the practice of sending children to adult prisons was abolished in preference for industrial schools and reformatories. Some of the child's unique developmental needs were catered for through compulsory education, beginning in 1880.

Successive legislation through the twentieth century has recognised the special identity of the child and consolidated the right of all children to be protected from cruelty (Ford 1978). The 1933 Children and Young Persons Act introduced the concept of the 'welfare of the child'. Care proceedings date primarily from this Act, with the institution of the 'Fit Persons Order' to be used where parents/guardians were deemed unable to care for their children. The 1948 Children Act charged local authorities with furthering the child's 'best interests' and the 1963 Children and Young Persons Act set out clearly the grounds upon which a child could be removed from home into local authority care. Most recently, these various pieces of legislation were replaced by the 1989 Children Act which promotes a partnership between parents and the local authority in pursuit of child care and protection.

Social attitudes to the family and its members

Parallel with these changing social attitudes to child care have been evolving views about the family (e.g. Ariès 1962; Poster 1978; Lewis 1986). Two areas seem particularly relevant to the issue of child abuse: one is the changing beliefs about the family as an identifiable social unit; the second is changing attitudes to the individual family members.

In feudal times, most people lived in village communities in which there was relatively little differentiation between family units. Life was more community centred and less focussed on the biological family. Furthermore, the serf was the property of the feudal lord, fully responsive to his dictates. Until the end of the seventeenth century, this communality meant that nobody was ever left alone. It was not until the eighteenth century that families of the big houses began to keep society at a distance, developing more of a private life from which servants and friends were excluded. Towards the end of that century, agricultural labourers tended to set up house on their own instead of lodging with their employers.

The industrial revolution produced a social as well as an economic transformation. Just as the wealthy withdrew further into their estates, each working family came closer together as a coherent social unit. Many moved to the cities and in the process became more detached from their extended families. Initially, economic survival depended on all members of the nuclear family working. Later, middle-class families emerged in which mothers remained at home looking after large numbers (by today's standards) of children. Thus, in Victorian times the nuclear family became the focus of economic and emotional life. The marital relationship was also changing, from an economic partnership between two working parents to one in which the husband was the sole financial provider while the mother remained at home. The grouping of biological parents and children came more and more to describe society's view of 'the family' and the welfare state related to them as the basic unit of living which provided the emotional, social and practical needs of its members.

However, the latter part of the twentieth century has witnessed a considerable change in views of the family as a social unit. Links with extended family have been progressively severed, except in certain communities (Young and Willmott 1957). Increased life expectancy of children, together with family planning, has meant that fewer children are being born. Marriages can be dissolved more easily and this has led in turn to greater acceptance of different family structures, such as single parent, reconstituted or homosexual families.

Within the family unit, the roles of men and women have gradually changed, sometimes in response to economic factors, but often as a result of wider public debate through the media. Two world wars and recurrent problems of male unemployment have encouraged renewed acceptance of women working outside the home and the feminist movement has challenged the long-established view of male domination. Although women over 21 years became entitled to vote in 1928, only recently has taxation law, for example, been changed to take account of the social transition in the male/female relationship. This issue of male domination is considered highly pertinent to child abuse by many contemporary writers (e.g. The Violence Against Children Study Group 1990) who argue that child maltreatment is one example of men exerting socially sanctioned power over others.

THEORETICAL INFLUENCES ON PROFESSIONAL PRACTICE

The earliest, organised, professional response to child abuse in Great Britain emerged with the birth of the British Society Against Cruelty to Children in Liverpool in 1883. A national society (the NSPCC) was established as an amalgamation of many societies in 1890 and by the end of the decade the NSPCC had a national network of officers. A strong sense of Victorian social and moral values pervaded the organisation, with an emphasis on forcing parents to accept and carry out their parental responsibilities to provide adequate standards of physical care. Professional effort was directed towards the parents and it was considered counterproductive to remove children from parental care, even for their own protection, as this would relieve parents of their responsibilities.

The twentieth century saw an upsurge of professional and academic interest in children, which did much to heighten awareness of their emotional, psychological, educational and social needs. Sigmund Freud (1905), for example, was one of the first to stress the importance of early childhood experiences for later adult life. Later psychoanalysts, such as Anna Freud (1927) and Melanie Klein (1932), began to draw attention to the inner world of the child which hitherto had not been recognised. Winnicott, through his radio broadcasts in the 1940s (1957) and Spock (1946) made the public more aware of the everyday needs of children. Piaget (1952) stressed the need for parents to stimulate their children in age-appropriate ways to enhance cognitive development.

It was within this context that the rediscovery of child abuse occurred. The broader definition of the needs of children brought with it a growing realisation that large numbers of children were not being provided with adequate care. Explanations were offered from theorists of the day and psychoanalysts, behaviourists, sociologists and, later, family therapists all proposed models which have influenced both the understanding of the phenomenon and intervention strategies.

Paradoxically, although the psychological theorists had first directed attention towards the needs of children, their attempts to explain child abuse have often directed professional attention almost exclusively onto the parents. At one time, psychoanalytic ideas dominated child abuse theory and practice and the work of Bowlby (1951) probably has been the most influential. He originally proposed that biological mothers are primed by their hormones to 'bond' to their infants and that there was a crucially sensitive period between 6 months and 5 years of age during which the infant has constant need of the presence of an 'attachment figure' (usually the mother). According to Bowlby, the unavailability of good attachment figures in early life leads to 'maternal deprivation', which in turn is manifested by an inability to parent the next generation. This was taken as evidence for a 'cycle of deprivation'.

Kempe took up the ideas of Bowlby and applied them enthusiastically to the field of child abuse (e.g. Kempe and Helfer 1972). His model involved encouraging long-term, nurturing therapeutic relationships with parents so that their dependency needs could be met and they would better be able to meet their children's needs. The NSPCC Battered Child Research Department (Denver House) was established in London in 1968 under Kempe's direction. Staff perceived parents as powerless to influence their own lives and consequently the NSPCC accepted responsibility on their behalf for promoting change. This was a dramatic contrast with the Society's earlier approach. The emphasis now was on the provision of nurturing care for the parents, whilst the establishment of controls and limits to behaviour was given little attention. A confusion often arose as to who was the client: the parents or the child.

The upsurge of behaviourism in the 1970s did little to alter this problem, even though this model proposed that child abuse resulted from poor learning experiences and inadequate controlling techniques. The behavioural therapy approach attempted to replace deficient parenting skills with those considered more socially acceptable and help parents develop self-control. Although responsibility was placed back with parents, in practice interventions were directed at the adults and children often ceased to be a focus of attention in their own right.

The behavioural approach never offered a serious challenge to the psychoanalytic model in the area of child abuse. The then Secretary of State for Social Services, Sir Keith Joseph (1972), popularised the notion of a cycle of deprivation and he funded research into it and initiated the publication of the first Departmental guidelines for the management of child abuse (Department of Health and Social Security and the Welsh Office 1970). 'At Risk Registers' were to be established to help the identification and monitoring of children believed to be at risk of harm, as well as local, multi-disciplinary 'Area Review Committees' to review practice and promote inter-agency training and co-operation.

Bowlby's notion of 'maternal deprivation' did much to promote the idea that preserving the 'blood-tie' was paramount in making decisions about the placement and care of children. However, after the death of **Maria Colwell** in 1973, the blood-tie policy began to be questioned and there was greater recognition that rehabilitation to the natural family after serious physical abuse was not always desirable. Local authorities operated with greater caution when considering rehabilitation and were concerned to test out the potential for change in the family of origin. More children were removed from their parents during the late 1970s as the social mood swung towards needing to protect the child at all costs. An emphasis on the importance of family life was maintained through permanent placement of children in substitute families: the 'permanency policy'.

Sociological theories, in their turn, have highlighted wider contextual factors surrounding child abuse. They have emphasised the role and responsibility of society as a whole and pointed to the need for political and social changes in order to address the problem (e.g. Gil 1970; Garberino and Sherman 1980; Gelles 1973). Meanwhile, a developing interest in applying systemic theory to the interactions of social groupings, such as families, led to family therapy being heralded as an exciting new approach for tackling this difficult problem. However, family therapy has also been criticised for taking attention away from children and their protection by emphasising the functioning of parents and families (e.g. Blom-Cooper 1986). Nevertheless, systemic theory has been very influential in the more recent attempts to find a method of intervention for families where abuse has occurred (e.g. Dale *et al.* 1986; Asen *et al.* 1989). Systemic ideas have also formed the basis for the review reported in this book, which both attempts to view the abuse within its wider context and give equal weight to the position of the child and other members of the family.

THE FAMILY AND THE STATE

The issue of child care highlights the complex and changing relationship between the family and the state over time and in particular the question of the state's right to intrude into family life. The tension between the view that the family's right to privacy is a sacrosanct civil liberty and the view that the state must continue to monitor and intervene into many facets of life has been voiced by many authors (e.g. Rosenfeld and Newberger 1979; Goldstein *et al.* 1979; Donzelot 1980; Freeman 1983a; Minuchin 1984; Parton 1985). Of course, the issue is one of degree. It is generally accepted that the state encroaches onto family life in many ways, such as guiding public health and compelling its citizens to be educated. The state proscribes certain behaviour and can imprison citizens whose actions are unacceptable or commit a person to psychiatric hospital under the Mental Health Act.

The state intervenes into family life on behalf of children in a number of ways. It offers help and support to parents so that the family's integrity might be maintained; it institutionalises some provisions on behalf of the family, such as health and education; and it may override the authority of parents and remove their children from the family. The history of state intervention where there has been concern for a child's welfare has swung between authoritarian state control and family rights. The Poor Law was concerned with abandoned or orphaned children. Children living with their parents, whatever the quality of their care, were considered in law to be the possessions of their parents and the rights of property prevented the state from intervening between the owner and his belongings. However, once kin support had failed, familial and citizen status was replaced by pauper status. It was under a revision of the Poor Law, the 1889 Poor Law (Children) Act, that Poor Law Guardians could assume parental rights over children already under their care if they considered the parents to be irresponsible. The twentieth century saw increasing legislation allowing the state to intervene in families. The Prevention of Cruelty to Children Act of 1904 first gave local authorities powers to remove children from their parents who, again, were seen as having failed morally and being in need of reform.

Successive Acts show how the pendulum has continued to swing between state powers and family rights. The 1933 Children and Young Persons Act increased committal powers and included a duty on local authorities to board out children in foster homes, thus removing them from their natural homes. However, the 1948 Children Act emphasised keeping families together and local authorities now had a duty to try to rehabilitate children with their families of origin. The 1963 Guardianship of Infants Act confirmed the state's intention to keep families together and local authorities were charged with undertaking preventative work towards this end. The 1969 Children and Young Persons Act most clearly set out the criteria by which local authorities could apply for care proceedings to the juvenile court, which had considerable powers to remove children from home. The 1975 Children Act emphasised children's need for permanency, even if this was in substitute families.

Practitioners' difficulty in knowing how to interpret child care law was demonstrated by two very different recent inquiries into child abuse. The **Kimberley Carlile** inquiry in 1987 demonstrated that the law allowing statutory professionals access to a child suspected of being abused was unclear and needed revision. However, the Cleveland Inquiry (1988) was prompted by public concern that professionals had too readily removed children from their families on suspicion of sexual abuse.

An ambivalence about the relationship between the family and the state persists in the latest legislation, the 1989 Children Act. At the time of writing, the Act has gained the Royal Assent but is awaiting implementation. It consolidates the notion of family responsibility and the belief that children are generally best looked after within their family. Local authorities will have a duty to promote the upbringing of children in need by their families so far as it is consistent with their welfare. The Act envisages a partnership between families and the state, so that if a local authority arranges for a child to live away from home this should preferably be under voluntary arrangements with the parents. On the other hand, the Act makes new powers available to courts to intervene to protect children at risk of harm within the family in the form of an Emergency Protection Order and a Child Assessment Order.

The present political climate is also one of considerable ambivalence to child protection and the means by which it can be achieved. The thrust of recent Acts has been for social workers to engage in preventative work to avoid children coming into care. However, funding for social services departments has been progressively cut, with the effect that social workers are unable to engage in long-term preventative work and only have the resources to do the minimum necessary. In practice, this means concentrating their efforts on crisis management and acting as agents of social control. Dingwall succinctly articulates the present social dilemma about state intervention:

> the child protection system contains an inherent bias against intervention anyway. If we wish to change that, then we must confront the social costs. If we do not consider that those costs are worth paying, then we must frankly acknowledge the human implications, that some children will die to preserve the freedom of others.
>
> (Dingwall 1986: 503)

PUBLIC INQUIRIES

The 1970s and 1980s witnessed a new phase in the history of child abuse with the explosion of public inquiries into certain cases of fatal abuse. An inquiry was held in 1945 into the death in foster care of **Denis O'Neill** (Home Office 1945) but the next one in Great Britain that we are aware of concerned **Graham Bagnall** in 1973. It is worth speculating about the reason for this quiescence and sudden intensification of interest. As we have shown, child abuse had been rediscovered in the 1960s at a time of transition in social attitudes to children, family life and the state. New legislation increased state powers to remove children from home for their own protection and the media reflected and encouraged public interest by monitoring situations where children had been harmed and questioning whether professionals had failed to fulfil their statutory responsibilities. From the time of the **Maria Colwell** inquiry in 1973/4, the media has focussed attention on child abuse tragedies and has helped to fuel public anxiety and anger that abuse should occur at all. It is clear from the introductions to many reports that the inquiries were set up as a result of public concern, often propelled by media interest.

Parton (1981) suggests that a moral panic ensues at the news of a child being severely abused. Representatives of society, such as social workers, easily become the receptacle of public upset and rage that these events have not stopped. Outcries in the media and recurrent public inquiries into professional practices help maintain the unreal beliefs that all child abuse and child manslaughter can be prevented and that it is only because of bad practice that professionals fail to eradicate it. The recurrent vilification of social workers probably helps calibrate public concern, allowing a sudden outpouring of anger so that the problem can then recede from social awareness.

Inquiry panels have tended to focus their investigations on professional practice and so the social or psychological circumstances surrounding the child's death are often missing from the reports. Hallett (1989) suggests that in criticising the actions of individuals, the basic social order remains unchallenged. She means by this that no consideration is given to the process of socialisation which leads adults to harm children, or to social values which sanction a power imbalance between men and women and children, or to the harsh and depriving conditions in which many of the families lived. In particular, inquiries may be used as a political expedient to allay public disquiet in the expectation that: 'attention and blame would be laid at the feet of individuals and political responsibility for the child-protection system, its modes of operation, its legislative framework and its resources would largely escape public scrutiny' (Hallett 1989: 144). Hill (1990) also argues that inquiries have had a disproportionate influence on policy-making since they serve as a means of policing and exerting authority over the professions involved.

Nonetheless, as Adcock (1989) has pointed out, three major changes in law have followed public inquiries. The **Denis O'Neill** inquiry in 1945 was followed by the Curtis Committee, which resulted in the 1948 Children Act. The 1974 inquiry report into **Maria Colwell**'s death was soon followed by the 1975 Children Act. The **Jasmine Beckford** inquiry in 1985 and the **Kimberley Carlile** inquiry in 1987 preceded the Cleveland Inquiry (1988). The **Kimberley Carlile** report highlighted how complex the child care laws had become and the Law Commission had also been working to rationalise the various Acts. The 1989 Children Act followed hard on the heels of these three inquiries.

SUMMARY

We have discussed how the concept of child abuse is an evolving one, with changes in its definition and recognition. Over the years, social attitudes towards children and the state's role in protecting them have varied and responses have needed to be consistent with prevailing societal and professional belief systems and existing laws. Professionals who become involved in child abuse cases operate at the confluence of many sensitive social issues, which fluctuate as knowledge and attitudes change. An appreciation of this wider context must be relevant to front-line professionals in their everyday work, to inquiry panels and to this review of recent tragedies.

Chapter 3

Tragedies revisited

In this chapter we shall present the theoretical principles which formed the basis of our approach and then describe how we applied them in our project to review the inquiry reports.

CONCEPTUAL FRAMEWORK

As a group of practitioners from varied professional backgrounds working in a child mental health team, we drew on a number of conceptual frameworks to guide our practice, including psychoanalytic, cognitive, communication and systemic theories. Systemic theory, as well as being an important body of ideas in its own right, also provided an overall framework linking the other theories and helped us make sense of interpersonal, group and institutional functioning.

Practitioners tend to refer to systemic *thinking*, or a systemic *approach*, rather than systemic *theory* as such. This is because von Bertalanffy's general systems theory (1968) primarily described mechanical and mathematical relationships between elements, which only went some way towards explaining the intricacies of human interaction. Furthermore, relationships between the family and others are as relevant to problem analysis as those within the family unit. Therefore, the more general term *systemic* approach is preferred to that of *family systems* approach.

Some tenets of the systemic approach

The systemic approach describes processes by which human groupings come together, interact, develop and transform over time. Some of the basic notions will be summarised here. Fuller explanations are given by Hoffman (1981), Gorell Barnes (1985), Simon *et al.* (1985), Barker (1986), Burnham (1986) and Campbell *et al.* (1989).

A *system* is considered to be any unit organised through feedback. The whole is qualitatively more than the sum of the individual parts because the properties of the whole derive from the properties of the *relationships* between the parts (Gorell Barnes 1985). Human systems are groups of people interacting around a common issue: for instance, a task group meeting intermittently, such as an amateur choir; the regular working concerns of a professional agency; or the daily living preoccupations of a family. A family functions together around multiple issues, including the need for child nurturance, desires for emotional and practical security, wishes to seek sexual and attachment gratification by the adults, and so on. Therefore, human systems are held together by the desire to meet the needs of its members and to fulfil particular tasks. The system may be transient or long-lasting and may either have overt rules of membership (such as criteria for acceptance into a club) or more blurred distinctions (for example, should the estranged father be considered as a member of the family system?). Hence, the limits, or *boundaries*, of human systems often depend on the observer's evaluation and the specific *context* under consideration.

Even so, it is useful to imagine the boundaries of human systems showing properties along a continuum of openness–closedness, depending on the degree to which members are free to enter or leave and information to be exchanged. For instance, prison systems have relatively impermeable boundaries, while hospital casualty departments are expected to have more permeable boundaries. The more open the system, the greater is its contact with the other systems and the more flexible it is and capable of adapting to change. Systems which find change and adaptation less easy tend to close off from contact with the outside world. Boundary permeability of human systems may need to change according to circumstance. Thus, traditional codes of confidentiality for doctors are required to change when child abuse is suspected in order to allow optimal information transfer between all agencies of the professional network and co-ordination of their plans. The boundary permeability of families can also vary and sometimes they may welcome contact with neighbours and helping professionals, while at other times they may attempt to keep their boundary closed to outside intrusion. Families must retain a balance between openness and closedness in their contact with the outside world.

Human systems show differentiation of skills, roles and tasks – that is, a *structure*. Parenting is provided by one or more caretakers, the parenting *subsystem*. According to Minuchin (1974), 'healthy' family functioning requires adequate inter-generational boundaries between the parenting subsystem and the sibling subsystem, since many of their needs and tasks are different. Families also exist in relation to larger *suprasystems*, such as their extended families and society's laws and cultural mores. Such suprasystems define a *context* within which family behaviour is observed and understood.

The concept of *circularity* is central to the systemic model, as it describes mutual influence between two or more people. Instead of a belief that one individual, A, can cause another, B, to do something ('linear causality'), the notion of *circular causality* proposes that A's behaviour receives a response from B, which *feeds back* to A, who responds to B's response, and so on (see Figure 3.1).

As an example, an infant's cry is likely to draw the caretaker nearer and evoke a comforting response. Eventually, the infant will stop crying and tolerate greater

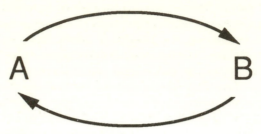

Figure 3.1 Circularity

distance from the caretaker. In addition, the episode will help reinforce the infant's sense of security. The behaviour of A and B is said to arise out of the circularity between them and neither is considered unilaterally responsible for what has happened. A systemic approach is characterised by a *non-blaming* stance and *mutual causality* is probably a more appropriate description of this sequence of interactions. The more intense the meaning that one person has for another the closer they will be bound by the feedback between them.

The mutual interaction between members of a system is described as showing *pattern* and some consistency over time. This allows an observer to describe common themes to the inter-relationship and to the group's behaviour as a whole, as though undeclared *rules* govern the system, both over time and in the present. These rules may be the manifestation of unconscious beliefs or myths about family life, such as 'Mothers should always look after children' or 'It's best to deal with loss by pretending it never happened.'

It is also possible to discern interactional patterns between loosely bound groups whose members only meet together occasionally. A good example of such a system is the network of professionals from different agencies working with a particular family. When children are at risk of abuse, the network must assess, monitor, protect and plan for the child's welfare. This shared set of tasks unites respective agencies and professionals into a system, whatever the degree of personal contact between them, and repetitive patterns of relationships will inevitably develop over time.

Human systems are required to remain sufficiently stable so that needs are met and tasks fulfilled and sufficiently flexible so that learning, growth and adaptation can occur. Figure 3.2 depicts a child growing up in a family, within the wider context of the external world. At any one time, patterns of interaction can be observed across all these systems. The family will evolve through a *life cycle*, involving births, deaths, inclusions of new members, leavings and natural changes such as puberty and adolescence. In addition, external influences, such as illnesses, will impinge on family life. These transitions affect all members of a family system because everyone must adapt. The role and meaning that each person has for the others must be modified and their relationships renegotiated. This period of adjustment may be stressful and become apparent as emotional, behavioural or relationship problems. It is therefore useful when considering families in which child abuse has occurred to focus attention on the effects of life cycle and transitional events. These might include a death, the arrival of a new partner or baby, a child returning home after a long period in care or the replacement of a professional who has been involved for a long time.

The systemic approach, child abuse, responsibility and power

The systemic approach proposes that abusive behaviour to children occurs at times of heightened tension in current relationships between vulnerable people against a background of chronic social and environmental stress. As Greenland

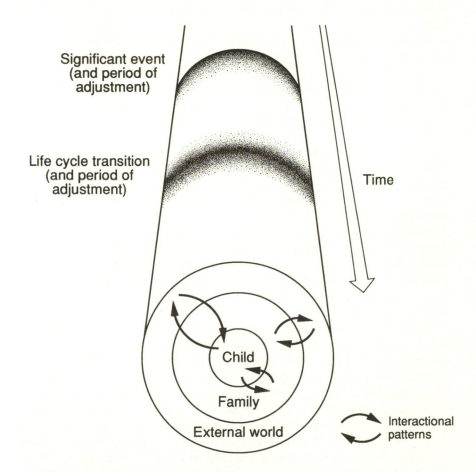

Figure 3.2 Historical and relationship influences on a child and family's development (after Hoffman 1982)

suggests: 'thinking about high-risk families in a "non-linear" way means becoming aware of the existence of "complex interacting variables" rather than, say, "one-shot" altercations between an aggressor and a victim' (1987: 156).

The non-blaming stance of the systemic approach raises a legitimate question about personal responsibility. By preferring a belief in mutual causality to notions of individual blame, do systems theorists try to dispense with the idea of personal responsibility? It is our opinion that no explanatory philosophy should deny the relevance of individual responsibility. Neither groups nor relationships can be held responsible for one person's behaviour and individuals must be seen to be responsible and accountable for their actions, as a social reality and as a philosophical belief. We would suggest that a systemic approach enables personal responsibility to be acknowledged and addressed because it helps analyse the covert, interactional and contextual constraints upon an individual. Once these unwitting processes are recognised it is possible for the individual more fully to accept responsibility for his/her actions. Thus, in disentangling the individual from the relationships of which s/he is a part, this approach can be seen to add to the notion of personal responsibility rather than detract from it.

The systemic approach has also been criticised for failing to acknowledge the operation of power in human relationships, especially when family violence and child abuse are concerned. The argument centres on whether, in describing mutual influences between members of a system, the theory denies how one person's will may be imposed upon another. This criticism has generated a creative and important debate amongst practitioners (e.g. Dell 1989; Perelberg 1990) which has clarified the need to distinguish between what Dell calls the domain of *experience* and the domain of *explanation*. The notion of power changes as one moves between these two perspectives and it is essential to articulate which frame of reference one is using.

Everyday encounters confirm the universality of power relationships, in which one person's assertion of power over another is defined by the context (such as hierarchies in the workplace) or implied through imbalances in strength (for example, between parent and infant). Therefore, within the domain of *experience*, power cannot be denied. However, it is when one goes on to analyse the nuances of such relationships that an alternative and equally valid understanding of power emerges. From the perspective afforded by the domain of *explanation*, behaviour occurs in a context and within a pattern of behavioural antecedents and feedback. For example, a child's crying can provoke irritation, then rage, in the parent, who may lash out in frustration. The parent's assault is unquestionably an abuse of power (as seen within the domain of experience) but the child also can be described as having the power to influence, however unwittingly, the outcome (from the domain of explanation). Such explanations do not deny the unequal power relationships in human interaction, nor do they attempt to excuse abuses of power. They seek a wide understanding of the behaviour, having first acknowledged, and if appropriate deplored, its existence. A wider understanding of the situation in which a parent assaults the crying child might also lead us to recognise the parent's sense of powerlessness in certain contexts. The crying of a distressed child or threats from professionals to impose controls over the family may exacerbate a profound sense of powerlessness in the adult who unconsciously attempts to redress it by assaulting the defenceless child.

The spirit of the project reported in this book was to examine child abuse tragedies primarily within the domain of explanation.

Evolution of systemic practice

Eastern culture has long been systemic in outlook, believing in pattern and harmony between people, groups and events. In the West, systemic thinking about human behaviour grew from a number of disparate roots. The origins can be traced back to the 1950s, a time when the physical sciences were moving away from a reductionist attitude (that is, analysing the properties of discrete elements in isolation) to explaining phenomena in terms of inter-relationships (Capra 1982). Concurrently, psychoanalysis was being influenced by object relations theorists (e.g. Fairbairn 1952; Winnicott 1965), who proposed that the primary motivational drive in humans was not to obtain instinctual gratification but to seek relationships with others. In addition, developments in group psychotherapy (e.g. Foulkes and Anthony 1957), conjoint marital therapy (e.g. Dick 1967), the therapeutic community movement (e.g. Main 1957; Jones 1962) and the realisation of the influence of institutions on psychiatric patients (e.g. Stanton and Schwartz 1954; Goffman 1968) all pointed towards a focus on interpersonal interaction.

Disenchantment with the biological preoccupations in psychiatry led to explanations for psychiatric disorder in terms of social and relationship disorder (e.g. Laing and Esterson 1964) or communicational confusions (e.g. Bateson *et al.* 1956). However, Laing's theories about relationship knots and Bateson's early description of the double bind were essentially blaming in nature, since they suggested that the family's behaviour caused the psychotic person's disorder. However, from the early 1960s, other psychiatrists such as Skynner, Minuchin, Ackerman and Whittaker began to translate their psychoanalytic experience into observations about family functioning and were able to demonstrate patterns of mutual interaction between family members. This history has been well documented by Guerin (1976), Hoffman (1981) and Broderick and Schrader (1981).

The development of one influential group, the Milan associates, illustrates how many other theories have become integrated into systemic ideas and practice. Selvini Palazzoli, Boscolo, Cecchin and Prata began working together in 1967, using a psychoanalytic basis for their treatment of couples and families (see Tomm 1984; Boscolo *et al.* 1987). Their practice was tranformed by the work of Watzlawick *et al.* (1967), and later Bateson (1972, 1979), who had been interested in the meaning people attribute to messages in particular contexts and the contradictory messages in interpersonal communication.

The Milan team came to see symptomatic families as being in a state of disequilibrium between the momentum for change brought about by life-cycle developments and a compulsion to retain old relationship patterns. All family members were understood to be caught in this core conflict. Before seeing referred families, the team developed *hypotheses* about the family's relationship dilemmas and attempted to understand the present conflict in the light of the family's history and development. Then, in the therapy session, they explored circular connections between individuals' beliefs, communications and behaviour (Selvini Palazzoli *et al.* 1978, 1980a).

The Milan team's, and particularly Boscolo and Cecchin's, work was further informed by the constructivist school (e.g. von Foerster 1981; Maturana and Varela 1987), with its recognition that our knowledge and sense of the world is built up subjectively. Hence,

> the problem does not exist independently of the 'observing systems' that are reciprocally and collectively defining the problem

and

> It is far better to do away with the concept of family system entirely and think of the treatment unit as a meaning system to which the treating professional is as active a contributor as anyone else. We would then not say *the system creates the problem* but would reverse the sentence: *the problem creates the system.*
>
> (Boscolo *et al.* 1987: 14)

Constructivist ideas have helped bring about important shifts in the systemic approach. First, emphasis is also given to the functioning of the individual within the group and not exclusively to the collective phenomena of the system. Second, greater attention is paid to the *meaning* that one person has for another and the cognitive, emotional and relationship factors which bind them together. Finally, it is recognised that the presence of an observer changes the context of the observations and therefore modifies the nature of the information gathered.

Practical application

Influences of the Milan associates have been immense, not just for those conducting therapy, but also practitioners requiring a framework to understand the behaviour of complex systems (see Campbell and Draper 1985). Professionals have learned to widen their perspective about a problem and consider who has been involved in its evolution and who is affected now. The Milan systemic approach has taught that each person in the system should be considered equally significant, since his/her beliefs and behaviour contribute to the overall 'gestalt'. Furthermore, suspending moral judgements prevents observers taking sides and helps them consider the part played by all members of the system. As a result, connections can be traced, or mapped, between people and events over time which show a pattern and suggest how the current problems might be understood.

In addition, consideration must be given to how an observer, such as a monitoring social worker, affects the nature of that which is observed.

Systemic maps guide consultants who need to gather and organise information about complex cases (Reder and Israelstam 1988). It is especially important to process information about situations of child abuse because they often involve large accumulations of facts and observations over the course of many years, held in different places by numerous people, which have been transmitted through a series of intermediaries, about anxiety-laden and life-threatening events in chaotically functioning families with fluctuating structures. The various professionals may also have distinct or overlapping responsibilities, skills and roles and operate within a complex legal and social context.

Table 3.1 summarises the categories of information that are most relevant to child abuse cases and build into multi-dimensional maps about the system of the family, its problems and the professional network. This framework directs the professional's thinking towards particular facts and patterns in the here and now and over time. Constructing a family genogram (or family tree) forces the worker to consider individuals within their interactional contexts and to ascertain who has been part of the family and how the structure and relationships have changed over time. In order to complete the drawing of the genogram, it becomes necessary to clarify the number of children in the household (all of whom will need protection), who is in a caretaking relationship to the children (and therefore their backgrounds must be known and their parenting capacities assessed), and so on. Once the history of problems in the family is arranged in chronological order, patterns may emerge which coincide with significant life cycle changes and suggest explanations for the difficulties. For instance, abuse or neglect of the children may have recurred whenever the parents separated. The family's relationship to professionals and the help they have offered guides the planning of interventions. The functioning of the professional network also has significance for the efficacy of child protective work, such as the organisation of its communications and decision taking.

Figure 3.3 shows the principal relationship constellations that need to be considered in cases of child abuse. It depicts a family in contact with a number of helping agencies. Within each organisational cluster there will be patterns of interaction between individuals which have built up over time. This is true for both the family and each professional agency. At the same time, there is a wider network of relationships operating between all the agencies concerned with the family's problems. Hence, we use the term 'case' in this book to recognise the relevance of relationships within the family, amongst members of the family's professional network and between the families and these professionals. For a comprehensive view, consideration must also be given to the wider socio-political context within which these organisational clusters operate, as discussed in the previous chapter.

We shall now describe how we applied these principles to our review of child abuse inquiry reports.

Table 3.1 Framework for constructing a systemic map of a family and its professional network

THE FAMILY

Family genogram
What is the legal status of the children, parents, etc.?
Who are the current members of the household?
Who is/are the child's caretaker/s?
What have been the significant life cycle changes?
What have been the significant relationships over time?

THE PROBLEMS

What is the history of problems in the family?
What help was attempted (and by whom)?
What was the effect of these attempts to help?
Who is/are worried now, and about what?
Does the family believe there are problems now?

THE PROFESSIONAL NETWORK

What is the history of professional contacts with the family?
Which professionals/agencies are currently involved?
What are their statutory/professional obligations?
What are the aims of their contacts?
What are they doing in pursuit of those aims?
What is the family's relationship to the professionals/agencies?
What is the family's reaction to professional attempts to help?
What are the significant relationships amongst the professional network?
What changes have there been/are expected in the professional network?
What case conferences have there been, and with what outcome?
Who is the allocated social worker/key worker?
What is his/her assessment of risk and is the child adequately protected?

REVIEW OF INQUIRY REPORTS

When we tried to obtain copies of all known and available inquiry reports it quickly became obvious that there is no central register and we had to turn to other publications as reference sources (Department of Health and Social Security 1982; the **Kimberley Carlile** Inquiry Report 1987). From time to time in our reading we found reference to another inquiry we had not known about and we were also surprised by a number of 'false trails' in which a publication mentioned a report but the relevant authority denied all knowledge of it when contacted. We only know of one public report which we did not obtain (the **Emma Hughes** Inquiry, Calderdale, 1981). BASW (1982) also lists three reports

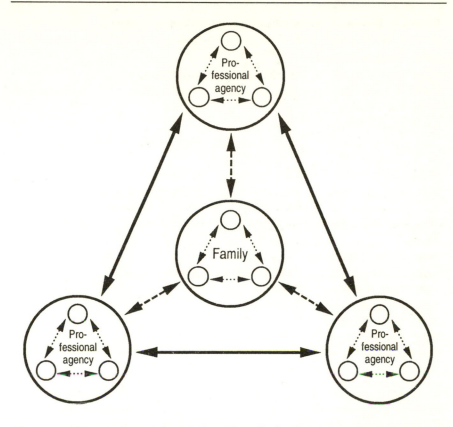

Figure 3.3 The intra- and inter-relationships of a family system and its wider professional network

which are not available to the general public – into sexual abuse in the **'H' family** in Surrey (1977) and the deaths of **Heidi Trott** in Humberside (1979) and of **Marie Delaney** in Walsall (1981).

In all we reviewed thirty-five inquiry reports, which are listed according to year of publication in Table 3.2. On average, the reports we obtained were published about two years after the child's death, although some took much longer (for example, three and a half years for the **Lucie Gates** inquiry and four and a half years in the case of **Richard Fraser**).

We included one child, **Richard Clark**, who was not fatally abused. He suffered a severe head injury with a massive cerebral haemorrhage and was reduced to an irrecoverable 'vegetable' state with a greatly reduced life expectancy. It seemed inappropriate to exclude this report from our review and all subsequent discussions which refer to a child's death include this case. Another case we might have excluded was **Stephen Menheniott**, who was aged 19 when his father killed him. However, Stephen had been in care for most of his

Table 3.2 The inquiry reports reviewed (by year of publication)

1973	Graham Bagnall		
1974	Maria Colwell	David Naseby	Max Piazzani
1975	Richard Clark	Susan Aukland	Lisa Godfrey	Steven Meurs
1976	Neil Howlett		
1977	Wayne Brewer		
1978	Karen Spencer	Simon Peacock	Stephen Menheniott
1979	Darryn Clarke	Lester Chapman	
1980	Claire Haddon	Carly Taylor	Paul Brown
1981	Malcolm Page	Maria Mehmedagi	Christopher Pinder/ Daniel Frankland
1982	Jason Caesar	Anonymous	Richard Fraser	Lucie Gates
1983			
1984	Shirley Woodcock		
1985	Jasmine Beckford	Reuben Carthy	Gemma Hartwell
1986	Heidi Koseda	Charlene Salt	
1987	Kimberley Carlile	Tyra Henry	
1988	Gavin Mabey		
1989	Doreen Aston		

life and this case, like that of **Richard Clark**, is always quoted amongst the list of child abuse inquiries. It also contained the same issues of professional decision-taking and family–professional interaction that interested us in the other cases.

We decided to complete our project with the **Doreen Aston** report, published in July 1989. Subsequent newspaper articles and the recently published Department of Health review (1991) alerted us that we could have added more cases in which children known to statutory agencies died at the hands of their caretakers: for example, **Karl McGoldrick** (Whitehaven, 1986), **Dean Scott** (Southwark, 1987), **Liam Johnson** (Islington, 1987), **Stephanie Fox** (Wandsworth, 1989), **Christopher Palmer** (Ealing, 1989) and **Danial Vergauwen** (Hackney, 1989).

The reports varied enormously in length and in detail. This may be a reflection of their somewhat different purposes, since a number seemed more concerned to review local procedures and check whether they had been followed, while others reviewed more comprehensively the development of the case. These differences may be accounted for by the various commissioning agents; see Table 3.3.

The reports ranged in length from 585 typed pages to just 13 and some hardly seemed to do justice to the life and death of a child. The child did not always seem central to the inquiry. For example, **Max Piazzani**'s age is never mentioned in the report on his death and the **Susan Aukland** inquiry was into 'the Provision of Services to J.G. Aukland', that is, the father who killed her. This was also

Table 3.3 Commissioners of the thirty-five reports

DHSS	Secretary of State for Scotland	Local Authority	Local Authority + Health Authority	Local Authority + Health Authority + Education Authority	Local Authority + Health Authority + Probation Service	Health Authority	Area Review Committee
5	1	6	11	1	2	1	8

reflected in the selected information contained in the reports and the way it was organised. In some cases, detail about the family and the chronology of events was sparse. Other reports contained much information but scattered about in various sections, so that we needed to make copious notes and interweave the events in our own write-ups in order to make coherent sense of the unfolding story. It was clear that the inquiry panels did not have a common framework as a basis for their task.

We were particularly surprised that so many of the reports lacked what was, for us, basic and essential information. For example, we had hoped to find details about the parents' upbringing which might help us understand their later behaviour. Instead, many reports began their account with the birth of the fatally abused child, as though previous history had no relevance for what followed. We do not know the ages of sixteen caretakers held responsible for a child's death and the ages of the child's siblings were often omitted so that we could not be sure of the structure of the family. We tended to find significantly less information about a non-abusing parent, as though that person was considered less relevant to the process.

We emphasised in the previous chapter how important the wider context is to understanding interpersonal behaviour. Unfortunately, much relevant contextual information about the families and professionals, such as their socio-economic status and racial and cultural backgrounds, was largely omitted from the reports. It was therefore not possible to explore these factors and include them in our review.

With each report, we organised whatever information it contained into a chronology of the events leading up to the child's death. In order to map out important, intra-familial relationships we constructed a genogram of the family as it was at the time of the child's death (see Appendix). We included such information as the ages of the parents and children, dates of separations, divorces, deaths, etc. as far as was possible from the available data. We studied the genogram and drew together preliminary ideas about the family. For example, we were interested in what was known about the parents' families of origin, about their own experience of caretaking and upbringing and the quality of their relationships with their own parents. We wondered how they had come to leave home, how the couple had come together and their emotional relationships as adults and as partners. As we read through each chronology we tried to piece together possible links between people and events to make a coherent, inter-actional story. We were especially interested to arrive at some overview of the interactional patterns between the family members, between professional groups and between the family and involved professionals.

We recognised that our review was subjective and did not have the more objective rigours of a 'scientific' study. However, within this limitation and guided by our systemic approach we attempted to draw inferences from a non-blaming position. In other words, we viewed all information as equally relevant to the overall picture of each case and no one person as solely responsible for the tragedy.

We were aware from the outset of the emotive nature of the material we would be reading. As we embarked on each report we knew that we were moving relentlessly towards the death of a child. We expected that this would provoke strong emotions in us despite our previous professional training and present academic interest. We were, perhaps, unprepared for the strength of feeling we experienced, of disgust, of anger and of sadness, together with a wish to criticise and to blame someone. At times, we felt flooded by painful material and at other times the cases seemed to merge together so that we forgot all details about individual families. We wondered how common this experience might be amongst workers in day-to-day contact with such cases.

We tried to start hypothesising afresh on each new case and not let ideas from previous discussions prejudice our views. Having read and discussed all thirty-five reports, the next stage was to look for patterns which seemed to be common to them. We were gradually able to condense these patterns down into a number of recurring themes, which we shall present and illustrate in the chapters which follow.

First, though, it is necessary to consider whether these thirty-five selected cases, occurring over a sixteen-year period, might be too atypical to provide lessons that can be applied to everyday practice. By contrast, the names of some 23,000 children are newly entered each year on Child Protection Registers in England (Creighton and Noyes 1989), over 41,000 children are registered at any one time (Department of Health 1990) and an estimated three children a week die from abuse or neglect at the hands of their caretakers (Creighton and Gallagher 1988). While recognising that the tragedies we reviewed were extraordinary, such extremes have always been the ultimate guide of professional practice. Professionals are not only expected to have the skills to deal with common problems but also an awareness of what might constitute dangerous develop-ments and the ability to respond appropriately to extreme crises if and when they occur. It is these skills of monitoring risks, minimising their likelihood but also knowing how to intervene when the situation is dangerous that distinguishes professional from other practice. Furthermore, we shall show that the thirty-five cases of child abuse deaths we reviewed had a number of significant features in common with all such deaths from a defined population (Greenland 1987) and it seems reasonable, therefore, to draw some general inferences from our study.

SUMMARY

The authors undertook a project to review thirty-five fatal child abuse inquiry reports published between 1973 and 1989. The cases at the centre of the inquiries were re-analysed using systemic and other relevant theories in order to discover whether new lessons could be learned about the tragedies. According to the systemic approach, events are most usefully understood in terms of their participation within a network of inter-related events. In practice, attempts are made to understand how historical and contextual factors influence an individual's current relationships and behaviour. This framework enabled us to re-examine the cases from a non-blaming perspective and identify themes common to them.

Chapter 4

The families

Our principal intention in reviewing the thirty-five inquiry reports was to look for common themes between the cases. We shall begin in this chapter by bringing together information about the families at the centre of the reports and describing their composition, relationships and parenting behaviour. We shall then suggest how the abuse of the children might be understood within the context of these family relationships.

We are not able to give a comprehensive picture of the thirty-five families because, as we have already noted, a number of the reports failed to record basic information. For example, some began the chronology of events with the birth of the child who was later killed, so that we were unable to obtain an impression of the historical influences on family relationships. When one caretaker was held responsible for the death there was often minimal information about the partner, as though the relationship between them was not relevant.

We are careful not to assume that the cases we reviewed are representative of the problem in general, because only a small number of children who are abused die and only a fraction of such deaths become the subject of a public inquiry. However, some data are available from a defined population which usefully can be compared with ours. They are from a study by Greenland (1987), who was able to collate information about all known child abuse deaths between 1973 and 1982 in Ontario, a cohort of 100 cases. We have processed some of his findings and shall present them alongside ours to show that there are a number of similarities between the two groups. Other studies in the United States (see Schloesser *et al.* 1991) are also consistent with this pattern.

FAMILY STRUCTURE

The structure of the families is most vividly illustrated by the genograms in the Appendix. One of the most striking features is the complex and often fluctuating nature of their membership, including multiple relationships, partners separating and coming together again and children conceived from a number of different liaisons.

As an example, **Paul Brown**'s mother, Pauline Brown, married David Brown in 1970 and, although she remained married to him, they only had intermittent contact through the years and did not live together for more than a few weeks until 1976. In the meantime, Pauline had liaisons with at least three other men, two of which resulted in the births of Paul and Liam. She always referred to David Brown as the father of the boys even though he took no parental role. Eventually, Pauline and David Brown removed the two boys from their foster home and placed them with David's parents and it was in this household that Paul was killed and Liam seriously physically abused.

The mothers of **Lester Chapman** and **Lucie Gates** had children from four different partners and the mothers of **Graham Bagnall, Kimberley Carlile, Maria Colwell** and **Gemma Hartwell** had children from three different relationships.

Although half (nineteen = 54 per cent) of the caretakers were married at the time of their child's death – see Table 4.1 – this is only an apparent stability, since the families tended to have histories of considerable mobility. In addition, many of the children were temporarily placed outside the household with the extended family, previous partners or in the care of social services. One of the most complex families was **Maria Colwell**'s, in which the mother had ten children from three different partners. Some of these children were placed with their maternal grandparents, others were taken into the care of social services, some lived permanently within the household and Maria was placed with her paternal aunt and uncle until finally returning to her mother and step-father where she was killed.

At the time of their death, most of the children (thirty = 86 per cent) had at least one natural parent involved in their care and over half (nineteen = 54 per cent) were cared for exclusively by their natural parent/s – see Table 4.2. Step-parents were involved in the care of eleven (31 per cent) of the children. **Paul Brown** was placed with his step-grandparents and four children were in foster or adoptive families: **Richard Clark, Gavin Mabey, Christopher Pinder/ Daniel Frankland** and **Shirley Woodcock**.

Table 4.3 shows the relationship between the child killed and the caretaker/s held responsible for the death. Natural parents were involved in the deaths of twenty-five (71 per cent) of the children and a natural parent was held exclusively responsible for nineteen (54 per cent). Step-parents were involved in a minority of the deaths (eleven = 31 per cent) and were held exclusively responsible for

Table 4.1 Marital status of the caretaker/s of the children who died (at the times of their birth and death)

Status	At time of child's birth	At time of child's death
Married	15 (43%)	19 (54%)
Cohabiting	11 (31%)	10 (29%)
Liaison	7 (20%)	N/A
Separated	0	6 (17%)
Not known	2 (6%)	0

only five (14 per cent). Table 4.3 also contains Greenland's figures for the caretakers held responsible for the children's deaths in Ontario and the similarity between the two groups is striking.

Table 4.2 Caretaker/s of the children at the times of their death

		Natural parent/s only	Natural parent/s involved	Step-parent only	Step-parent involved	Substitute caretaker/s
Father	2	} 54%				
Mother	4					
Moter and father	13		} 86%			
Mother and step-father	10					
Father and step-mother	1				} 31%	
Step-father only	0			} 0%		
Step-mother only	0					
Substitute caretaker/s	5					14%

Table 4.3 Relationship between the children and the caretaker/s held responsible for their deaths (equivalent figures from Greenland's Ontario study, 1987, given in parentheses)

		Natural parent/s only	Natural parent/s involved	Step-parent only	Step-parent involved	Substitute caretaker/s
Father	7	} 54% (63%)				
Mother	8					
Mother and father	4		} 71% (71%)			
Mother and step-father	5					
Father and step-mother	1				} 31% (29%)	
Step-father only	5			} 14% (18%)		
Step-mother only	0					
Substitute caretaker/s	5					14% (9%)

THE CHILDREN

Information about the children themselves was sometimes very sketchy as the reports concentrated on the events leading up to and surrounding their deaths.

Of the thirty-five children, nineteen were boys and sixteen were girls. The majority of the children were pre-schoolers. The youngest was **Claire Haddon**, aged 10 weeks when she died, and the oldest child was **Lester Chapman**, aged 8 years 9 months – see Figure 4.1. Six (18 per cent) of the children were below the age of 1 year and thirty-one (91 per cent) were younger than 6 years. **Max Piazzani**'s age was not given but the description is of a baby or toddler. **Stephen Menheniott** was included in our project despite the fact that he was 19 years old when he died. Excluding **Max Piazzani** and **Stephen Menheniott**, the mean age of the children at the time of their death was 2 years 7 months, and including **Stephen Menheniott** the mean was 3 years 1 month. The Ontario group were somewhat younger, with 57 per cent of the victims aged below 1 year and 95 per cent younger than 6 years.

Because the composition of these families often fluctuated over time, we worked out the sibling position of the child who died in relation to the household at the time of death. This was not known for three of the five children who were killed in substitute families. Table 4.4 shows that a majority (66 per cent) of the children who died were the youngest or only child of the household. Of the Ontario children 88 per cent were the youngest of the family.

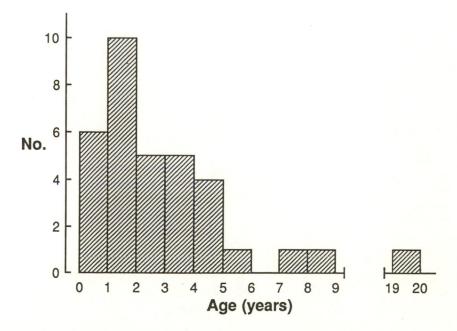

Figure 4.1 Age of the fatally abused children (known for 34 children)

Table 4.4 Position in the household of the children who died (household composition at the time of death only known in 32 cases)

Eldest	*'Middle'*	*Youngest*	*Only child*
5	6	10	11

21
(66%)

THE CARETAKERS

Most of the caretakers were aged between 20 and 29 years at the time of the child's death (71 per cent, compared with 67 per cent in Ontario) with an average age of 24.6 years – see Figure 4.2.

The **Shirley Woodcock** report does not make it clear who was charged with her death. With this exception, twenty-five men and twenty-one women were held legally responsible for a child's death.

The family background or personal characteristics of the caretakers were not always given. Some of the abusing parents had themselves clearly experienced severe abuse and deprivation as children. A typical example was **Jasmine Beckford**'s mother who had been deserted by her mother when aged only 6 months and her father and step-mother punished her so excessively that she ran

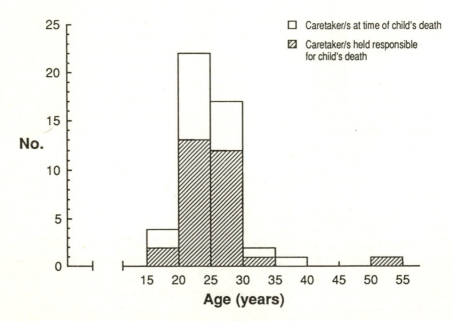

Figure 4.2 Age of the caretaker/s at the time of the children's death

away from home. In addition, Jasmine's step-father was looked after by his grandmother for most of the first nine years of his life and when he rejoined his nuclear family he was severely beaten and neglected and forced to sleep in the woodshed. He was taken into care at the age of 13. **Lisa Godfrey**'s mother was from a family of twelve children and when her parents divorced she lived in a children's home for three years. Her mother remarried and when they were reunited her mother caused her to become partially deaf through repeated blows to the head.

However, we believed that the absence of such a history in some of the reports was misleading. For example, at her criminal trial, **Doreen Aston**'s mother gave evidence that she had been sexually abused by her own father (*Guardian* 22 December 1988) but this history is not contained in the inquiry report (see Chapter 10).

We do know that some of the parents were of limited intelligence. **Graham Bagnall**'s step-father and **Jasmine Beckford**'s mother and step-father had attended schools for educationally subnormal children. **Paul Brown**'s mother was described as having a mental age of 10 following meningitis as a child and **Simon Peacock**'s mother had learning difficulties. Similar descriptions are made of the mothers of **Richard Fraser** and **Malcolm Page**, the mothers and fathers of **Karen Spencer** and the **anonymous** baby and the foster-mother of **Richard Clark**.

Dependent relationships

Parents who show difficulty parenting their children have been described as having had their caring and dependency needs unmet in earlier life so that they are easily overwhelmed by demands for care from others (e.g. Steele 1970). The thirty-five case histories suggested that most of the caretakers suffered from conflicts about unmet dependency, which became manifest in various ways. Sometimes this was evident from professionals' assessments of them: for example, a health visitor reported that **Lucie Gates**' mother 'needed a grandma figure 24 hours a day' and the official inquiry report refers to **Paul Brown**'s mother as 'an emotionally immature wayward girl'.

For other caretakers, the pattern of their relationships gives an impression of their dependency conflicts. For example, **Tyra Henry**'s mother, Claudette Henry, seemed to sustain an ambivalently dependent contact with her mother and an ambiguous attitude to her own role as a parent. Claudette began to truant from school when her mother started to work and it may be that she found herself precipitated into a parentified role towards her younger siblings. She became pregnant soon after. Later, she made efforts to acquire a flat of her own yet spent much of her time back with her mother or living with Tyra's father, Andrew Neil, and his family, taking Tyra with her. Andrew Neil mirrored many of her own conflicts, for he had lost his mother at the age of 7 and as a child had shown severe separation anxieties.

Unresolved separation from family of origin appears in many of the histories. **Doreen Aston**'s mother and step-father periodically fought, separated and went back to live with their own parents. They then returned to each other, only to repeat the cycle. **Simon Peacock**'s parents were neighbours in a small village but there was a strained relationship between their families. Christina and Colin Peacock married when she was already pregnant with Simon but for a while after the marriage each still lived with his or her own parents. They eventually accepted an offer of a home close to Colin's family, which Colin's father had requested from the local authority. Simon was killed three weeks after the young family moved in but his injuries were consistent with abuse of three to four weeks' duration. We conjectured that the pregnancy with Simon was an attempted solution to his parents' 'leaving home' dilemma, as described by Haley (1980). However, his birth followed by their move placed them in a new conflict between being autonomous adults with a dependent baby to look after as opposed to dependent children themselves who were still attached to their families of origin.

Many of the mothers started to have children at a young age. Unfortunately, only twenty-two of the reports contained information which allowed us to calculate when the natural mothers first bore a child. In those cases, the average age of the mothers was 18.5 years. The youngest was **Lester Chapman**'s mother who bore her first child at the age of 14; **Claire Haddon**'s mother was 15 years old; **Wayne Brewer**'s and **Tyra Henry**'s mothers were aged 16 and the mothers of **Steven Meurs, Malcolm Page** and the **anonymous** child were 17 when they had their first baby.

There are various possible explanations for this. Becoming pregnant can be an attempt to leave home and escape from a conflictual, abusive or deprived family life. For example, **Claire Haddon**'s mother was a 15-year-old who had lost her own mother through parental separation and whose father seems to have been emotionally absent. She refused to go to school and then ran away with her older sister and was later found cohabiting with a 20-year-old man by whom she was pregnant.

Pregnancies can be the unplanned consequence of sexual contacts that are meant to satisfy wishes for cuddles and physical affection (Pines 1972). There was evidence of considerable ambivalence to or rejection of some pregnancies, possibly because the expectation of the baby's dependency was too threatening. **Maria Mehmedagi** was reported to be an unplanned pregnancy. **Wayne Brewer**'s mother considered termination of her pregnancy with him and **Lisa Godfrey**'s mother wanted termination of the baby she was carrying when she killed Lisa. **Lucie Gates'** mother had her first child adopted and considered adoption for her second baby. The mothers of **Neil Howlett, Doreen Aston, Simon Peacock, Charlene Salt, Carly Taylor** and **Shirley Woodcock** had minimal or no ante-natal care during those pregnancies and **Richard Fraser**'s step-mother refused ante-natal care during a subsequent pregnancy. **Carly Taylor**'s mother discharged herself from hospital, leaving the twins in the special care baby unit, and the prematurely born **Claire Haddon** was left in hospital by her mother who gave a false home address. The mothers of **Doreen Aston**, **Maria Mehmedagi** and **Shirley Woodcock** also discharged themselves from the post-natal ward against advice.

Alternatively, pregnancies can be planned with the unacknowledged expectation that the baby will provide the loving care that the mother felt that she had not received herself as a child and still longs for (Pines 1972). Of course, in reality a baby can never fulfil such hopes and this might be why some mothers have baby after baby, such as **Maria Colwell**'s who had ten children and **Malcolm Page**'s mother who was pregnant with her fifth child when Malcolm died.

Parents who are already suffering from unmet dependency needs are likely to find that the actual presence of a dependent infant readily reawakens their underlying sense of deprivation. In addition, we noted that some of the children had special needs that placed even greater demands on their caretakers. **Susan Aukland**, **Wayne Brewer**, **Kimberley Carlile** and **Claire Haddon** were premature babies and **Carly Taylor** was of low birth weight because she was a twin. Feeding difficulties were shown by **Stephen Menheniott**, **Simon Peacock**, **Christopher Pinder/Daniel Frankland**, **Karen Spencer** and the **anonymous** baby. **Maria Mehmedagi** had pyloric stenosis, as did **Paul Brown**'s younger brother and **Reuben Carthy**'s younger brother. The extra demands that the young children made on the parents are likely to have provoked intolerable feelings of helplessness, frustration and anger, leading to physical abuse. In nearly two-thirds of the households (twenty-two = 63 per cent) there was a child below the age of 2 years when the fatal abuse occurred and in ten (29 per cent) there was a child under 12 months – see Figure 4.3. In three households (9 per cent) the mother was pregnant again when the child was killed, compared with 4 per cent in Ontario.

We believe that some parents showed their sense of deprivation by requesting to have their children returned home from care after someone else declared a strong interest in looking after them. This desire did not appear to be for the children in their own right but more as a 'piece of property' that would otherwise be lost. The threatened loss may have reawakened the parents' own sense of deprivation and been a reminder of their wish for the children to provide them with love and affection. **Graham Bagnall**'s mother and step-father successfully requested his return home from voluntary care when the social worker and the NSPCC officer raised the possibility of his being adopted and he was killed four weeks later. **Lucie Gates'** mother said she wanted her children back from care after their foster parents raised the possibility of adoption. The childminder who looked after **Carly Taylor** and her twin sister during their placement with their grandmother wanted to pay the mother so that she could keep them. Their mother responded by taking the children home again. The **Maria Colwell** and **Karen Spencer** cases are examples of fostering couples showing a strong attachment to the child which seemed to provoke the mothers' competitiveness and wish to have them back.

Presumably, a crisis was precipitated when these children returned home

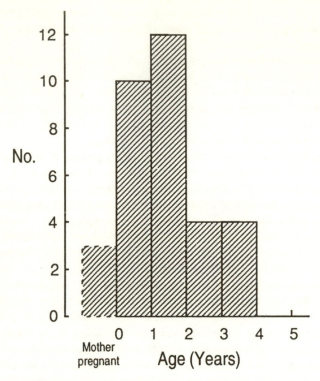

Figure 4.3 Age of the youngest child in the households at the time of the
children's death (including the dead child if s/he was also the
youngest – age not known in 2 cases)

because they were upset and anxious at the change and were in need of extra
security and dependability. **Kimberley Carlile**, for example, showed a marked
reaction to being moved from foster care to her mother and step-father, beginning
to foul and wet herself, eat faeces, make herself sick and refuse food. In addition,
children making real demands for care in their own right would have contrasted
dramatically with the fantasised children who were meant to satisfy the parents'
needs and who had become idealised objects to be acquired.

A hasty move of children can also generate stresses for both the children and
caretakers alike, with the children suddenly uprooted and the caretakers unprepared to meet their needs. **Gemma Hartwell** was returned home because her
prospective adoptive parents split up and she was killed within two weeks. **Gavin
Mabey** and his brother were placed with foster parents just three days after they
had been approved by the fostering panel. **Shirley Woodcock**'s mother
abandoned her children when the father was sent to prison and they were placed
with three different sets of foster parents over a short space of time because all
found them too difficult to manage. The final placement, where Shirley was

killed, was arranged at short notice and the couple had not been fully assessed. When he was 9 days old, **Christopher Pinder/Daniel Frankland** was placed with a childless couple who had been approved for adoption just four days previously. They had been told initially that their chances of getting a baby were very remote. They had no time to prepare for him and the mother had difficulty adapting to his needs, especially his feeding problems. Despite her expressed anxieties, the adoption was pushed forward and he was killed two days before the adoption hearing.

Many of the family histories suggested that the parental couples were mutually dependent individuals who came together seeking dependency on each other. Finding that this was frustrated, they recurrently fought with each other, separated and then came back together or attempted a new relationship with an equally dependent partner. Possibly, they also looked to the children to satisfy their needs and attacked them when this was not forthcoming.

The children were particularly in danger at times of crisis in the couples' relationships and especially when dependency was threatened by loss, separation or withdrawal of support. For example, **Susan Aukland**'s mother was considered immature and incompetent by her husband, while he in turn behaved as a chronic invalid and had long periods off work being cared for by his wife. After many separations, Susan's mother finally left the family and Susan was killed by her father four months later. **Steven Meurs'** father was imprisoned three months before Stephen died and **Reuben Carthy**'s father had left home about two months before his mother killed Reuben. **Karen Spencer**'s parents, Marilyn and David Spencer, were of low intelligence, described as emotionally immature and had a stormy and violent marriage. They separated a number of times but came back together again. Marilyn took two overdoses during the first two years of their marriage and became increasingly depressed, turning to her general practitioner, a paediatrician, her father and the social worker for help. Karen was fatally assaulted by her mother two weeks after her official return home on trial from care, on the day David Spencer left Marilyn early in the morning to go fishing after they had had a row the previous day.

An additional way that some parents seek to satisfy dependency needs is through reliance on drugs or alcohol. However, this usually exacerbates tensions in the family, including increasing the likelihood of violence. There were histories of drug or alcohol dependency in the families of **Jason Caesar** (his mother and father), **Wayne Brewer** (his step-father), **Paul Brown** (his mother), **Richard Clark** (his mother and foster mother were drinking partners), **Carly Taylor** (her mother and father), **Susan Aukland** (her father) and the **anonymous baby** (his father).

Violent relationships

A second theme recurring through the caretakers' histories was a proneness to violence. A number of them had previously subjected other children of theirs to physical abuse. **Susan Aukland**'s father had been imprisoned for killing his first daughter aged 9 weeks and he scalded his next child so badly that he required two months hospitalisation. **Doreen Aston**'s mother admitted smothering her first baby and **Tyra Henry**'s father previously had been charged with an assault on the couple's first child, which had left him severely mentally handicapped and blind. **Stephen Menheniott**'s father had been imprisoned for neglect of his first two children and then imprisoned for ill-treatment of his next two. He was described as 'bitterly anti-authority' and 'an aggressive psychopath' and had beaten up a number of his sons and a boyfriend of one of his daughters. **Gemma Hartwell**'s father had first been imprisoned for assault to his daughter by his first wife when she was aged 3 weeks and again for harming his second wife's 2½-year-old daughter from a previous marriage. **Maria Mehmedagi**'s father had previously been convicted of actual bodily harm to her.

Even more common than histories of aggression to children was recurrent violence between the partners, which was reported in at least half of the cases. Often it was aggression by the male partner who was known to have an unpredictably violent temper. Some parents seemed particularly prone to choose partners with propensity to violence. **Lester Chapman**'s mother had previously had a miscarriage following physical assault by a man friend. **Lucie Gates'** mother was badly beaten up by the boyfriend she was hoping to marry. **Kimberley Carlile**'s mother had had two previous marriages with violent men and then cohabited with Nigel Hall. **Tyra Henry**'s father not only had a history of sudden rages towards children but had been convicted of actual bodily harm to adults: Tyra's mother repeatedly returned to live with him and in the final weeks of Tyra's life he was violent to the two of them. The first husband of **Richard Clark**'s mother was killed in a brawl and she later stabbed Richard's father and was charged with attempted murder.

Only a few reports gave an indication of the precursors of parental violence but what evidence there was suggested that it was an attempt to control or punish anyone perceived as a threat to self-esteem. **Lester Chapman**'s father assaulted Lester's mother after she had revealed to him that she had started divorce proceedings. A social work report on **Richard Fraser**'s family commented: 'potential violence, especially when pressure from other agencies' and the social worker undertook 'low profile' visiting because she feared violence to herself. Richard's father was twice imprisoned for violence, once to a woman police constable who returned Richard to hospital on a Place of Safety Order after the father and the step-mother had forcibly removed him. He also beat up the step-mother when she threatened to leave him. The mother of the **anonymous** baby was reported to have a history of violence when feeling unsupported and later assaulted the social worker. Other parents assaulted professionals, including **David Naseby**'s father (nursing staff), **Carly Taylor**'s mother (staff of a homeless families hostel), **Darryn Clarke**'s step-father (a police officer) and **Jason Caesar**'s mother (a police officer). **Maria Colwell**'s step-father threatened violence to a visiting educational welfare officer.

There were occasional stories of apparent rages of frustration by parents who experienced events happening out of their control. This frustration was particularly pronounced when the mother and child were in hospital and it was as though the partner was desperate for them to return home to within his ambit of control. **Heidi Koseda**'s step-father banged his head against the wall of the hospital when told his wife's pregnancy would be induced: he had previously had a violent outburst on the ante-natal ward. **Shirley Woodcock**'s father created a disturbance on the post-natal ward when he found his wife had discharged herself. **Simon Peacock**'s father angrily demanded both mother and baby's discharge from hospital and **Charlene Salt**'s father insisted on taking the mother and baby home ten hours after the birth. Later, when Charlene was in hospital on a Place of Safety Order, he refused to let her mother stay visiting alone.

PATTERNS OF ABUSE

We can describe three principal patterns of abuse occurring in the families which resulted in the children's deaths. We have designated them: 'Violence', 'Neglect' and 'Not Existing'. These patterns were not mutually exclusive and most children who died as a result of parental violence also experienced considerable neglect and emotional abuse. A few children were chronically neglected without accompanying violence. Three children died when they were shut away as though they no longer existed in their parents' minds and they perished from malnutrition and hypothermia. Thirty (86 per cent) of the children died from violence, compared with 76 per cent in the Ontario study.

Violent abuse

The majority of the children we read about had been beaten, bruised and sometimes tortured for a long time prior to their deaths. In some instances their injuries had already led to hospital admissions. **Jasmine Beckford** and her sister Louise were taken into care following admission to hospital with fractures but they were later returned to their family. This also occurred with **Graham Bagnall** and his brother Neil, **Karen Spencer** and **Maria Mehmedagi**. **Jason Caesar** and **Reuben Carthy** had both been treated for fractures prior to their deaths and **Kimberley Carlile**'s mother and step-father actively concealed her fractured leg from the visiting social worker. The commonest evidence of this abuse was recurrent bruising around the child's head or body. **Darryn Clarke**'s physical injuries were particularly horrifying and included severe burns to his legs. Darryn's step-father also locked him in a cupboard, forced him to drink lager and tied up his penis and put a cork in his anus to stop his incontinence and forced Darryn to sit on the potty for hours.

Most of these children also had been subjected to emotional abuse and neglect, including malnutrition, being left alone, lying unchanged in filthy nappies when a baby and living in squalid conditions. **Jasmine Beckford** and her sister showed significant failure to thrive with slow physical growth and poor weight gain and a number of the children and their siblings wet or soiled themselves, another common indicator of emotional stress. **Kimberley Carlile** had experienced a long period of starvation leading up to her death and **Maria Colwell** was often left locked in her bedroom and she lost a considerable amount of weight in the last months of her life as well as looking listless, apathetic and withdrawn.

When the children were in temporary alternative care there was often a contrast between their growth, development and contentment with the foster parents compared with at home: for example, **Jasmine Beckford** and **Maria Colwell**. This sometimes showed when they went home from foster care for weekends on trial. **Karen Spencer** twice returned to her foster parents after such a weekend with her bottom sore and bleeding from urine burns.

We postulated that psychologically these children's existence was acknowledged by their caretakers but not through the giving of care. It seems likely that the children subjected to violent parenting repeatedly asserted their needs and their dependency only to find their caretakers unable to meet them. The children's immaturity would have been experienced by the parents as an intolerable extra demand that competed with the parents' own dependency wishes. Frustration and violence to the children then resulted. For example, **Wayne Brewer**'s step-father hit him for wetting his nappy twice in quick succession and wetting the settee, while **Darryn Clarke**'s step-father could not even tolerate him playing with toys in the flat. **Lisa Godfrey** regressed in her bladder and bowel control after an operation and her mother repeatedly assaulted her over subsequent months.

Neglect

Severe and chronic neglect was the predominant form of abuse by a number of caretakers, including those of **Paul Brown, Lester Chapman, Lucie Gates** and **Max Piazzani**. In addition, **Shirley Woodcock** was neglected by her natural mother before being taken into foster care, where she died of physical abuse. **Neil Howlett**'s story is typical, with repeated calls to the NSPCC about the Howlett children living in filthy conditions, looking starved and being left alone at home and Neil showed a typical sign of emotional deprivation in his head-banging.

These caretakers showed the same deprived and dependent characteristics as those who abused physically but their customary response to their children's demands appeared to be dismissal of them rather than violent frustration and subordination of the children's emotional and physical needs to their own. As an example, **Charlene Salt**'s parents were often in bed when professionals called in the late mornings and baby Charlene was left dirty, hungry and bruised. Their social worker gave the parents money for baby food, blankets and clothing but they used it to buy themselves a car.

In this pattern of chronic neglect, the acute fatal episode was sometimes extreme violence, perhaps when the child did assert his/her presence and needs.

For example, **Paul Brown** and his brother Liam were both severely neglected by their step-paternal grandparents with whom their mother had left them. Although Paul died from severe violence, his body was emaciated and filthy and Liam was found to be verminous and ravenously hungry, unsteady on his legs and below the third percentile for physical development.

Two cases of chronic neglect ended with fatal accidents that could have been avoided. **Lester Chapman** was physically abused as well as emotionally neglected and rejected and his parents repeatedly asked for him to be taken into care or adopted. He threatened to kill himself at least twice. Lester ran away from home a number of times and on the final occasion he fell into sewage sludge and died from exposure and suffocation. **Lucie Gates** was the youngest of three children remaining with their single mother. All of them were hospitalised suffering from recurrent chest infections, weight loss, ingestion of rat poison or their mother's pills, having fallen from scaffolding or with burns, cuts or fractures from other accidents. They were often left alone in a house without food, were under-stimulated, had infected scabies and nits and their nappies were changed infrequently. Their mother often failed to collect them from school and when they were babies she tried to feed them with crisps, pepsi-cola and congealed milk (see Chapter 8). One evening the children were left at home alone and Lucie, aged 2, died when an electric fire fell on her.

Unfortunately, the inquiry reports give little information that might allow us to understand what precipitated the fatal episodes in these cases. However, we do know something about **Lucie Gates**. The evening that Lucie and her siblings were left alone again, the family had just returned from a visit to the zoo. In studying the whole case we found a pattern of Lucie's mother reacting to 'idealised' family occasions (such as Christmas gatherings) with a sense of let-down, following which her neglect of the children increased. Perhaps these idealised family occasions reawakened in the mother her own sense of deprivation and neglect and she was then unable to put her children's needs before her own.

Not existing

Three cases involved complete absence of child caretaking that is the most difficult to understand psychologically (see Chapter 9). Some of the children described above who were severely neglected or assaulted were also left locked in their rooms for long periods (for example, **Maria Colwell**), but here the children were completely shut away from the world outside and from the family indoors, as though their very existence was unacceptable. Basic human needs of food and warmth were denied them until life ceased. The children must surely have asserted their existence by crying for nurturance which the parents must have ignored, both practically and psychologically. This not existing pattern did not occur throughout the children's lives but a transitional event in the family heralded its onset. Of the three, **Steven Meurs** and **Malcolm Page** had been previously neglected but the earlier caretaking of **Heidi Koseda** was apparently unremarkable.

Heidi Koseda began to be neglected when her parents separated and her mother started to cohabit with Nicholas Price. The new family became more and more reclusive over the next year and Heidi was rarely seen by the neighbours. She died of starvation when her mother was eight months pregnant and the chronology of events suggests that Heidi was increasingly shut away from the onset of that pregnancy. Heidi's body lay in her bedroom for two months after her death, ignored by her mother and step-father who told concerned workers that she was staying with friends.

Steven Meurs' mother recurrently left her children alone for long periods or let others look after them. Her profound neglect of Steven entered the phase of not existing coincident with two events: Steven's father was imprisoned and simultaneously his mother agreed to look after two older children of a distant relative. At times, she left all the children alone at night but Steven was left alone in an upstairs room most of the time, filthy, unfed and understimulated and he died of malnutrition. The closest we can conjecture about this case is that, in the absence of her husband, Steven's mother felt deprived and abandoned and when she agreed to take in the two older children it was so that they might support her. However, this sudden change in their lives upset them (they had begun to wet the bed and refused to go to school) so that they needed to make large demands of her. The mother's sense of deprivation would have been exacerbated, leaving her more preoccupied by her own needs instead of being able to keep her youngest child in mind.

In the **Malcolm Page** case, all four children were severely neglected: their bedrooms were full of faeces and their beds soaked with urine. However Malcolm, the youngest child, experienced the worst neglect; he suffered a number of weeks of malnutrition followed by acute starvation and he died of malnutrition and hypothermia. His mother was about one month pregnant at the time of Malcolm's death and we estimated that the acute period of complete starvation began when she learned that she was pregnant. Malcolm was the youngest child (14 months old when he died) and it may be that his existence was totally ignored when his mother had a new pregnancy to deal with.

SYNTHESIS

We can now condense our observations and ideas about the thirty-five families into an overall framework which allows an understanding of the abusive behaviour – see Figure 4.4.

A general principle of good-enough parenting is that it requires appropriate demonstrations of 'care' and 'control', as well as an adequate balance between the two. Care involves anticipating the child's age-appropriate needs and providing for them through ante-natal care, feeding, warmth and protection (Kelmer Pringle 1978). The child must be wanted and treated as a person in his/her own right, whose feelings are respected and are of concern to the parent.

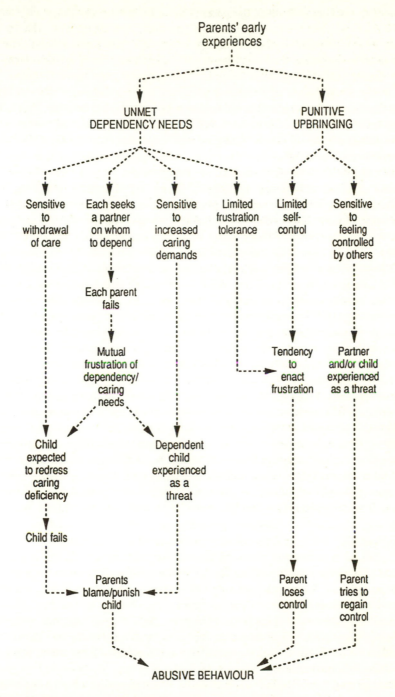

Figure 4.4 Care and control conflicts in abusive behaviour

In order to provide such care, the parents must be able to put the child's needs above their own and tolerate the child's immaturity and dependency (Reder and Lucey 1991). Control involves ensuring the child's safety and setting limits to behaviour in a caring way consistent with the child's level of development. Control must avoid being punitive and the parent must exercise self-control.

Clearly, these facets of parenting are inter-related and parenting problems often can be seen as an inability to maintain an equilibrium between them. This is particularly so for adults who have suffered punitive controls and unmet caring needs during childhood. Their frustrated care experiences make them especially vulnerable to threatened losses of supportive relationships, threats to self-esteem or extra dependency demands made on them by others. Any of these stresses can provoke extreme anxiety and feelings of being out of control, resulting in an explosion of anger or attempts to punish or control the person evoking the insecurity. Usually, this is through impulsive violence but in addition the parent may try to prevent such feelings being stirred up by distancing the source of the threats, either by removing themselves and neglecting the child or by shutting the child away. Hence, violent, neglectful or not existing forms of child abuse occur.

The relationships we have described in the thirty-five families suggest such care and control conflicts in many of the caretakers, although they showed in different ways. For instance, leaving home in a crisis as an attempted solution to caring problems in the families of origin which were experienced as depriving or rejecting; young parents who recurrently returned to live with their original families as they struggled to resolve feelings that their caring needs had still not been met; or repeated changes of partners to avoid becoming dependent on anyone who might later leave or to prevent others becoming dependent on them. It is possible that mothers who became pregnant at an early age were unwittingly seeking to satisfy unmet dependency needs by looking for love and care from the children. However, absence of ante- or post-natal care indicated considerable ambivalence to the babies and their vulnerability, as did intolerance of the young infants' demands. Drug and alcohol abuse not only implied dependency conflicts but also problems with control, since the parents' self-control was recurrently impaired and responsibility and the locus of control externalised. Proneness to violence, whether to children, partners or professionals and sometimes exaggerated by drink, again pointed to problems of impulse control.

Contributory stresses in many of the families may have been the caretakers' limited intelligence or poverty but factors in the children themselves added to the problems. Some children had feeding difficulties or were born into a household already containing young and dependent children. Others regressed as a result of stressful experiences in their lives. However, their chronic neglect must have increased their anxiety and demands for security and dependency. This in turn added to the difficulties of their caretakers and generated even more neglectful and abusive behaviour.

This general formulation leads inevitably to the questions of why one child of a family was killed rather than another and whether there was anything specific about the children who died. We shall address these questions in the following chapter.

SUMMARY

Our underlying premise has been that child abuse occurs at times of critical stress in the relationships of vulnerable parents. There was much to support this in the histories of the thirty-five families, in which the parents showed emotional immaturity and/or dependency, often combined with problems about frustration tolerance and impulse control. Violence, neglect and not existing were the three patterns of abuse we identified, with some overlap between them. All were chronic patterns of parenting which ended either in a fatal episode of extreme violence, an avoidable accident or the child's actual existence ceasing. The fatal episodes were probably precipitated by extra dependency demands placed upon the parents, such as threatened separation between the couple, regression of the child or the presence of a young and needy infant in the family. Some parents gave warning signals of an impending crisis but the link is only clearly evident in retrospect. Greenland's Ontario study (1987) of 100 child abuse deaths shows similarities in a number of areas to the thirty-five cases reviewed.

Chapter 5

The meaning of the child

A child can mean different things to different parents. Traditionally, a child is considered to carry the hopes and aspirations of the parents, who are prepared to sacrifice some of their own personal gratifications to further the child's development. However, the vicissitudes of family life always colour the picture and many factors can influence the meaning that parents attribute to children generally, or to one child in particular. As a result of these influences, but without the family necessarily being aware of it, the child acquires an undeclared 'script' or 'blueprint' for his/her life that is consistent with the themes of the family but may submerge his/her personal characteristics. This has been described by Britton (personal communication) as: 'being an actor in someone else's play'.

Family therapists have discussed how influences from a family's past may distort the meaning of relationships in the present and examples of the therapeutic use of such theories can be found in the writings of Byng-Hall (1979, 1985) and Lieberman (1979), amongst others. In particular, a significant interest of the Milan associates (e.g. Selvini Palazzoli *et al.* 1978; Boscolo *et al.* 1987) has been the hidden meanings attributed to family members that are built up from historical and contemporary relationship patterns.

One example of such influences might be a child who becomes associated with the emotions accompanying a particular event, having been born at the same time. For instance, a child may be born just after a grandparent dies, an experience which leaves the parent/s devastated and unable to invest emotionally in a baby. The parents might blame the child for their feelings of loss and unhappiness. Alternatively, the child may be expected to support the parent/s and fill the emotional void, even by replacing the role of the lost figure and taking on the grandparent's identity. Of course, this task is not only impossible for the child but is the reverse of the support and dependability needed from the parent. The child is both allotted a specific meaning within the family and is doomed to fail in that role.

THE MEANING OF THE CHILD IN ABUSING FAMILIES

There is a popular belief that one child in a family is singled out and maltreated, probably as a result of the **Maria Colwell** case in which Maria was said to be rejected, scapegoated and treated very differently from her siblings. In fact, all the children in the Colwell household were severely neglected and Maria's 5-year-old half-sister was also physically abused. Our review suggests that violence or neglect was often a general caretaking pattern. There were twenty-three households known to have contained other children at the time of the fatality and in twelve of these at least one other sibling was reported as also having been abused. In some instances the abuse was severe and might itself have proved fatal. **Jasmine Beckford**'s younger half-sister Louise was the first to be admitted to hospital suffering from a broken arm and retinal haemorrhages. It was the care of **Paul Brown**'s younger brother, Liam, which exercised the professionals so much, right up to the time of Paul's death. The mother's care of **Neil Howlett**'s elder brother, Stephen, had been the principal focus of professional concern. **Tyra Henry**'s father had previously assaulted Tyra's elder brother, Tyrone, so severely that Tyrone was left blind and mentally handicapped. The father of **Susan Aukland** and the mother of **Doreen Aston** were known to have killed a previous child of theirs.

Our review of these cases, therefore, does not support a contention that one child is invariably singled out for abuse. However, we are left with the questions: why were there cases in which only one child was abused; and in the households where many children were abused, why was one mistreated so badly that s/he died? Was it just chance that one child died instead of another or was there something specific about the unfortunate child which did, indeed, single him/her out?

A small number of the fatalities might be considered chance. **Lucie Gates'** mother left all of her children alone the night that she died and presumably the electric fire could have fallen on any one of them. **Malcolm Page**'s death also might have been unrelated to any specific meaning he had for his parents. He was the youngest of four children under 6 years of age and all of them were virtually forgotten about when their mother learned she was pregnant again. However, the effects of the neglect would have been most severe for Malcolm (aged 14 months when he died) and his sister Suzanne (then aged 23 months) because they were the youngest and most vulnerable.

Nevertheless, with other children we can propose certain meanings that they had for their caretakers which contributed to their deaths. Some of the meanings we shall describe are non-specific and could arise from relationship conflicts experienced within many families. Others are specific to that particular family and reflect idiosyncrasies of their experiences. Once again, we must acknowledge that our comments are speculative and limited to the information available in the reports. Even so, we hope we shall be able to demonstrate that such conjectures have validity and value in making further sense of the cases.

MEANING RELATED TO DEPENDENCY CONFLICTS

In some families, the meaning attributed to the child can be considered within the context of the adults' unmet dependency needs. In the previous chapter we suggested that the equilibrium between care and control was precarious for many of the caretakers and that they were easily upset by anything that endangered their sense of security. They appeared to experience the children as threats in various ways.

We believe that children born to mutually interdependent parents were experienced by them as competitors for limited caring resources. The youngest and most immature child was felt to be the greatest threat and even more of a competitor at times of crisis in the couple's relationship. For example, when **Susan Aukland**'s father, John Aukland, was 3 years old, his legs were injured and he needed to be wheeled around in a pram until the age of 9. He married a woman whom he denigrated and regarded as incompetent and immature. The couple lost contact with their parents because both families disapproved of the marriage and they became emotionally dependent on each other. Throughout his adult life, John Aukland relied on prescribed drugs, alcohol, sick notes and his wife. He suffered from chronic anxiety which became even more severe at the birth of each of the couple's children. He killed Susan, the youngest child, four months after the mother finally separated from him and we infer that he experienced the 15-month-old Susan as making intolerable demands on him at a time when he felt unsupported. Six years previously, he had killed the couple's first child, aged 2 months.

Other children had special problems which must have increased their caring needs, such as **Claire Haddon**, who was born prematurely, and **Maria Mehmedagi**, who required surgery for pyloric stenosis.

We also considered that the meaning of some children was to be the unwanted consequences of sexual liaisons primarily sought to satisfy the parents' desires for physical affection. Other family histories suggested that the children had been conceived as an attempted solution to the parents' conflicts about leaving home (for example, **Simon Peacock**). Some children's significance appeared to be as 'property', wanted back by parents who refused to be deprived of them when other prospective caretakers wished to 'have' them (for example, **Graham Bagnall**, **Karen Spencer** and **Carly Taylor**).

Other babies may have been conceived in the hope that they would provide the affection that the parent had never received. Thus, before **Gemma Hartwell** was born, her mother had already had two children and each time that they were a year old she placed them with relatives. An explanation is that, as babies, they validated the mother's precarious self-esteem but when they showed early signs of autonomy, she needed to give them up and replace them with a new baby. This might also have happened to Gemma, if she had not been removed into the care of social services when only a few months old. Over the succeeding months, her mother tried to gain access to her but also became pregnant with a fourth baby. The cycle could well have restarted with this replacement child but Gemma's prospective adoptive parents split up when she was 22 months old. Gemma therefore returned to live with her mother and she was killed within a few days.

These are all variations on the theme of the child acquiring meaning within the context of dependency conflicts. Their importance is that the children's identities and infantile needs apparently were overlooked because of the roles attributed to them. Rather than being able to give consistent primacy to the children's demands for care, their caretakers perceived them as having failed to provide the expected solution and instead were experienced as an added drain on scarce emotional resources.

MEANING ASSOCIATED WITH SPECIFIC THEMES IN THE FAMILY'S LIFE

The child associated with marital stress

Sometimes, children are conceived in the unspoken hope that they will repair a deteriorating relationship between a couple. This is not only an awesome responsibility for the babies but places them in considerable danger of being blamed when they fail in the task. The children are then seen as the cause of the couple's disharmony. For example, **Lisa Godfrey**'s parents separated and reunited repeatedly during a marriage that produced three children. The eldest and youngest child were born during a phase of reconciliation between the parents but they separated for nine months following Lisa's birth. Their mother abused Lisa more persistently and severely than she did her two other children.

The child as a marital-distance regulator

Byng-Hall (1980) has described how a child can be caught up in the parents' conflicts about emotional intimacy by becoming a 'marital-distance regulator'. Parents who fear both being too close or too separate from each other tend to go through oscillating cycles in their relationship. They come together seeking mutual support but when this is frustrated they create more emotional distance between themselves. However, now feeling unsupported they try to come closer together again. If the child happens to do something that does bring the parents together (for example, being ill, so that the parents unite in their concern) followed by something that helps them separate (for example, behaving uncontrollably, so that the parents argue about how to handle it), repetitive cycles occur that maintain the distance in the parents' relationship.

We believe that **Karen Spencer** was a marital-distance regulator between her parents. Their marriage was stormy from the outset and they separated and reunited on a number of occasions. After Karen was born, she seems to have become caught up in this cycle. While Karen was living with her parents, they argued. When Karen was removed from home to a place of safety, their fighting subsided and they came closer together again. At this point they asked for Karen to be returned to them. The visiting professionals were impressed at the improvement in their relationship and agreed that this was an indication that Karen could return home. However, once she was back, her father increasingly accused her mother of incompetent care and their rows increased again. Karen was killed two weeks after her return home from care. With hindsight, we infer that her parents' renewed closeness was only possible because Karen was *not* there but as soon as they were in danger of becoming too intimate they needed her back to increase their emotional distance again.

Another example of children becoming entangled in their parents' oscillating relationship is **Lester Chapman** and his sister, Wendy. Lester and Wendy were already in care because of neglect when their mother began to live with a new partner. As soon as their mother's decree nisi was granted, she asked for the Care Orders to be revoked and the two children returned home on trial four days after the decree absolute. We wonder whether Lester and Wendy were expected to confirm for their mother that a 'better' family life had begun. However, the couple argued repeatedly about Lester and the step-father once accused the mother of hitting Lester to make his bruises worse so that she could get a divorce. On another occasion, the mother asked a social worker to visit because her husband had hit Lester: the social worker considered that she was trying to find ways to get her husband out of the house. Later, the mother instituted divorce proceedings but then withdrew them. Lester's step-father repeatedly asked for him to be taken into care, yet four months after the birth of the couple's first child they applied for the step-father to adopt Lester and Wendy.

The child associated with a life-cycle transition

Families progress through a series of life-cycle changes: for example, births, deaths, separations and psychological milestones such as adolescence and leaving home. Each change affects all members of the family system, who must adjust and adapt to the new circumstances. Inevitably, there will be stress during the period of transitional adaptation which may take time to dissipate. However, some families are overwhelmed by the effects of the changes and a child can acquire a particular meaning associated with the impact of the events.

It is very likely that **Maria Colwell** had a special significance to her mother, Pauline Kepple, because her birth coincided with her father's death. Pauline's first child was from an unmarried liaison and she placed her with the maternal grandmother from birth. The father of Pauline's next five children was Raymond Colwell and Maria was the youngest of that family. Raymond left the household one month after Maria's birth and he died three months later. This coincided with the development of a rift between Pauline and her own mother and Pauline became very depressed and neglected all her children. However, she treated Maria differently from the others and just a few weeks after Raymond's death she decided to take Maria to Raymond's sister's family (the Coopers), who agreed to look after her. Eventually, the remaining children were taken into care because of neglect and two were also placed by social services with their maternal grand-mother. However, Maria was the only one of the children with whom Pauline kept in contact and the only one of her absent children whom she insisted remain Catholic, her own religion.

Over the next six years, Pauline made a number of requests for Maria to return to her, always at times of transition in her own life. These attempts to be reunited with Maria occurred when Pauline was planning to settle down with and then marry William Kepple and again when she became pregnant by him. She made yet another request to have Maria back when her youngest baby was three months old, the age Maria had been when she gave her up. Maria was eventually returned when aged 6 years and she was neglected, assaulted and rejected over the next year until dying from violent abuse by William Kepple.

This suggests that Maria had a special meaning for her mother because her birth was associated with the loss of Raymond Colwell and the breakdown in Pauline's relationship with her own mother. Pauline was then unable to let Maria go as she had done the other children, clinging on to the memory of the 3-month-old Maria and wanting to be reunited with her as a way of dealing with her unresolved reactions to the loss of Raymond. However, Maria's actual identity when she did return must have contrasted dramatically with the fantasised meaning that predominated in her mother's mind. She was not the 3-month-old baby who could help her mother resolve the loss of the father but a 6-year-old, very upset and regressed after being displaced from caring foster parents and who continued to reject both her new caretakers in preference for the old ones.

In a number of other cases, a family loss coincided with the birth of the child who was later killed and it may be that their parents found their presence intolerable because it reminded them of the loss. Alternatively, the child was meant to make up for the loss and failed. The **Kimberley Carlile** report indicates that her parents separated when she was 4 months old and her father died of a cerebral haemorrhage three months later. Kimberley's mother was noted to be depressed around that time and although Kimberley had two elder siblings, it was she who was deprived from a very young age. **Tyra Henry**'s mother, Claudette Henry, fell pregnant with Tyra in the same month that her own father died. Claudette had been her father's favourite child and she was extremely upset by his death. In addition, Claudette's first-born child, Tyrone, had been taken into care the previous month, having been severely injured by her partner, Andrew Neil. Therefore, Claudette had lost her son and her father in quick succession and may well have tried to replace them with Tyra. We would also speculate that the grandfather's death had a profound effect on Claudette's mother and that this would have complicated Claudette's attempts to leave home. Indeed, the relationship between Claudette, her mother and Tyra developed very ambiguously, with Claudette hovering between staying with her mother and living independently. During that time, Tyra was sometimes 'mothered' by Claudette and at other times by her grandmother and probably took on a special meaning to both 'mothers' by acting as a bond between them.

The step-child

It is commonly believed that step-children are the most vulnerable of all to abuse and neglect. However, step-parents were held exclusively responsible for the deaths of only five of the thirty-five children and jointly responsible for a further six (see Table 4.3). The report on **Jasmine Beckford**'s death makes great emphasis of the fact that her mother, Beverley Lorrington, cohabited with Morris Beckford when she was already pregnant with Jasmine, who was registered as Beckford even though Morris knew he was not her natural father. Although this might appear to have been a denial of Beverley's previous relationship, it should be noted that the natural child of Beverley and Morris' cohabitation was also severely abused.

Nonetheless, we surmise that parents with vulnerable self-esteem would perceive a step-child as a constant reminder that the partner once had an intimate relationship with someone else. Furthermore, if the child has a close relationship with the natural parent, this can be interpreted as the natural parent having something that the step-parent does not, which compounds a sense of deprivation.

Wayne Brewer's step-father found his infantile needs intolerable and he hit him repeatedly from the time of his cohabitation with Wayne's mother. Wayne was taken into care but his mother and step-father applied successfully for revocation of the Care Order (but unsuccessfully for adoption) coincidentally with the mother becoming pregnant again. However, following the birth of the baby, Wayne's rejection by both parents increased and the physical abuse by his step-father worsened. Other examples of step-children include **Maria Colwell**, who was mistreated even more severely than her half-siblings and killed by her step-father, and **Heidi Koseda**, who was neglected and shut away when her mother remarried, while the son of that new partnership was better looked after.

CHILDREN WITH SPECIFIC MEANINGS

In a few cases, we inferred that the child who was abused acquired a meaning that was idiosyncratic to the family. For example, the Duncan family who looked after **Richard Clark** and his elder brother in an unofficial fostering arrangement might have been hoping that the two children would prove what 'good' parents they were. Two of the Duncans' own children had previously been taken into care because of severe neglect and some professionals had been dubious about their parenting capacity.

A very different example is that of **Christopher Pinder/Daniel Frankland**. Christopher was placed for adoption as a 2-month-old baby with the Franklands, four days after they were approved as adoptive parents. They not only changed his surname to Frankland but also his first name to Daniel and we wonder whether this represented their idealisation of him and expectation that he should be a perfect, new child who totally belonged to them. However, in reality he proved to be a very difficult feeder and the new mother found severe problems adjusting to his demands and needs as a young baby, especially without any time to prepare for his arrival.

Darryn Clarke may have held different and complex meanings for his mother, Kathryn Clarke, and step-father, Charles Courtney. Kathryn's pregnancy with Darryn was probably associated with her struggles to separate from her family and coincided with the death of her own mother. Kathryn tried to leave home at the age of 19, became pregnant three months later and returned home again. Then, five months after Darryn's birth, the maternal grandmother died and Kathryn had to run the home in her place, because the grandfather was disabled. Within a few months she made a successful housing application for herself and Darryn to the local authority. Darryn also seems to have held a special meaning for Charles Courtney, who abused him appallingly. Charles was an illegitimate child of a Ghanaian seaman and a Liverpool woman and from infancy he was looked after by various relatives. After he came together with Kathryn and Darryn, Darryn, too, was passed round to different relatives to be cared for. One incident in particular seems to have been symbolic of their relationship. Darryn and his mother were very proud of Darryn's curly hair but one day, when Kathryn was absent, Charles brutally chopped it. We wonder whether Charles identified curly-headed children with himself (he was of mixed race) and could not bear being reminded of his own deprived background. Cropping Darryn's hair can also be seen to symbolise an attack on the close bond between the mother and son.

SUMMARY

We have cited a number of examples in which we infer that the children who died had special meanings to the caretaker/s who killed them. If valid, these hypotheses go some way towards explaining why those particular children died rather than others in the household. It appeared that in those families dominated by excessive dependency conflicts, the children either were blamed for the conflicts or used as a means by which the parents tried to overcome them. Other children may have been associated in their parents' minds with the emotional turmoil that accompanied critical family events. They were either blamed for the events or expected to help parents overcome their distress. A common theme was parents relating to children as property and requesting their return home from care in order to overcome their own sense of deprivation. The children therefore were not related to as persons in their own right but as objects to satisfy their parents' needs.

Chapter 6

Inter-professional communication

If one feature of the thirty-five inquiries stands out above all others, it is the panels' repeated conclusions that inter-agency communication was flawed. Report after report highlights how crucially relevant information was not passed on to new workers or agencies and that information was not shared amongst concurrently involved professionals. For example, a child's new school remained unaware of the existence of a Care Order or, when a family moved, reports were not sent on to the social services department of the new borough. Sometimes, records of emergency telephone calls could not be found. Consequently, professionals were left working in isolation or ignorance and planning for the child's welfare remained uncoordinated.

For many years, Stevenson (1963, 1988) had reported that problems of inter-professional communication and co-operation play a crucial part in child abuse tragedies and she re-emphasised this when she sat as a member of the **Maria Colwell** inquiry panel. Amongst this panel's conclusions were that: 'Maria, despite an elaborate system of "welfare provisions", fell through the net primarily because of communications failures' (**Maria Colwell** Inquiry Report 1974: 62). Since then, many other inquiries have highlighted similar issues:

> We do not minimise the problem of consultation and indeed communication. This case (and many others in the country) has underlined how difficult this was . . .
>
> (**Max Piazzani** Inquiry Report 1974: 16)

> It is immediately apparent that there were failures of communication in several directions.
>
> (**Steven Meurs** Inquiry Report 1975: 11)

> There can be no doubt . . . that if co-ordination and communication between these services had been effective, then, on the information and evidence available to one or more of the services, the risk of repeated serious non-accidental injury to Lisa should have been clearly recognised and acted upon.
>
> (**Lisa Godfrey** Inquiry Report 1975: 27)

A fundamental problem here was that the full picture was not really known to any one agency.

(**Neil Howlett** Inquiry Report 1976: 10)

As a result of the circumstances of this investigation we were able to compile a picture of the family which no one of the authorities which held parental responsibility ever constructed.

(**Stephen Menheniott** Inquiry Report 1978: 24)

The Committee concluded that there was an unfortunate combination of weaknesses in communication.

(**Simon Peacock** Inquiry Report 1978: 19)

The problems of communication which existed within, to, and from the Social Services Department are, to a large extent, self-evident in the text of this report.

(**Darryn Clarke** Inquiry Report 1979: 56)

This decision required an assessment of all the information available to the Social Services Department and other agencies. We find that such an assessment was not made . . .

(**Paul Brown** Inquiry Report 1980: 34)

The senior social worker, the health visitor and the probation officer consulted each other frequently and exchanged information, but they seem to have taken refuge in this consultation rather than action, for which it is no substitute.

(**Carly Taylor** Inquiry Report 1980: 23)

We have instanced many examples of inadequate communication...

(**Maria Mehmedagi** Inquiry Report 1981: 46)

This inquiry, like others which have preceded it, came across numerous instances of information which was known to one agency not being known to another.

(**Lucie Gates** Inquiry Report 1982 Vol. 1: 288)

there does appear to have been some failure of communication between agencies . . .

(**Shirley Woodcock** Inquiry Report 1984: 63)

we . . . noted a degree of inaccuracy in recorded telephone messages which had profoundly serious consequences in this instance.

(**Heidi Koseda** Inquiry Report 1986: 40)

the report of the Panel of Inquiry into the circumstances surrounding the death of **Jasmine Beckford** in December 1985 showed clearly that no system of exchanging information among the relevant agencies existed . . . Throughout this report we have pointed to a number of instances where the principles of an information service were breached.

(**Kimberley Carlile** Inquiry Report 1987: 158)

It is here that the breakdown of effective communication between social services and housing appears to have occurred.

(**Tyra Henry** Inquiry Report 1987: 122)

The Panel were concerned about the shifts in emphasis which appeared to occur between verbal and written communication between workers in different disciplines.

(**Doreen Aston** Inquiry Report 1989: 105)

Over the years, the various reports have contained valuable recommendations about improving structures for inter-agency communication and co-operation, including more prompt case conferences, improved note-keeping and closer monitoring of procedural guidelines by Area Review Committees (now called Child Protection Committees). However, although these recommendations have been useful in themselves, they clearly have not been sufficient, since the same issues of communication failure have occurred time and time again.

In search of an explanation, Dingwall (1986) argues that the inquiries are failing to make any lasting impact on the everyday practice of the professionals because of fundamental limitations in the legal approach utilised by the panels. Clearly, the subtleties of inter-personal communication are more readily examined during learning exercises and training workshops than in quasi-legalistic inquiries. In addition, we suggest that the panels have not appreciated that communication is much more than the structured handling of information and its mechanical transfer from one person to another. It is a complex process, an integral component of all human behaviour and of inter-personal interaction. By restricting their investigation to the organisational structures for professional inter-communication, the panels have not addressed the relational processes.

We therefore made a particular effort in our review to focus on psychological factors in inter-professional communication to see whether it might be possible to learn additional lessons from the cases. Here, we shall discuss some general principles of communication and in the two chapters which follow shall discuss how we believe they became manifest between members of the professional networks in the thirty-five cases.

SOME GENERAL PRINCIPLES OF COMMUNICATION

When we speak of 'communication', we imply notions of exchanges of information between two or more persons using language that is common to them in ways that permit receipt by those to whom the information is intended and to which they attribute meaning (e.g. Reusch and Bateson 1951). According to Simon *et al.*:

Wherever information is exchanged, one can speak of a communication system. The amount of information that the behaviour of one interactional partner has for another depends first of all on whether both have access to the same code and, secondly, on the quality of transmission . . . Information is not an inherent, static attribute of some object, but an aspect of interaction between a 'sender' and a 'receiver'.

(Simon *et al.* 1985: 198)

Thus, 'information' is not synonymous with 'meaning' and 'every interpersonal communication is not only an exchange of information about some subject matter, but also concurrently contains a message regarding the relationship between the interactional partners' (Simon *et al.* 1985: 53). This second, relational aspect of communication is said to belong to a higher logical type and to represent a form of metacommunication (that is, communication about the communication).

Watzlawick *et al.* (1967) have written extensively on the relationship aspect of communication, beginning with the premise that all behaviour has message value and therefore is communication, whether that behaviour is activity or inactivity, words or silence, attention or inattention. The behaviour of 'ignoring' a message can convey a great deal about the recipient's attitude to the information and the sender and is itself a communication. In a sense, then, the concept of communication embraces the whole of human behaviour and interaction. As Pearce and Cronen remark: 'persons are seen as living within a world of symbolic meanings . . . These symbolic meanings are negotiated and exchanged by persons through communication' (Pearce and Cronen 1980: 14).

Furthermore, it is crucial to distinguish two components of this communication: the message content and, at a different level, the relationship context which classifies it and adds colour and meaning to it. Although various theorists have coined different terms for these two components, the basic concept remains the same. Watzlawick *et al.* (1967) distinguish 'digital' from 'analogic' communication where the analogic includes non-verbal and affective cues which accompany the digital elements of the message. Morris (1946) discusses the 'syntax' and 'semantics' of language, with syntax referring to the word content of the message and its grammatical construction and semantics to the connotation which gives meaning to the words. Reusch and Bateson (1951) differentiate between 'report' and 'command' aspects to communication.

More recently, Cronen and Pearce have proposed that messages must be understood within multiple levels of context (Pearce and Cronen 1980; Cronen *et al.* 1982; Cronen and Pearce 1985). In this theory of communication, which they call the 'Coordinated Management of Meaning', every specific speech act is interpreted according to a number of relationship contexts within which it is embedded. Thus, there are the recurrent patterns of interaction between the participants, which themselves are manifestations of the overall relationship between them. This relationship will have evolved within the context of each person's life script (or sense of self), for which there is an even higher order conception of how society, personal roles and family relationships work. Cronen and Pearce realised that a further complexity arises because levels of context are interchangeable. Sometimes, a relationship context accords meaning to a particular message but, at other times, it is the message itself which helps clarify the relationship. Contradictions between these levels will lead to confusion, paradoxical communications, etc.

Haley (1959) considers that when one person communicates a message to another, s/he is manoeuvring to define the relationship and the other person is thereby posed the problem of accepting or rejecting the relationship offered. Watzlawick *et al.* (1967) agree that relationship problems may distort communication, particularly when the participants constantly struggle about the nature of their relationship so that the content aspect of the message becomes less and less important. The frequent problem is that communicators fail to identify or define their metacommunications.

The practical implication of these ideas is that, for workers to attribute relevant meaning to their communication, they must not only identify the message content but also the multiple levels of context within which it is embedded. For example, the way that one worker receives information from another is influenced by the affective tone of voice (such as level of anxiety), non-verbal cues (which might suggest that the message should not be taken seriously), preconceptions about the other person's profession, previous patterns of interaction between them and so on. There must be sufficient synchrony between the message-giver and the message-receiver so that the intention, content and associated feelings become shared property.

An example of the lack of synchrony between communicators is when the intention behind the message remains obscure. The message might be intended to convey that: 'I am worried and would like to offload my anxieties onto you so that I can stop worrying.' However, this remains covert and undeclared as the initial imbalance in anxiety between the communicators becomes exaggerated during the conversation. The more that one person expresses anxiety, the more the other one backs away. A message-initiator may fail to realise that the content has triggered personal anxiety in the receiver who has responded with distancing and denial, leaving the information unheard. Alternatively, the contextual message: 'I feel helpless with this case and would appreciate someone taking it off my hands' is received as: 'I had better take on this case and do something immediately, whatever it is.' An apparent referral from one agency to another may contain the undeclared metacommunication: 'We don't trust that you will handle this sensitively and, although we are obliged to inform you, we don't want you to act upon it.' Ignorance or inexperience can prevent either communicator from differentiating between the elements of the message which are of crucial importance from those of less relevance. Weighing up such issues is the responsibility of both parties and needs to be acknowledged jointly.

Furthermore, social institutions develop their own structures for internal communication and, while these structures will be set up with the intention of handling the mechanics of information exchange, they will also reflect the relationships between the institution's members. Commonly, these relationship components are completely denied, even though they have a major impact on the effectiveness of the agency's functioning. For example, a social work department may have developed a clear and straightforward system for the receipt of telephone messages. However, the office clerk who is designated as the first person of contact is often inexperienced, overworked, poorly paid and feeling undervalued and unsupported in a very stressful job where s/he hears of children's lives being at risk. All these factors interplay with his/her ability to attend to and record anxiety-laden messages.

There are added complications when the communications encompass a multi-agency network. Baker (personal communication) has estimated that up to seventy-two different professionals can become involved when there are suspicions of child abuse. This large network of professionals includes social workers, NSPCC officers, home helps, nursery staff, health visitors, police, magistrates, solicitors, barristers, judges, probation officers, teachers, educational social workers, general practitioners, nurses, paediatricians, school medical officers, psychologists, psychiatrists, etc. Some professionals work together regularly in multi-disciplinary teams but the majority operate from uni-disciplinary agencies, each of which has its own rules of practice, and they only come together around specific tasks or cases. Even when members of the various professional agencies have previously worked together, every new case produces a unique system of the workers' relationships to the family and to each other.

There will need to be a great deal of information exchange between members of this professional network by letter, telephone, formal or informal face-to-face contact, through intermediaries and so on. At every contact there is the potential for distortion or loss of message content. The Chinese Whispers party game aptly demonstrates how the content of messages becomes distorted unintentionally as it is passed around a group of people. Each person has the possibility of subtly distorting the message. As communication between professionals tends to progress through a series of intermediaries (for example, secretaries or an on-call worker) the potential for distortion is multiplied. In addition, one worker may concurrently receive messages from different sources which apparently contradict each other (Reder and Kraemer 1980).

PROFESSIONAL INTERACTION

It is evident that inter-professional communications are embedded within multiple relationship contexts and that during every professional interchange personal, professional, institutional and inter-agency factors colour how the messages are relayed and received.

Personally, workers bring into their contacts with families and colleagues their 'personal luggage': beliefs, prejudices, moral and social standards, investments, sensitivities, blind-spots, previous experiences and so on (Hallett and Stevenson 1980). Even though professional training and personal reflection allow workers to become more aware of these influences, each professional encounter is likely to bring forth some aspect of this luggage and workers will feel uneasy when responding to certain types of situations that resonate with them. For example, those who lack self-esteem in making judgements tend to submit to someone else's opinion or they may try to compensate for insecurities by presenting themselves as infallible. These are variations of human make-up and are not in themselves problematic. However, some people show such self-assurance and self-belief that they deny the possibility of others having something useful to contribute. Over-investment in wanting to help can lead workers to fear losing the case to other professionals and they compete to demonstrate that their help is most valued by the client.

Professionally, different workers have particular responsibilities which determine their role. There are certain core functions associated with specific professions which afford them a unique identity and for which they receive special training. Examples are the statutory role of social workers or medical examinations by doctors. In addition, some overlap exists between workers' skills so that similar interventions (such as parental counselling) may be undertaken by a number of different professionals. As child protection involves so many workers, there is a need for clarity of function between them so that role differentiation and role complementarity can occur. However, dormant professional rivalries may surface in a network whereby workers lose sight of their primary function and intrude upon the tasks of other agencies. Alternatively, professional stereotypes and prejudices can colour relations between agencies. For instance, lack of trust often results in minimal cross-referral between agencies and, if they happen to be involved concurrently with the same family, each group of workers resists giving up their role to the other and co-operation remains poor (for example, see the Cleveland Inquiry 1988).

At the institutional level, the agency structure, as well as its perceptions, beliefs and customs, will affect how the staff interact with each other and with those of other agencies. As Menzies (1970) has described, agency systems develop their own internal patterns of relationships which act as defences against the anxieties inherent in the work. The stress of being responsible for people's lives can generate a tradition that all decisions are passed up a chain of command and, as a result, those at the bottom come to be defined as incompetent and incapable of deciding anything.

Alternatively, some agencies operate without clear structures for decision-taking, so that its staff feel anxious and confused about their work. In response to the demands of their job, senior staff become increasingly remote from their juniors, disappearing into the routine of administration and being virtually unavailable for supervision and support. Inevitably, juniors will experience greater stress but in trying to communicate this to their seniors they discover that it pushes them even further away. The demands of the work often lead staff to institute procedures that are followed routinely, inflexibly and without thought. Satisfactory work within an agency also depends on seniors and juniors having sufficiently congruent views, since the juniors may find it impossible to carry out prescribed tasks with which they disagree.

An agency's staff may hold to a collective view that they should be all things to all people: they never filter incoming requests, are always in danger of being overwhelmed with work and only have time for superficial assessments and crisis management. However, the knowledge that *someone* is doing *something* reduces anxiety for other members of the network and the case becomes less of a priority for them.

CASE CONFERENCES

Over the years, the advisability of convening case conferences as a means of improving inter-professional co-operation and communication has become en-shrined in procedural guidelines (e.g. Department of Health and Social Security 1974, 1976; Department of Health and Social Security and the Welsh Office 1988) and this forum is now central to the inter-disciplinary management of child protection. The **Wayne Brewer** inquiry put the arguments for case conferences persuasively:

> We see as the advantage of case conferences the pooling of information relevant to the care and safety of the child. The total information yielded is likely to be a great deal more than the sum of the individual parts. Many professionals are inclined – erroneously – to assume that they know what another's contribution will be. An opportunity exists for each participant to offer his interpretation of particular aspects of the situation and to contribute to the decision finally reached. Not only is each participant directly aware of the decision but because it is collectively arrived at he will have a fuller under-standing of it and a greater sense of commitment towards its implementation.
>
> (**Wayne Brewer** Inquiry Report 1977: 30)

There is no doubt that holding case conferences can advance planning and co-operative work and that their absence usually signals a failure in the network's functioning (in fourteen of the thirty-five cases we reviewed, no case conferences occurred). While not wanting to challenge this basic assumption about the value of conferences, like Hallett and Stevenson (1980), we would suggest that un-realistically high expectations of them may have evolved. Although the principle of bringing people together around a shared task is a good one, the process is by no means straightforward. Conferences are subject to the same group processes as any other type of meeting, during which such issues as attendances and absences, chairing, alliances, hierarchy and projection (Bion 1961; Main 1975) will influence the final decision.

When professionals meet together in a case conference, they bring with them much more than just information about the particular family. Some will have a history of previous contacts around other cases as well as the current one. Others will be meeting for the first time. Prior to the conference, the professionals within the network will also have developed attitudes and beliefs about one another and their respective roles in the case. The conference is a brief episode in the continuous inter-relationships between members of the network. Hence, not only is that conference prone to enact the usual dynamics of groups but it is also a coming together of all professional relationships that have evolved in the course of work with that family.

There can be little doubt, then, that issues of inter-professional communication are complicated and any review of how these processes operate during a particular case requires in-depth study. Unfortunately, such information was not available in sufficient detail from any of the inquiry reports for us to be able to build up a comprehensive picture. As we have observed, the primary concern of the panels in this area was the mechanics of information recording and transfer. Therefore, in our review there were limitations on the extent to which we could apply the psychology of communications to the thirty-five cases and make further sense of communication breakdown in so many of them. However, we were able to discern a number of patterns of inter-professional communication which we believe have implications for practice. We shall describe these in the following chapter (Chapter 7). In Chapter 8 we shall consider how professionals organised information about their cases during the assessment process.

SUMMARY

Serious problems in the transmission of information between members of the professional networks occurred in the majority of cases. In order to examine these problems it is first necessary to review aspects of the psychology of communication. Communication is the inevitable accompaniment of human interaction and involves the exchange of a message component and a relational component. The relational element qualifies and gives meaning to the message content. In addition, inter-personal communications are embedded in multiple levels of relationships. Therefore, any analysis of communications between professionals in child abuse cases must consider the relationships between individual workers and their agencies, as well as the organisational structures available to them for information recording and transfer.

Chapter 7

The professional networks

Effective communication is fundamental to the practice of child protection and considerable attention needs to be paid to the process of information transfer within a multi-agency network. We have discussed how communication between members of professional networks involves mechanical procedures as well as relationship issues at a number of levels. To take this further, in this chapter we shall first consider the working context within which professionals operated during their involvement with the thirty-five cases. We go on to discuss the overall relationships which evolved between members of the professional networks and then the way communication seemed to be impeded during workers' absences or at weekends.

SECURE WORK SETTING

At a general level, every professional requires a 'secure setting' in order to undertake the demanding work of child protection. Anxieties about the child can be monitored more readily when stresses within agencies and organisations are minimised. Many factors contribute to a secure setting, including adequate training, regular supervision and support, clear procedural guidelines, adequate funding and staffing, low staff turnover, an optimal case load, continuity in management, a stable organisational structure, good secretarial back-up, requisite facilities and so on. All these elements combine to provide the mechanical means for effective communication and also a context within which the workers feel valued, respected and supported. As Dale *et al.* (1986) emphasise, professionals operating from a position of chronic stress are excessively prone to commit errors of judgement and action, even becoming 'dangerous professionals'.

It is salutary to reflect that the years covered by our review have been characterised by repeated reorganisations in health, social services, education and local government. They have been accompanied by shifts in priorities, policies, procedures, managerial relationships, funding and resourcing. These socio-political changes are bound to have created an overall uncertainty and insecurity for all involved professionals. We shall cite just a few specific examples from the cases.

At least one-third of the inquiries report that the allocated key worker was unqualified, a student or only recently qualified. Most of them did not receive the supervision which might have partially compensated for their inexperience and lack of knowledge. At the time of the **Shirley Woodcock** case, the area office was in the middle of reorganisation, the social workers all carried excessive case loads, there was a high staff sickness rate (itself an indication of staff stress) and there were delays appointing into vacant senior posts. As a result of a local reorganisation of services, the unqualified social worker involved with **Susan Aukland** lost his Team Leader and had to go to a new Area Officer for supervision. The reorganisation also resulted in the health visitor relating to new nursing officers who gave her less supervision and to the loss of the social services case file. **Lester Chapman**'s social workers were short-staffed and overworked, with poor secretarial assistance and supervision. Their early contact with the family coincided with the 1971 Seebohm reorganisation of social services and when the key worker left she was not replaced for three months. Similarly, four months after **Steven Meurs** was born, the health visitor retired and was not replaced because of staff shortages. **David Naseby** was admitted to hospital under a general physician because no paediatrician had been able to be appointed to the paediatric department for six years. Social services went on strike during the **Maria Mehmedagi** case and this left the health visitor and probation officer as the only monitoring workers. As a final example, the Senior social worker was on maternity leave for six months at a crucial stage in the **Jasmine Beckford** case, during which time the Basic social worker had to act up as her own, and others', senior and she therefore had extra responsibilities and no supervision of her own work.

PROFESSIONAL NETWORK RELATIONSHIPS

Effective communication also depends on relationships at the inter-professional and inter-agency level. In reviewing the thirty-five inquiry reports, we were able to describe patterns of inter-professional contacts along a continuum of system boundary permeability. That is, just like a family, a professional system must maintain an optimal level of inter-personal contacts with outside systems in order to fulfil its purpose. Too much permeability across the boundary can be overwhelming, flooding the workers with information and producing chaotic thinking. In addition, it may produce a lack of identity and confusion between agencies. Insufficient contact leads to isolation, poor responsiveness and inflexibility. Hence we conceptualise an optimal balance of boundary permeability in which all relevant systems inter-communicate at a level which does not overwhelm, confuse identities or isolate.

We inferred from the reports that, within the networks, some professional groupings (or subsystems) were very open, others extremely closed. The significance of the relatively closed subsystems was that their workers' ideas remained unchallenged by others in the networks. Discrepant ideas or observations appeared to be disregarded because they were incompatible with those held within the subsystems. It was therefore impossible for all relevant professionals to obtain a coherent overview of the cases. Where there were excessively open subsystems, workers' thinking capacity seemed impaired and it was difficult for them to develop and hold on to autonomous ideas.

We have called the principal patterns of relationships within the professional networks which we were able to identify: 'Closed Professional System', 'Polarisation', 'Exaggeration of Hierarchy' and 'Role Confusion'.

CLOSED PROFESSIONAL SYSTEM

In this pattern, a group of workers developed a fixed view about a case and was inaccessible to contrary information or observations. This closed subsystem of the network may have comprised a whole agency or a number of professionals from different agencies or, occasionally, a single worker.

Our own experience is that closed professional systems arise in a number of ways. For example, workers may be so conscientious that they are unable to take a step back and instead they resolutely continue with the same focus. Furthermore, the stress of child protection work can drive staff to seek allies to share their anxieties or confirm their beliefs. Some workers hold a passionate conviction that their views are right, so that they become even more dogmatic when challenged by possible alternatives. A past history of poor relationships with other agencies or a stereotypical mistrust of them can result in a positive wish to exclude those workers from the case. Such attitudes may also occur alongside a fear of losing control of the case to another agency were it to become involved.

Alternatively, the pervading influence of a core belief (for example, that the child is bound to return home from care) can bind together the workers' thinking so that they understand everything within that framework. The relevance of observations inconsistent with that belief are minimised and the workers' thinking remains unchallenged. A pervasive belief influenced the course of many of the cases and the **Jasmine Beckford** report provides a clear example. Soon after Jasmine and her sister had been taken into care following serious injuries, the social worker and her Senior began to work towards their rehabilitation home. This approach was endorsed when a magistrate renewed the Care Order but expressed the hope that the children would return home, which they eventually did. However, no criteria were set for what would constitute failure of the plan, as though that alternative course of events was not considered possible. By now the two social workers appeared to be functioning as a closed system implementing the rehabilitation decision, since they did not check regularly with other professionals about the children's well-being nor did they translate conflicting evidence (Jasmine's absence from nursery school and their inability ever to see her) into its relevant meaning.

There were many other examples. The first social worker involved with **Lucie Gates'** family was convinced that Lucie's mother could adequately care for her children given support, practical help and a chance to prove her capabilities. The social worker did not waver from this path despite many reports of child neglect from diverse sources (see Chapter 8). In the **Malcolm Page** case, the social worker, health visitor and home help collectively maintained a view that all was satisfactory and only practical help and encouragement was needed. Once again, this was sustained despite evidence to the contrary. The **Carly Taylor** and **Maria Colwell** cases are examples of professionals being inaccessible to messages from lay people. Neighbours and relatives kept trying to convey their concern to health visitors or social workers but found that their anxieties were not taken up or acted upon. In both cases, the professionals felt optimistic about their plans to keep the children and their parents together and their thinking remained unchallenged by contradictory evidence of the children's suffering. Since Maria's mother also believed that Maria would return and remain with her (see Chapter 5), it could be said that the mother and social worker also functioned together as a closed thinking system.

Closure emerged in a different way in the **Karen Spencer** case. The police had been present at early case conferences but once the plan to rehabilitate Karen home was implemented they were not invited to the next one. Previously, the police had questioned some gaps in assessment and it was as though they had taken on the role of reality testers. The day before Karen died, a police detective telephoned social services to inquire when the next case conference would be and he was told that it had taken place two months previously.

Charlene Salt had been admitted to hospital on a Place of Safety Order with unexplained bruising. In granting a Supervision Order, the magistrate asked to hear of any further evidence of lack of parental co-operation with professionals. In fact, the family shunned contact with almost everybody, although they did permit the health visitor and social worker access. These two practitioners worked harder and harder to teach the couple parenting skills but repeatedly resorted to completing the tasks themselves. For example, having encouraged the parents to take responsibility for obtaining their social security benefits, the social worker eventually took them to the office herself. She also loaned them money and brought them baby food, blankets and clothing. We would infer that, within this relationship, the social worker and health visitor functioned like a closed system, failing to acknowledge the parents' lack of co-operation with them and other agencies nor appreciating the increasing danger to Charlene.

POLARISATION

In this pattern of interaction a schism developed between two groups of workers and, over time, two subsystems of the network emerged whose points of view progressively diverged. Groups sometimes consisted of just one person or else comprised several workers or agencies. Although communication within the groups was often satisfactory, information or ideas were rarely exchanged between them and the families usually received contradictory messages from different sources.

It is likely that polarisation between members of a professional network has the same precursors as in the development of closed professional systems. For example, fixed beliefs or mistrust of other agencies tend to inhibit co-operative work and promote alliances between workers. Where differences of opinion fail to be resolved, opposing attitudes become entrenched. Sometimes, incompatible emphases lie behind the polarisation, in which workers identify with different parts of the family system and take sides on their behalf. An example is when some workers make the child's protection their primary focus while others give primacy to the parents and their needs.

It is important to clarify that in polarisation, as with all the patterns we are describing, the interaction between workers was not engineered deliberately or maliciously. As we would see it, the workers inadvertently interacted together in a way that gradually became more polarised. The problem was not so much that the schism was developing but that the participants did not realise it and so were unable to take steps to reverse the process.

We have already suggested that the social workers involved with **Jasmine Beckford** functioned as a closed professional system. In addition, polarisation developed when Jasmine and her sister were taken into care. They were placed with foster parents who had been assessed by the Principal Fostering Officer but he had many clashes with the key social worker about future planning over the months that followed. Indeed, it may be that the social worker turned to her Senior as an ally and this encouraged the two social workers into a progressively closed thinking system. While the social worker and her Senior were advocating a policy of rehabilitation, the fostering officer was informing the foster parents that they had been approved as long-term foster parents. As tension grew between the workers, the foster parents' complaints about the condition of the children when they returned from weekend access visits were not followed up by the social workers and the foster parents felt uninformed about plans for the children.

Similar disagreements were reported between the fostering officer and social worker in the **Shirley Woodcock** case. Shirley and her brother had been placed at short notice with inexperienced foster parents after the breakdown of a previous placement. The social worker did not want them disrupted by a further move, while the fostering officer wanted the decison referred back to the fostering panel. It remained unclear to the foster parents whether the placement was short-term or long-term, which compounded the stress they experienced of looking after severely deprived children. The foster mother's growing tension, which culminated in a fatal assault, was not noticed by the workers.

After **Maria Mehmedagi** was admitted to hospital with extensive injuries, serious disagreements about procedure arose between the police and other care workers. For example, the police were concerned that the doctors and social workers had disregarded rules of evidence in interviewing the family and later they disagreed about whether the father should be charged. In court, the police opposed bail for him, while the social worker spoke in favour. The mother was then also charged with child neglect, again contrary to the wishes of the social worker and paediatrician. The police received their invitation to the next case conference too late for them to attend and this exemplifies the rift that had developed between the two entrenched groups, one becoming advocates for the parents (the social worker, probation officer, health visitor and paediatrician), the other (the police) being seen as hostile to them. In the middle of this polarisation was Maria and plans to return her to her parents continued even though she was observed to be bruised and injured. It seems that, as these processes develop, the great wealth of feeling generated by the professional interaction interferes with thinking about the child.

An officer from the Royal Scottish Society for the Prevention of Cruelty to Children and a social worker were both visiting the Duncan family with whom **Richard Clark** and his brother were fostered. The two workers had differing views about the ability of these parents to care adequately for children. Social services considered them to be unsuitable as official foster parents but approved them in an unofficial capacity and the social worker worked harder and harder to confirm her optimism. Although the social worker and the RSSPCC officer did retain some contact together, it did not lead to a change in planning or to a different social work response when information was received that Richard was being injured within that home.

EXAGGERATION OF HIERARCHY

In some cases, workers' assumed positions in an inter-professional hierarchy became exaggerated. Professionals with a lower perceived status deferred to the opinions of others who were perceived as hierarchically superior. Alternatively, the power or status associated with a particular role dominated the case and overshadowed the thinking of other workers. Those seen as having the greatest importance often paradoxically had only fleeting contact with the child and family, such as medical consultants, magistrates or judges. People seen as less important included health visitors, social workers, neighbours or relatives of the family. Usually, those apparently lower in the hierarchy were the most closely involved with the family and so the information they held remained unheard. Exaggeration of hierarchy was most clearly manifest at case conferences or in court and it was as though an undeclared 'pecking order' regulated who might speak and who would be listened to.

There were a number of examples. The first social worker involved with **Lucie Gates** was impressed by her mother's potential to improve her standards of caretaking and cleanliness. At the initial case conference, the social worker's report strongly in favour of leaving the children at home held sway, even though she was not present to speak to it. A health visitor who was present and very concerned about that proposal did not speak out. The midwife who found **Charlene Salt** at home dirty, hungry and bruised felt unable to express her disquiet at the first case conference's decision to return Charlene home. Similarly, at the first case conference held on **Jasmine Beckford**, the health visitor did not impress upon those present the significance of her height and weight recordings (which indicated that Jasmine was failing to thrive). In the early phases of the **Neil Howlett** case, a student social worker and health visitor separately reported their strong suspicions of parental neglect and cruelty. However, their views were not taken up with any degree of urgency, maybe because of the low hierarchical status attributed to them. Neighbours' and relatives' worries were equally unable to redirect the professional approach later in this case, as in the **Steven Meurs** and **Carly Taylor** cases.

Courts wield considerable power in child abuse cases but we found instances in which it was exaggerated and unduly skewed the course of events. For example, the magistrate who granted a Care Order on **Jasmine Beckford** and her sister added the hope that they would be reunited with their parents. Not only was the expression of this opinion beyond the remit of the court but it also added greater weight to the plans of the social worker and her Senior, who favoured returning the children home. These views contrasted with the considerable pessimism about rehabilitation expressed by the social services Area Manager and the majority of those who had attended the recent case conference.

Wayne Brewer had been taken into care following physical and emotional abuse. When his mother and step-father applied for revocation of the Care Order, the social worker gave evidence that there had been no change in his step-father's unpredictable and violent temper, nor improvement in his mother's immaturity and lack of warmth towards Wayne. In dismissing the parents' application at that time, the Chairman of the Bench reminded them that they could re-apply in due course. This they did, successfully, just three months later, despite contrary recommendations by the social worker and Consultant paediatrician. The main reasons given for the decision to revoke the Care Order were that the couple had decorated and refurnished their flat and borrowed books on child care from the library (as their solicitor had advised them to do). At that hearing, the Chairman of the Bench recommended that Wayne should be visited three or four times a week, ignoring the Assistant Prinicpal social worker's plea that they did not have the resources to do so.

The magistrates court hearing which returned the **anonymous** baby home on a Supervision Order was unusual. A previous case conference had unanimously recommended a Care Order because of the mother's history of unpredictable violence. In court, social services were not allowed to submit a Consultant paediatrician's hearsay evidence supporting a Care Order. However, when the general practitioner began to read from the report of a Consultant psychiatrist, who saw no objection to the baby returning home, this hearsay was allowed. The psychiatrist had only seen the mother once, at her solicitor's request, and neither he nor the general practitioner had attended case conferences. Social services were represented in court by a solicitor who had not previously handled a contested Care Order. The baby was killed by his mother four months later.

ROLE CONFUSION

Some overlap is inevitable between the skills and responsibilities of the various professions. For example, social services, the NSPCC and the police all have statutory powers and both social workers and health visitors are well placed to observe a child at home. Frequently, it is possible for workers to share over-lapping roles without difficulty, so long as they remain in communication together and are clear about who is doing what. Problems arise when there is ambiguity about professionals' tasks or one worker tries to adopt the role and responsibilities appropriate to another profession, denying that there is any difference between their training or statutory powers.

In some cases, a professional whose primary task was to work with adults assumed the role of a child care worker and displaced someone who carried that specific, statutory responsibility. For instance, **Lisa Godfrey**'s mother was placed on probation for defrauding the Department of Health and Social Security and she turned increasingly to her probation officer for emotional support. The probation officer effectively became a communication switchboard between the family and all other agencies. When the family were allocated a social worker, the probation officer increased her contact and suggested that social services did not have a relevant role. Social services decided to keep their file open but to take no further action. When social services later planned a case conference, the probation officer suggested that, since housing was a major issue, the conference should not take place if the housing directorate could not be represented. When the health visitor informed social services that Lisa was bruised, social services told her to inform the probation officer, whose reaction was to contact the housing directorate.

The **Graham Bagnall** inquiry report records a series of role contradictions. The paediatrician wrote to the general practitioner that the family's main prob-lems were social, yet the contents of his letter were not shared with social services (contrary to a very recent joint circular between the local health and social services departments). When Graham's brother was also admitted to hospital with non-accidental injuries, it was the hospital and the NSPCC who arranged for him to be returned home on trial and social services only received notice after his discharge. Although there was telephone contact between the NSPCC officer and the social worker, the social worker tended to postpone home visits whenever she knew the NSPCC officer was visiting. The social worker ended up dealing with practical arrangements, such as obtaining a cot, in readiness for Graham to return home from care, while the NSPCC officer undertook to supervise the return home and to submit monthly reports to social services. No case conference was called, perhaps because it was unclear who would take responsibility.

The social worker involved with **Steven Meurs** had previously been worried about the care of the other children in the household but was also concerned about the mother's angry resentment of professionals. When the social worker first saw Steven to be 'pasty, understimulated and dirty', she consulted her Senior, who suggested getting the health visitor to call surreptitiously to observe him. However, Steven's mother would not co-operate and, as the health visitor had no statutory powers, she was unable to insist on seeing him. Neither the health visitor nor the social worker saw Steven alive again.

Role confusion can be precipitated by prescribing tasks to people who are not present at a meeting, so that they are not in a position to own the task or comment on its appropriateness. For example, the health visitor had not been invited to the first case conference on **Jasmine Beckford** and her sister which decided to return the children to their parents. Yet she was prescribed to visit fortnightly, with her monitoring used to help determine whether long-term fostering would be needed as an alternative to rehabilitation home. From then on, the social workers concentrated on parental help instead of their statutory role of child monitoring and protection.

Confusion about roles can also lead to inaction, with each worker believing that responsibility lies with someone else. For example, during the early phases of the **Lucie Gates** case, the NSPCC received three complaints within two months about neglect of the children but each time they withdrew immediately because of the involvement of a social worker. It was only after a fourth complaint, during the social worker's absence on leave, that an NSPCC officer undertook an assessment. In the **Lester Chapman** case, the health visitor decided that the case was not serious because it was not active on social services' books.

We would suggest a personal confusion about roles faced the social worker involved with **Jason Caesar**'s family. He had previously known both parents in their own right when working in a drug dependency unit. When Jason was born, the social worker visited occasionally to help with practical problems and he was later appointed key worker when Jason was admitted to hospital with fractures. The social worker agreed to give 'maximal support' to the family and it seems possible that he was unable to switch roles from supporting dependent young adults to being a statutory agent whose primary focus should have been the child. The effect seems to have been that other workers remained satisfied that the new situation (child abuse) was under control. When Jason was reported to be bruised again, social services only held a case conference of their own staff without inviting the health visitor and general practitioner who had examined Jason. The conference decided that there was no need to take further action.

Another possible example of personal role confusion is in the **Kimberley Carlile** case. The social worker who dealt with the case when it was transferred from another part of the country was the Area Team Manager. He had very recently been promoted to that position and we wonder whether he still experienced himself to be in transition from a field worker to a manager. He decided not to allocate the case for specific work to be undertaken, perhaps to protect his busy junior staff, but ended up working harder and harder himself. However, since the case remained unallocated, his involvement was only in response to demand and this precluded the possibility of a planned assessment. In addition, during the final phases of the case, he realised that the parents were not allowing him to examine the children and he concluded that the position was one of stalemate. He then asked the health visitor and school Head to maintain a watch over the family. However, this also proved ineffective, since these two workers possessed no statutory powers. The family managed to neutralise their monitoring attempts by declining access to the health visitor and transferring the children to a new school.

INTRA-AGENCY ORGANISATION

Much has already been written about the way that organisational procedures within agencies impeded communication and the Department of Health and Social Security review of child abuse inquiry reports (1982) summarises the many difficulties that occurred in the recording, storage and retrieval of information. As well as these issues, we would add two other relevant factors at the intra-agency level, which we have called 'Pivotal Worker Absent' and 'Weekend Phenomenon'. Although they depended on organisational arrangements within an agency, they also affected communication across the professional network.

Pivotal worker absent

In approximately one-third of the cases, a centrally involved professional was unavailable for some reason at a critical phase of the case and not infrequently in the crucial terminal stages when the abuse escalated and the child died. The practitioner's unavailability was most often an actual absence on leave or because of illness but we also include under this heading an inferred psychological unavailability, such as imminent plans to leave the post.

Clearly, a pivotal worker's absence raises many issues. Parents who have become dependent on a worker may feel abandoned or others may have to shoulder an increased burden of responsibility. However, we believe that a pivotal worker's absence is most relevant because information about the case needs to be passed on to a colleague. The pivotal worker has to decide which pieces of information are the most important, must arrange to convey them to a relevant other person and must transmit the information in a way that allows the required action to be clear and agreed. Confusions can arise from contradictions between the message content and the metacommunications. For example, the pivotal worker might pass on the case file in such a way as to convey: 'Please accept responsibility for my case but don't change anything before I get back.' Unscheduled absences do not allow for any handover to occur and this makes greater demands on the covering worker, who inherits the case but not the absent worker's knowledge and relationship to it.

Before **Shirley Woodcock** was fostered into the family where she died, there had been a number of crisis alerts at a time when the key social worker was away. The first was on a Friday and was taken by the stand-by duty team. Then, the nursery staff found marks on Shirley's brother's buttocks. A case conference was called for the following day but the social worker and Assistant Area Officer were both on leave and decisions, including whether to register the children as 'at risk', were deferred until they returned. The social worker subsequently misunderstood that the conference had concluded that there was insufficient evidence to consider the children to be at risk. A month later, the neighbours complained that the children were being left unattended, again when the key social worker was on leave. Shirley was placed with foster parents but was still noted to be bruised. During that time, her social worker was recurrently on sick leave and meetings intended to discuss Shirley's placement did not take place. Shirley was killed during the social worker's protracted sick leave.

There were a number of other examples. In the **Tyra Henry** case, the social worker had to take compassionate leave within a few weeks of the case conference decision to apply for a full Care Order. Thereafter, she kept minimal records. It is also likely that Tyra's mother secretly moved back to live with Tyra's father, who eventually killed her, around the time that the social worker went on a month's annual leave. Tyra was progressively assaulted during that month. A health visitor was the main professional monitoring **Max Piazzani**'s development but she was herself suddenly admitted to hospital and no one visited for about five months. Soon after the health visitor returned to work the family went on holiday and then so did she and on her return she left the service. No key worker was available when, three weeks later, the parents initiated contact with the health clinic at a time of crisis and Max was killed two days later before anyone could intervene effectively. Not only were social services on strike during the final months of **Maria Mehmedagi**'s life but the health visitor was also away on a week's course. This was immediately followed by the social worker's absence on a week's leave and she returned the day before Maria's father fatally assaulted her. **Richard Fraser** was killed during his social worker's month-long summer leave but that leave was also the interlude between the social worker finishing work in one area office and moving to another. **Karen Spencer**'s social worker obtained a new job three months after Karen returned home from foster care. She had made a joint visit with her successor as a preliminary to handing over a month later but, before that could happen, Karen was killed by her mother.

The **Lucie Gates** case illustrates actual problems of information transfer between a worker who is leaving and her successor. The first social worker had been key worker for three years, up to the time that she left the department. She had had an intense involvement with the family, actively supporting and encouraging Lucie's mother to improve her parenting skills and she carried the greatest optimism that the family could stay together. She left without forwarding a promised case summary or the file to the new social worker and she continued visiting informally over the next year. The new social worker was left with little knowledge of the case and neither her Senior nor Divisional Officer was familiar with it. The file was never located and it took many months before the new social worker was able to meet her predecessor to reconstruct the history. Clearly, the old social worker's investment in the case and difficulty giving it up significantly affected the transfer of information between workers.

Weekend phenomenon

We observed that some significant turning points in the cases had occurred out of office hours. Exploring this further, we found that in about one-third of the reports there was evidence that critical events had coincided with weekends or public holidays. We have called this the 'weekend phenomenon'.

It must be of some significance that at weekends agencies are staffed by duty teams who usually have no direct knowledge of the case and have few contemporary records. Another factor must be that at weekends or public holidays a worker tends to respond with a 'least that needs to be done' approach, waiting for the knowledgeable team to pick up the case again. On-call workers have difficulty obtaining a coherent overview of the situation and weighing up the relevance of available information because of their unfamiliarity with the background. They usually work alone and without full back-up support, so that anxiety may well colour their responses to emergencies. Should the regular worker have anticipated problems and attempted to convey this to the duty team, their communications are prey to all the difficulties discussed previously.

There were two cases in which an infant was discharged home from hospital at a weekend in apparent disregard of a decision to keep him/her on the ward. **Charlene Salt** was readmitted to hospital aged 2 weeks when the midwife found her dirty, hungry and bruised at home. The next day, a Place of Safety Order was taken out because of unexplained bruising. Following a case conference, the parents were told that if they were to spend the next Saturday at the hospital learning how to look after Charlene, they would be allowed to take her home on the Monday. It is unclear from this brief inquiry report how the decision was made to discharge Charlene but even though her parents did not visit the hospital at all over the weekend, she was still discharged from that 'place of safety' on the Monday. It was left to the duty social worker to inform her Team Leader that the contract had been broken. From that time onwards, Charlene's parents allowed professional staff less and less access to her.

Similarly, **Simon Peacock** was transferred to the hospital special care baby unit for assessment of his jaundice and feeding difficulties when only a few weeks old. The hospital staff had been concerned about his father's verbal and physical violence to the mother and they referred the case to social services, who took out a Place of Safety Order because of Simon's failure to thrive. The social worker discussed the Order with the medical staff but the following Saturday a doctor confirmed that the mother and baby were fit for discharge. An apparent lack of clarity over the reasons for taking out the Place of Safety Order is exemplified by the conclusions of the case conference five days later, in which the Order was allowed to lapse and social services decided only to be involved again on request. Thereafter, case transfer notices contained no indication of the seriousness of risk to the baby.

Louise, younger sister of **Jasmine Beckford**, was first admitted to hospital with severe physical injuries on a Saturday. The admitting junior doctor did not inform the hospital social worker and so Jasmine, still at home, remained un-protected. On the Monday, the hospital social worker informed social services, who made an unsuccessful attempt at a home visit. The next day, Jasmine, too, was taken to hospital with non-accidental injuries. **Darryn Clarke** was severely maltreated over many years but crises arose on a number of holidays and weekends, during which the strength of concern was not clarified or transmitted between professionals. On a Boxing Day, his mother's family told the police of their worry that they had not seen Darryn, his mother or his step-father. The police believed that this represented a family dispute but did contact social services. However, their records were not available until 28 December, the day the social worker started leave. The extended family's concern was renewed on 30 December (a Friday, leading up to the New Year's Eve weekend) when they saw Darryn with severe scalds and they telephoned the NSPCC, who contacted social services. Although the social worker and the health visitor attempted to visit, neither had managed to understand the nature of the anxiety or the degree of risk involved. A few weeks later, again on a Friday, the extended family felt it necessary to contact the NSPCC but, once again, messages between the NSPCC, social services and the police diluted the concern. Darryn died seven days later.

Some cases included more overt crisis alerts at weekends. The social services department responsible for **Kimberley Carlile** received an anonymous telephone call on a Friday about a little girl being beaten. The duty officer and duty Team Manager made a home visit but were refused sight of the children. It was not until Monday that the social worker with knowledge of the case was able to pick it up. He decided to adopt a more authoritarian approach than he had done previously and wrote a confronting letter to the parents insisting that the children must be seen. Even though the family eventually undermined this approach, it is interesting to speculate whether the intervening time lapse made a difference. The **Heidi Koseda** case is noted for the NSPCC officer who recorded in the notes an emergency home visit that he had not made. We discovered that this crisis and the fabricated note of a visit had occurred on a Friday and just two weeks prior to that officer leaving the NSPCC for a full-time course.

After **Maria Colwell** had been returned home to her mother and step-father, professionals received a number of reports of her mistreatment. One report to the NSPCC of bruising occurred on a Friday and the officer was eventually able to examine Maria, although she accepted the family's explanation that it was an accident. That Sunday, the police were called during an argument between the parents and, although the police knew of the social services' and the NSPCC's involvement, they made no contact with them. Later that Sunday, a neighbour overheard the parents arguing and blaming each other for hitting Maria. The neighbour contacted the NSPCC officer by a hand-delivered letter. These concerns were picked up by the NSPCC officer and social worker on the Monday but without the full knowledge of the weekend events, so that these incidents, as with many others, did not alter the course of the case.

Lester Chapman ran away from home repeatedly and on the final occasion he died of exposure. The first time he ran away was on a Friday. His mother had beaten him with a belt and later both parents went out to the pub and when they returned Lester was missing. They contacted the police, who already had found him. There was considerable bruising and weals to his buttocks but neither the police surgeon nor the duty social worker considered that a Place of Safety Order was required and Lester went home. Lester ran away again that Monday and one wonders whether a different assessment might have occurred at a time other than a weekend.

In the final two months between the placement of **Gavin Mabey** and his brother with new foster parents and Gavin's death, statutory agencies received five anonymous telephone calls alleging abuse of the children. The first four were made by the same caller and the final one, on the day of Gavin's fatal injuries, was by a different person:

17 July 1987 (Friday) – to social services
24 July 1987 (Friday) – to social services
29 July 1987   – to social services
31 July 1987 (Friday) – to the NSPCC
20 August 1987   – to social services

The only call which received an immediate response was that on the Friday evening to the NSPCC, when an officer visited and examined Gavin but accepted the foster parents' explanation for his bruising. Social services' response to the other calls during July was to wait until the children were due to be seen for supervised access visits or paediatric appointments a few days later.

Claire Haddon's mother telephoned social services on a Thursday in response to the social worker's note saying she had made an unsuccessful visit the previous day. Claire's mother said she would remake contact after the weekend but that Sunday Claire was fatally assaulted by both her parents. **Maria Colwell** and **Richard Fraser** also died on a Sunday, **Karen Spencer** on a Saturday and the **anonymous** baby on a Friday.

SUMMARY

Relationship issues at a number of levels qualified the content of communications between professionals and restricted their effectiveness. Sometimes, over-rigid boundaries developed between groups of workers, preventing the exchange of information between them or co-operative planning. We refer to these relationship patterns as: closed professional system, polarisation and exaggeration of hierarchy. Where the boundary between practitioners became too diffuse, there was a lack of differentiation between roles and role confusion. The absence of a pivotal worker or critical events coinciding with weekends or public holidays also influenced communication between workers.

Chapter 8

The assessment process

We shall now consider the central place of assessment in child protection work and illustrate how problems in the assessment process influenced decisions and interventions in the cases. Sometimes, children were returned home without appraisal of their parents' ability to look after them or case conferences decided to return children home and only afterwards to undertake an assessment of the parents. In other cases, decisions were made on partial information without considering the significance of a parent's new partner or the relationship between a couple.

In order to address these issues we must first pose the question: what is the purpose of assessment? The aim of assessment is to guide action. All professionals working with children and families may, at times, need to take action to protect a child, if only to pass their concerns on to another worker. Information received from others or direct observations made during ongoing contact must be weighed up and organised in order to suggest the most appropriate response. This assessment process includes identifying the problems and their severity and gathering other relevant information to help form an opinion about the degree of risk to the child. Assessment, therefore, is an ongoing process and at each step new information needs to be evaluated and given meaning. In this way, a picture emerges of the possible origins of the problems and how they might be resolved or contained. Assessment is thus both an activity in itself and a process of understanding. Without it, workers are left to react to events and intervene in an unplanned way.

The assessment process depends on individual professional practice and collective inter-professional collaboration. Individual workers need to monitor their observations constantly and ask themselves questions such as: 'Should I be worried about this?' and 'What should I do now?' They need to have acquired from their training a framework for thinking about and organising information, upon which is built confidence in making judgements. They must also be able to tolerate uncertainty and a degree of anxiety. Relevant anxiety about a child's safety in a confident and supported worker promotes appropriate protective measures. However, excessive anxiety is disabling and often leads to precipitate and ill-considered action in order to get rid of the discomforting tension.

Alternatively, it may produce an inability to think, paralysis and inaction. Furthermore, the observations and appraisals made by one individual only constitute a partial picture and need to be integrated with those made by other workers. Out of context, one worker's concerns about a problem may remain at a moderate level of anxiety. When all the observations are brought together, their cumulative effect can reach a critical threshold which demands a different response.

Assessment, then, is a process by which professionals acquire and process information, communicate about it and determine what action to take. Dingwall (1986) suggests that information needs to be available at an appropriate time in a usable form and he classifies four types of information, each of which requires a different response. First, when information is completely unknown, procedures are required for locating and developing new knowledge. Second, information may be known but not fully appreciated or interpreted, perhaps because of a false sense of security, pressure from competing tasks, distrust of the information source, distraction by a different problem or an inability to distinguish what is relevant or irrelevant. Third, information may not be fully assembled because no one person sees enough of the picture to recognise its significance. Or, fourth, information may be available but does not fit current modes of understanding.

Over the thirty-five cases, we saw a number of recurrent themes in the way that the assessment process was approached, which equate well with Dingwall's classification. They suggest that workers often did not have available to them a framework within which to organise information and observations about the family or consider their implications. We shall discuss these themes under the following headings: 'Information Treated Discretely', 'Selective Interpretations', 'Pervasive Belief Systems' and 'Concrete Solutions'.

INFORMATION TREATED DISCRETELY

The assessment process only has meaning when all information is pooled together and allowed to contribute to an overall and multi-dimensional picture. Details about the past history and the present circumstances need to be integrated to provide a context for understanding all new knowledge. For example, a bruise observed by a teacher takes on greater significance in the context of a child on the Child Protection Register who has just been returned home on trial. It acquires even more meaning when considered together with a health visitor's awareness of increasing violence between the parental couple and the social worker's realisation that s/he is unable to gain access to the house. Taken separately, each of these items of information might be viewed as unremarkable. Considered together, they produce a very worrying picture.

One striking observation that we made in a large number of the cases was how events were considered in isolation from each other so that no coherent overview emerged. In some instances we found that, over time, an individual worker treated discretely the successive pieces of information that were available. In other examples, workers did not integrate information known to them with that concurrently held by others in the network. Therefore, information was treated discretely either individually or collectively to the detriment of the assessment process.

The **Richard Clark** case was a graphic example. Richard and his elder brother were looked after by the Duncans as an informal arrangement after Mrs Clark had stabbed Mr Clark in a fight. However, the Duncans were already known to social services and the Royal Scottish Society for the Prevention of Cruelty to Children because of neglect of their own children, for which Mr Duncan had been imprisoned for three months and Mrs Duncan placed on two years' probation. When the RSSPCC worker expressed concern that the boys would be an unfair burden on Mrs Duncan, the social worker responded that it would be unfair to condemn the Duncans because of their past history. The social services department concluded that the Duncans were unsuitable as *official* foster parents but they arranged for Mr Clark to increase his maintenance payment to the Duncans by one pound a week and they accepted them as *unofficial* foster parents. Each subsequent report of Richard's bruising and listlessness was treated as a discrete event, out of context of this history and no changes were made to the plan.

The **Susan Aukland** case is an illustration of current information remaining dissociated from past history and although many assessments took place they were not integrated into a relevant, contemporary picture. The father, John Aukland, had a history of chronic emotional dependency and was reliant on alcohol, prescribed drugs, sick notes and his wife, Barbara Aukland (see Chapters 4 and 5). He killed their first child, Marianne, when she was 9 weeks old and a psychiatrist's report at that time identified that Marianne's birth had exacerbated his recurrent anxieties and depression. A pattern continued of heightened anxiety and psychosomatic complaints around the births of each child, followed by abusive behaviour and John Roy, the second child was severely scalded as a young baby. However, recognition of this cycle was probably impeded by misleading information from the family and inadequate communication between professionals about the background. For example, when John Roy was born, the hospital informed social services but did not pass on the history, so that the social worker believed that Barbara Aukland had been responsible for Marianne's death. The health visitor was also unaware of the family history. During his wife's pregnancy with their next child, John Aukland was referred with a psychosomatic skin complaint to the same psychiatrist who had seen him just before he had killed Marianne. His assessment concluded that the father was an 'irresponsible psychopath who lacked self-criticism' but the case lapsed when John Aukland failed to return for the next appointment and no integration was made with previous assessments. After John Roy was admitted to hospital with scalds, Barbara Aukland told the social worker that Marianne had died from an accident. The case was transferred to a new social services office after Susan was born and the new social worker only visited once before agreeing to close the case. When Susan was 1 year old, Barbara Aukland left the home because of her husband's cruelty and heavy drinking and Susan was received into voluntary care. Seen in the light of John Aukland's chronic dependency, the loss of his wife was a critical stressor and could have been expected to decrease his tolerance of dependent children and heighten the risk of his abusing them. However, when John Aukland asked for Susan to be returned to live with him and his two elder children, social services agreed provided that his own mother supported him. Barbara Aukland then called at her local social services office to seek advice on having her children back with her and she recounted the history of Marianne's death. This alarmed the duty social worker, who telephoned the family social worker. However, Susan remained at home until John Aukland fatally assaulted her two weeks later.

Throughout the **Lester Chapman** case, evidence was available and accumulating about the danger to Lester and his sister, Wendy, following their return home from care. This becomes clear when the events are listed:

- the social worker records that Lester 'sets himself up to be smacked';
- Lester is taken to casualty with an injured finger and Wendy with a broken nose;
- Lester is taken to casualty with a laceration to his eyebrow;
- Lester sustains a laceration to his forehead;
- Lester and Wendy are difficult to handle at school and the school believe that Lester is blamed for family problems;
- Lester is kept off school because of a black eye sustained when his step-father lost his temper;
- the mother complains that the step-father is bruising Lester;
- the mother calls the NSPCC about bruising on Lester's buttocks;
- the mother asks the social worker to visit because the step-father has hit Lester;
- the step-father accuses the mother of hitting Lester;
- the step-father asks the social worker to visit;
- an NSPCC inspector visits because Lester is lighting fires in the living room;
- Wendy goes to school alone and is knocked down by a car;
- a nursery officer sees bruises on Wendy and her sister Marie and although this is reported to social services, no link is made with Lester and Wendy's file;
- Lester is admitted to hospital with stomach pains and vomiting and he is reluctant to go home;
- Wendy and Lester are admitted to hospital with stomach pains and are frightened about supernatural monsters;
- Wendy is discharged but she is 'hysterical' at home and is readmitted;
- Lester is discharged from hospital and is reluctant to go home;
- the children's names are taken off the At Risk Register by the review panel but no case conference is held;
- the health visitor notes bruising to Marie's eye and contacts social services but finds the case is inactive there;

- Wendy is referred to the school nurse with marks on her upper arm;
- Wendy's tooth is kicked out, allegedly during horseplay with her mother;
- after Lester is beaten by his mother, the parents go to a pub and Lester is missing when they return;
- Lester runs away and threatens to jump into the canal;
- Lester runs away;
- the step-father asks the social worker to take Lester into care;
- Lester goes missing and is reported to have said that he was going to the railway to get killed by a train;
- Lester's body is found in sewage mud.

These events cover over a six-year period but when they are considered together the degree of suffering and risk becomes unmistakable. Integration of the history in this way to create an overall picture is a specific component of assessment and must be undertaken consciously and deliberately and this case contains many lost opportunities to do so. For example, a case conference, at which the available knowledge could have integrated, did not take place until after Lester went missing for the final time and the NSPCC officer was unaware of the family history when he made his assessment. Also, when the health visitor observed that Marie was bruised she allowed her anxiety to be assuaged by the fact that the case was not active within social services. So, on an individual and collective basis, workers related discretely to separate items of information and an overall picture did not emerge.

A summary of eight years of the **Lucie Gates** case, during which time the mother, Linda Gates, had four children from four different fathers, indicates similar problems in the assessment process:

- Linda's first baby is adopted at birth;
- Linda initially intends to place her second baby, William, for adoption;
- William is treated in hospital after ingestion of rat poison;
- William is treated in hospital for a chest infection and bruising;
- William is treated in hospital for an ear infection and nappy rash;
- William is seen in hospital for a suspected fit, which is diagnosed as a temper tantrum;
- Mary is born without any ante-natal care;
- William is treated for a fractured elbow after falling down stairs;
- the home help reports that the mother hits her children excessively;
- Mary is treated in hospital for a chest infection and neglect is suspected;
- William is taken to hospital with a cut head after falling from scaffolding;
- William is admitted to hospital having fallen from a slide and inadequate supervision is suspected;
- William falls and fractures his nose;
- the home help reports that Linda punches her baby Mary and feeds her crisps and Pepsi-Cola;
- the NSPCC receive a complaint that the children are being left alone;

- the health visitor notes a burn on William's abdomen;
- Mary is taken to hospital with a cut leg after falling out of her cot;
- the NSPCC receive a referral that Mary is underweight and her nappy is not changed regularly;
- Mary is seen at the health clinic with a gaping eye wound and facial and chest bruising;
- the NSPCC receive a complaint about Linda throwing Mary downstairs;
- the health visitor and neighbours express concern about standards of care in the home;
- the NSPCC receive a complaint that the children are being left alone for long periods and their mother is hitting them excessively and when an inspector visits he finds the flat and the children very dirty;
- William and Mary are taken into care for one year;
- two weeks after their return home Mary swallows her mother's anti-depressant tablets;
- the health visitor reports that things are as bad as before;
- the previous foster mother sees Mary and reports loss of weight and bruising to the social worker;
- Mary is noted to be very dirty, bruised and scratched at the play group;
- William is taken to casualty with a head injury;
- Lucie is born and hospital staff are concerned about Linda's lack of interest in her;
- William and Mary are placed in foster care during their mother's confinement and William says that he does not want to go home;
- Mary returns from a visit to her mother with a split lip;
- Lucie is admitted to hospital three times with gastro-enteritis;
- William swallows some tablets;
- at the hospital check-up Linda is noted to be feeding solids to the new-born baby Lucie;
- Lucie is admitted to hospital having been dropped on her head 'by a child', there are unexplained blisters on her hand and the health visitor finds no food at home;
- neighbours complain that the children are being left alone in the home;
- the social worker finds the children left unattended at home;
- Mary is admitted to hospital with a cut head having fallen from her bunk-bed;
- the home help reports that Mary has fallen downstairs, Lucie is underweight and her mother is feeding her congealed milk;
- William is treated for infected scabies;
- a neighbour complains that the children are being left unattended;
- the health visitor reports concerns about Lucie's weight;
- a friend reports that Linda has given William a black eye;
- Lucie is admitted to hospital with an ear infection and is noted to be bruised;
- Lucie puts on weight in hospital;
- Lucie is admitted to hospital with a respiratory infection;

- a neighbour tells social services that the flat is unheated and when the social worker visits she sees scratches on Lucie's face;
- the home help sees that Lucie has two black eyes;
- the social worker writes to Linda about her failure to attend the health clinic;
- there are numerous reports of cuts, bruises and nits on the children;
- Lucie's two-year check shows that she is underweight and understimulated;
- at a case conference all the children are reported to be dirty and smelling of urine, Lucie has lost weight and has had numerous infections;
- a lodger hits William during an argument with Linda;
- Lucie hits her head at a party and the hospital social worker is concerned about the number of reported accidents;
- neighbours worry about the children being left alone and being beaten by their mother;
- Linda beats Mary in front of her teacher;
- Lucie falls out of her pushchair and sustains a large bruise;
- Lucie is taken to casualty having 'fallen off a record player';
- a volunteer worker finds Lucie alone in the flat;
- Linda goes out to a pub leaving the children alone and an electric fire falls on Lucie and fatally burns her.

Many opportunities arose during those eight years for information to be synthesised and considered in total. Indeed, each time the children presented to hospital or each time a complaint was received there was a crucial need to link it to other knowledge about the family. On a number of occasions, a worker visited and made an assessment or report about the single complaint that had most recently been received. When a new social worker assumed responsibility for the case, the file was missing and her predecessor took six months to agree to a meeting in order to reconstruct the history. On one occasion, a health visitor reported that Lucie was gaining weight while at another health clinic she was described as underweight and a 'poor specimen'. A percentile chart, which diagrammatically portrays a child's weight and height over time and compares it with norms, would have integrated the discrete measurements that were made and translated them into information of relevance. Although both the NSPCC and social services received numerous complaints about the family, no NSPCC representative was present at the four case conferences held by social services. At one time, Mary was referred to a child guidance clinic because of slow development but their report only addressed her ability to cope in an ordinary school. Care proceedings were considered at various times but professionals always concluded that there were insufficient grounds.

In the **Neil Howlett** case, the general practitioner, health visitor, the NSPCC officer, a parent and child centre, the police and the social worker were all aware of signs or complaints of maltreatment but the individual incidents were not considered together as a whole. In addition, workers visited in response to a complaint but at the time could find little apparent evidence of neglect and they reported that Neil appeared to be 'in good spirits'. Professionals' anxiety then abated because they had only considered that one incident.

SELECTIVE INTERPRETATIONS

We have already discussed the fact that assessment involves the monitoring of observations in order to discriminate whether the information is relevant or serious. In a majority of cases, recurrent bruising or injuries to the children were observed but not interpreted by the workers as indicative of risk. We wonder whether professionals unwittingly resisted acknowledging the significance of what they were seeing because of insecurity about committing themselves to a definitive point of view or because they feared taking responsibility for initiating the child protection procedures this would have demanded.

Dingwall *et al.* (1983) have shown that front-line professionals, such as social workers and health visitors, make assumptions about the qualities of care that can be expected from the different families they visit. They adjust their sights accordingly and apply a 'rule of optimism' in which they always think the best of parents. The meaning they attribute to observations about the family tends to be organised by that optimistic presumption. Undue optimism seems to have interfered with the assessment of **Christopher Pinder/Daniel Frankland**'s safety. He was placed with the Franklands just four days after they were approved as adoptive parents. They had been expecting to wait a long time for a baby and almost immediately Mrs Frankland began pleading that she could not cope with his screaming demands and changeable needs. However, the professionals focussed on the child and saw a 'bright, alert baby' who was reaching his developmental milestones. While the adoptive mother spoke of 'not coping' and 'sending him back', they described him as a 'happy, bouncing, outgoing child'. The Franklands' difficulties were underestimated as a result of the professionals' optimism that, with a little reassurance and extra help, all would be well. This idea was reinforced when Mrs Frankland regained 'her usual efficient manner' after a brief contact with the social worker.

Sometimes, workers became desensitised to poor standards of caretaking in the family and, over time, they tolerated conditions of hygiene and care that were later described as appalling. By accommodating in this way, their threshold of concern, which might have led them to take protective action, was progressively raised. The most vivid example was the **Malcolm Page** case. The social worker and health visitor visited the family regularly and from time to time exhorted the parents to clean up their flat. Occasionally, the parents made minor improvements but they were always temporary and below the standards originally demanded. The workers probably accommodated to these conditions because the parents appeared to be co-operating. Sometimes, the workers confronted the parents but then they undermined their own intervention by taking over the home care themselves. The overall effect was a status quo between the family and workers within which the child and home care conditions progressively deteriorated. Following Malcolm's death from neglect and malnutrition, the police found piles of excrement, urine soaked bed-clothes, milk bottles and dirty clothes in his freezing cold room.

As summarised above, the caretaking ability of **Lucie Gates'** mother progressively deteriorated over many years with all her children repeatedly showing evidence of dirty, chaotic, neglectful and abusive upbringing. She was considered immature and in constant need of support. Although one of the social workers and a health visitor considered the possibility of taking Lucie into care, professional concern never reached the critical level which would have demanded protective action. Instead, the case conferences decided to increase home help support, influenced by the occasions when temporary improvement followed confrontation by a worker. Undue optimism also contributed to this process. Despite all the available evidence that Linda Gates' care of her children was inadequate, her flair for making Christmas preparations and attempts to create 'ideal' family events, such as outings to the zoo, made everyone believe that she was fundamentally a good mother. However, they did not recognise a pattern in which Linda Gates became seriously depressed after each 'idealised' event, as though let down, and the number of accidents to the children increased. Lucie died after a family outing to the zoo.

Menzies (1970) reports that professional groups may relieve the stress of decision-taking by applying ritualised routines for the acquisition and processing of information. These routines are followed mechanically and thoughtlessly so that even if relevant information is obtained no meaningful sense is made of it. These processes could have been behind some of the incidents in which we noted that observations about children's safety were made routinely and not weighed up for their significance. For instance, the health visitor regularly recorded **Jasmine Beckford**'s height and weight but did not interpret from them that she was failing to thrive at home. Again, the infant **Maria Mehmedagi** lost 11½ oz. in one week after returning home to her natural mother from care but the health visitor was not concerned because she considered Maria to have been overweight in the first place.

Some parents gave hints in a disguised way that abuse was escalating, so that the practitioner first needed to translate the information in order to become aware of its significance. For example, only a week before he was killed, **Jason Caesar**'s mother asked the hospital to admit him in order to investigate his 'tendency to fall'. **Lester Chapman**'s step-father asked for Lester to be taken into care several times. Two days before **Max Piazzani** was fatally assaulted, his mother telephoned the health clinic and asked for him to be taken into residential care and a few days before **Reuben Carthy** died, his mother again asked for day care for him. In the weeks preceding **Shirley Woodcock**'s death, her foster mother repeatedly told the childminder and general practitioner about her severe headaches. Only a few days before **Tyra Henry**'s elder brother, Tyrone, was seriously injured by their father, Tyrone had been admitted to hospital with gastro-intestinal problems. His parents volunteered to hospital staff that he had sustained two recent accidents: they said that he had fallen off the bed and that the bathstand had collapsed when his father was bathing him and he had dropped Tyrone in panic. The week before **Richard Clark** sustained near fatal injuries his 'foster' mother stopped the health visitor in the street and asked what medical condition caused bruising, saying that she was being accused of beating her children.

PERVASIVE BELIEF SYSTEMS

Professional thinking can be organised by overriding beliefs about a case. These beliefs may be determined by socio-political attitudes (as discussed in Chapter 2), strong personal or professional views (see Chapter 6) or inferences drawn from ongoing work with a family which develop into automatic thinking about them. Once a case becomes dominated by a fixed view, workers' selective attention is likely to distort their observations and any contradictory information becomes difficult to acknowledge. We have referred to this process in Chapter 7 in the section on closed professional systems. We found a number of cases in which pervasive beliefs seemed to dominate most decisions and actions.

In the 1970s, the prevalent social belief was that children were better off living with their natural parent/s. **Maria Colwell** had only spent the first five months of her life with her mother and for the next six years had been looked after by her aunt and uncle, with just two brief interludes in alternative placements. However, Maria probably had a special meaning to her mother (as discussed in Chapter 5), who never fully lost contact with her and she recurrently asked to have her returned. This corresponded with the social services' policy and long-term plan to return Maria to her natural mother, formulated when Maria was taken into care at the age of 1 year. They also assumed that the court would rule in favour of rehabilitation. Maria returned home on trial aged 6 years 7 months and this decision was so clearly viewed as desirable and inevitable that no assessment took place of the mother's new family circumstances and little was known about her new husband. All subsequent evidence of Maria's plight, such as her failure to thrive, weight loss, bruising, running away, her step-father's drunkenness and aggressiveness and her mother's neglect of her, had to be discounted in order to confirm the validity of the plan.

Although social workers applied for a Care Order on **Maria Mehmedagi** following her non-accidental injuries, they assumed that sooner or later she would return home. When the local social workers went on strike, their Director of Social Services introduced a rule that no child should be returned home without the consent of the Assistant Director. In reviewing the case, the Assistant Director had grave doubts about Maria's rehabilitation, based on the history of injuries, the father's violence to both Maria and her mother, the precarious marital relationship, Maria's special needs (she had suffered from pyloric stenosis and was considered a sickly baby) and her parents' denial of responsibility for her injuries. Even though this reassessment contained many contra-indications to rehabilitation, the plan went ahead with just a number of conditions specified for measuring possible future concern.

We shall cite two examples where initial impressions about a family led to the creation of fixed beliefs which came to dominate subsequent decisions. **Karen Spencer**'s mother was described as being of limited intelligence and lacking in confidence and Karen's father was said to be almost illiterate and immature. The couple had repeated fights in which he tried to assert his dominance over her. Karen was taken into care as a baby when her mother admitted dropping her and a case conference decided to allow Karen home for weekends if her father was present. This decision seems to have mirrored the father's conviction that he was capable and the mother incompetent. From that case conference onwards, Karen was gradually reintroduced home despite returning from weekends with a sore bottom through lack of care or clearly having been neglected when her father was the only parent at home to look after her. The idea that Karen was only safe when her father was present became an assumption that influenced everyone's thinking and it precluded an appreciation of the couple's fluctuating relationship and the role Karen played in this (see Chapter 5). Karen was killed by her mother following a marital argument.

The **Richard Fraser** case shows many parallels. Richard's father was repeatedly violent, dismissive and critical of Richard's mother. He often threatened her physically for neglecting Richard and eventually he beat her up and took Richard to a crisis reception centre. Richard's mother left the area and his father was then joined in the centre by a cohabitee. While the father was in prison for violence, Richard was seen to have sustained non-accidental injuries and was taken into care. A case conference decided not to return Richard to his father while he remained with his cohabitee but at the subsequent care proceedings the solicitors representing both parties came to an agreement for Richard to go home on trial provided that his father was present in the household. The early belief that Richard was safe when his father was there was reinforced by the legal process and continued despite contradictory evidence, such as his father's reimprisonment for violence and both parents' hostility to the social worker when he visited. It was Richard's father who was eventually charged with his murder.

CONCRETE SOLUTIONS

At some point in at least half of the cases we were able to note an attempt to resolve problems through what we have called 'concrete solutions'. We mean by this that undue reliance was placed on very practical measures as a means of dealing with or monitoring problems which were essentially emotional. While we recognise the value of practical assistance, we were struck by how often it became the main intervention to some families. In other cases, practical indicators were taken as the sole measure of whether caretaking had improved.

One example of concrete solutions has already been mentioned in Chapter 7, in which the magistrate ruled in favour of revoking **Wayne Brewer**'s Care Order because his mother and step-father had cleaned up and decorated their flat and borrowed books on child care from the library. In the **Lester Chapman** case, Lester and his sister had spent two and a half years in care because of parental neglect and during divorce proceedings their mother applied for custody of both children. The presiding judge was impressed by their mother's new partner and especially the fact that he was in employment and presented 'good prospects for a home life'. Lester and his sister were returned home on trial and when the couple later applied for full custody, it was granted without the social worker being invited to give evidence.

Rehousing was sometimes relied on as the main intervention to improve child care: for example, in the **Jasmine Beckford**, **Maria Colwell**, **Lucie Gates**, **Lisa Godfrey**, **Claire Haddon**, **Tyra Henry**, **Karen Spencer** and **Carly Taylor** cases. The psychiatrist who saw **Karen Spencer**'s mother following her overdose wrote a court report commenting on lack of incentives for the parents. He recommended rehousing as a 'carrot' for Mr Spencer to become more involved with his wife and in the treatment. In addition, during a court hearing the police agreed to access arrangements being dependent on rehousing. The social worker pressed for **Lucie Gates'** mother to be given a chance to prove herself by being rehoused and she used the physical appearance of the flat to measure the mother's caretaking capacity. When Lucie's sister was seen to be bruised, the social worker thought that the injuries were unfortunate because her mother had been working hard to clean up the flat. This family also received tremendous practical help and support through home helps, health visiting and social work but without sustained improvements in self-reliance or parenting behaviour and all the children continued to show signs of abuse and neglect. Standards of hygiene were also used as the principal measure of good parenting in other cases, such as **Richard Clark** and **Malcolm Page**.

Undue reliance on concrete solutions can lull professionals into a false sense of security because they believe that work is being done but fail to assess whether it has an effect on the emotional and relationship problems contributing to the abuse. What is being highlighted here is the need to offer practical help as part of a broader intervention rather than it being an end in itself.

SUMMARY

Effective child protection work depends on professionals having a framework for thinking which enables them to bring together information from many sources. We have considered problems in the way information was organised, both individually and collectively, during the assessment process which impeded planning and decision-taking on the cases. Difficulties arose in various ways, which we have grouped together under the headings: information treated discretely, selective interpretations, pervasive belief systems and concrete solutions.

Chapter 9

The family–professional systems

A number of authors have described a family and its professional network as one large, interacting system (e.g. Britton 1981; Furniss 1983, 1991; Reder 1983, 1986; Dale and Davies 1985; Dimmock and Dungworth 1985; Dale *et al*. 1986; Imber-Black 1988; Hardwick 1991). Such systems arise in various ways. The family may keep turning to new sources of help without completing the treatment originally offered or is successively referred on by therapists who feel defeated by its problems. Sometimes, workers become so strongly entangled in the emotional life of the family that, when they refer to another agency, they remain involved in an attempt to influence the new worker (Main 1957; Selvini Palazzoli *et al*. 1980b). Specialisation of skills also means that various aspects of a problem need to be addressed by different professionals in a number of agencies. In the case of child abuse, it is primarily the nature of the problem that activates a large network of statutory and other workers who are deemed relevant to its solution. Anderson *et al*. (1986) refer to this as a 'problem-determined system'.

As workers become engaged in the family–professional system, they develop relationships not only with the family but also with other members of the professional network. When a family turns from one agency to another, there is the potential for competition between them as to who is able to offer the 'best' help. Alternatively, members of various agencies may identify with different members of the family and unwittingly re-enact their relationships and thus the network's interactions come to mirror those of the family. Britton (1981) has observed how this unconscious process is revealed by dogmatic opinions, the pressure to take drastic or urgent measures, inappropriate concern, surprising ignorance, undue complacency, uncharacteristic insensitivity or professional inertia. Britton describes examples in which:

> quarrels are pursued between workers who seem as incompatible in their views as are the parents; highhanded intervention by senior colleagues echoes the domination of a family by the intrusions of an opinionated grandparent. In another case a succession of professional agencies not only failed to accept responsibility but uncharacteristically failed to communicate with each other or acknowledge other workers' existence, thus echoing the family pattern of a

child who had been at different times abandoned by both his parents, long since separated, who related to him independently without acknowledging each other's existence.

(Britton 1981: 51)

This mirroring could explain some of the professional network problems discussed in Chapter 7, including polarisation and role confusion.

Hardwick (1991) characterises two extremes of family–professional interaction. Some families attract professionals in an attempt to overcome dependency needs and experiences of deprivation, while others resent what they view as intrusion and persecution. Between these two polarities are the families who develop an ambivalent relationship with the network and both attract and repel professionals. We understand Hardwick to be suggesting that some families are dominated by severe dependency/caring conflicts, some by extreme conflicts over control, while others show ambivalence in care and control relationships.

For their part, professional workers implicitly carry a mixture of these roles. For instance, the police, whose primary function is a controlling one, also perform community duties and caring professionals, such as nurses and doctors, also monitor and report suspicions of child abuse. It is in the social work profession that these dual roles are most overt, with social workers carrying both caring and statutory responsibilites. Taking a child 'into care' is the most obvious example.

A family's emotional or social problems will, at different times, evoke a varying combination of caring and controlling responses from practitioners, who need to find a balance that suits the particular circumstance. Changing situations also require the workers to alter the emphasis of their response, such as more towards care following a bereavement or more towards control when intrafamilial violence erupts.

We believe that problems of care and control are central in child abusing situations, with regard to relationships within the family and in the family's interactions with concerned professionals. We shall therefore review the main ideas that we formulated about the families in earlier chapters and then illustrate how care or control issues seemed to dominate many of the families' relationships with professionals.

CARE AND CONTROL CONFLICTS IN ABUSIVE BEHAVIOUR

Figure 4.4 brought together our views on the care and control conflicts underlying abusive behaviour in the thirty-five families. As far as could be judged from the reports, many parents had themselves been subjected to emotionally depriving care and/or physically abusive punishment when they were children. We would therefore expect that they grew up with unresolved dependency needs and severe conflicts about control. In adult life, they tended to seek partners on whom they could depend but instead found someone with similar problems. Each partner then frustrated the other's expectations of care so that they recurrently fought or moved on to new partners. When children were born, the parents apparently hoped that they would redress their longstanding, unmet needs for care. However, children are not only unable to look after their parents but also assert their own dependency demands. In such circumstances, this would have increased the prospect of the children being blamed or punished for failing in their expected role. All this was compounded by the parents' limited self-control and sensitivity to feeling controlled by others. We inferred that parents repeatedly experienced their partner and/or children as a threat to their self-esteem or as trying to control them: for example, when the partner threatened to leave or when a child cried. Violent episodes probably occurred when the parents enacted their frustration, lost self-control or punitively tried to control those experienced as a threat.

CARE AND CONTROL IMBALANCES IN THE FAMILY–PROFESSIONAL RELATIONSHIPS

We believe that where the parents could not resolve their care and control conflicts within the family, the same issues were played out in their relationships with others, including professionals. In some instances, the workers already knew the family or became involved because of reported suspicion of child abuse. Some parents invited workers to provide practical and emotional support and developed increasing reliance on it. Others tried to retain a sense of control over their lives by keeping workers at a distance. Members of the professional networks needed to find the appropriate balance between care and control. With some families, workers found themselves providing long-term and intensive support, while with others they were relentlessly trying to track down the elusive family. As the family–professional relationships progressed, they became dominated by these dependency or control issues which had taken on a life of their own. The imbalances which had emerged also interfered with the professionals' attempts to work together or to protect the child.

We found a number of recurrent patterns in the family–professional relationships centering around care–control imbalances, which we have termed: 'Dependency', 'Closure', 'Flight' and 'Disguised Compliance'.

DEPENDENCY

In this pattern of relationships, the imbalance was skewed towards care, sometimes with professionals trying to meet parental dependency needs as a way of improving their ability to look after their children. The usual philosophy behind such an approach was that provisions of material resources and help for adults with their parenting skills and with their self-esteem should also assist them in caring for their children more effectively. However, these professionals were then unwittingly drawn into meeting more and more demands from the parents for practical and emotional support and became as much stuck in the process of giving as the families did in asking. Attention to the parents often obscured the children's needs and the parents sometimes subtly vied with their children to be the main focus of input and concern.

The **Jasmine Beckford** inquiry report concluded that the social services department focussed their intervention on providing help and guidance to Jasmine's parents rather than child monitoring and protection. Both the parents had experienced deprivation and abuse as children and they severely assaulted Jasmine and her sister, who had to be removed into care. Social services then planned to return them home and to commence intensive visiting. The social worker and her Senior felt optimistic about the children's return and they provided a family aide and parenting skills advice for their mother. They kept up regular home visits but their preoccupation with the parents appears to have prevented them realising that over many months they had failed to see the children, who were still being abused.

The **Lucie Gates** case illustrates professionals being drawn into a pattern of trying to meet dependency needs over extended periods of time without being able to effect a change in parenting. In the previous chapter, we summarised the eight years of injuries, accidents and illnesses suffered by all three of Linda Gates' children. During that time, Linda received regular social work visits to provide her with emotional and financial support, intensive home help and rehousing, as well as nursery placements, holidays, respite care and relief fostering for the children. At one point, when the children returned home from voluntary care, the social worker and health visitor spent several hours each day helping Linda 'get on top of things' again. The home help eventually left because she felt that Linda was taking advantage of her and she described her as childish, moody, prone to temper tantrums and in need of someone with her twenty-four hours a day to stop the situation deteriorating. The health visitor also felt that Linda needed 'a grandma figure twenty-four hours a day'. A case conference on all three children recommended massive support to keep the family intact and envisaged a minimum of ten further years of social work input. The first social worker involved with the Gates family visited them weekly for a further year after she had left the social work department and the case had been reallocated. There is a danger in these situations of front-line professionals sharing a conviction with parents that they are essential to the family's well-being and that the family would collapse without their regular input. This belief can lead to the development of a closed system which excludes other workers who might adopt a more controlling approach. The NSPCC were called by neighbours to the Gates home on several occasions but withdrew after discussion with the social worker. It was only when the social worker was on leave that the NSPCC requested a case conference which resulted in the children temporarily going into care.

CLOSURE

This was a striking phenomenon, noted in over half of the thirty-five cases, in which the family attempted to tighten the boundary around themselves so that they reduced their contact with the external world and few people were able to meet or speak to them. For example, their curtains were always drawn, the children stopped playing outside and no longer attended school or nursery. The parents failed appointments with professionals, the children were not taken to scheduled visits to health clinics and social workers and health visitors could not obtain entry to the home when they called.

We found 'persistent closure' in only one case, **Heidi Koseda**, in which the family shunned all contact with professionals from the outset. In the majority of other cases, there was a cyclical 'intermittent closure', each recurrence coinciding with periods of increased stress originating from either within or outside the family, together with escalating abuse of the children. In about one-third of the cases the death of the child was preceded by a period of closure. Usually, this 'terminal closure' followed repeated episodes of intermittent closure but in some instances it arose as a new phenomenon.

We understood closure to be primarily an issue about control, with parents feeling that they were in precarious control of their lives and that outsiders were unwelcome intruders who would further undermine them. Past family histories often provided indications of control conflicts in their relationships with the authorities or helping professionals. This included refusal of ante-natal care, premature discharge from hospital against advice with threats of actual violence (see Chapter 4) and failure to register with a general practitioner. It would seem that the parents' tenuous sense of control over their lives was threatened when they were obliged to engage in relationships outside the family and they responded by distancing themselves and withdrawing. When professionals had to assume an investigative or monitoring role following allegations of abuse, their stance probably acted as one of the external stressors that exaggerated the parents' conflicts about being controlled. Therefore, not only would the parents experience their family life as being in turmoil but also that their conflicts were compounded by the professionals' response. We believe that they attempted to regain control by shutting out the professionals.

For example, when **Heidi Koseda**'s mother, Rosemary Koseda, was admitted to hospital for the birth of another baby and the father was told that the birth would be induced, he banged his head against the wall in rage. The baby was neither registered with the Registrar of Births nor with a general practitioner and the health visitor and the social worker failed to receive replies to their numerous visits. At the one child health clinic appointment that was kept, Rosemary Koseda said that they planned to move and this led to the family records being closed. The family also stopped contact with the maternal grandmother who had previously given them financial and other support and the neighbours noted that their curtains were always drawn.

Charlene Salt's mother defaulted from ante-natal care and Charlene's father threatened violence to a number of workers. The family was not registered with a general practitioner and the house curtains were usually closed. When Charlene was born, her father insisted on the mother's and baby's discharge less than ten hours after the birth and the health visitor was not admitted to the home when she called, although the midwife and social worker were. When these workers later found Charlene to be bruised, her father only agreed to her removal to hospital when he saw a police car outside. Once she was admitted, he threatened to snatch the baby and refused to let her mother stay with Charlene alone. Charlene was returned home on a Supervision Order but at times her parents did not allow the health visitor or nursery staff to examine her. The parents were not in when the social worker called and they failed the next developmental check and refused to attend it with the health visitor when she called. Six weeks before Charlene's death, her father told the social worker and nursery staff that he would no longer allow access to the health visitor and three weeks later the nursery noted lack of attendance and uncooperative parents. One week after that, the health visitor was replaced, partly because of reorganization but also because of the parents' lack of cooperation. The social worker became increasingly worried about Charlene's weight loss but the parents did not attend the social services review as requested and again the social worker was unable to gain access. The parents had been told that the social worker's heightened concern would be discussed at the review and this, together with attempts to increase surveillance, may well have been experienced by them as greater attempts to control them. Charlene was killed seven days after the review. We shall further consider the effect of professionals' increased attempts to monitor in these situations below.

There were many similarities in the **Simon Peacock** case. His mother was not registered with a general practitioner and made only one ante-natal visit prior to his birth. Even though Simon was in the post-natal ward on a Place of Safety Order, his father successfully demanded their discharge from hospital and, when the health visitor called, Simon's mother expressed reluctance to have further visits, refused to register with a general practitioner or visit the health clinic and said that they planned to move. The family complied with some of the subsequent arrangements made by the social worker and health visitor but were often out when they called. The family moved to a new area four weeks before Simon died but, when the new health visitor tried to introduce herself, she, too, failed to gain access. Although this was a planned move, post-mortem examination of Simon indicated that his injuries were of approximately three to four weeks' duration: in other words, his abuse had escalated from the time of that move to an area where the family were not known to professionals.

In most instances, the family withdrew from contact with all professionals but occasionally the closure was partial and one worker was allowed to keep in touch with them. This was so for **Maria Colwell**'s social worker, who shared a belief with Maria's mother that Maria would eventually return permanently to live with her (see Chapter 8). It is likely that the social worker was allowed within the family's boundary because she did not threaten change or undermine the parents' sense of control. Maria had stopped going to school two months before she died and, by contrast with the social worker who successfully visited during this time, an education welfare officer made six visits without being allowed to see her. At the first visit she was told that Maria had the 'flu; the second time she obtained no reply; the third time Maria's step-father said she had diarrhoea and vomiting and when the education welfare officer asked to see her she was told that Maria had gone shopping; the fourth time the step-father refused to let her see Maria and intimidated her with a strap; she obtained no reply to her next two visits.

Terminal closure

Only in retrospect was it possible to know that the closure was terminal. It manifested itself in the same way as other episodes and we believe that all closure should be considered as indicative of increased risk of fatal abuse. The length of time of such closure varied across the cases, ranging from a few days or weeks to ten months.

For example, **Lisa Godfrey**'s mother had regular contact with her probation officer, who became the central professional in the case. However, six weeks before the mother killed Lisa, she began to default from her appointments. At one visit she spoke of going to Ireland and leaving her two younger children in England. Then, Lisa's mother had an angry confrontation with staff at the day nursery about Lisa not wearing a sling for her fractured arm and Lisa stopped attending the nursery for the last three weeks of her life.

Jasmine Beckford's attendance at nursery school dropped significantly and she stopped attending altogether ten months before she died. The social workers continued to visit but hardly ever saw the children, often being told that they were staying with their grandmother. At one visit, four months before Jasmine's death, the parents carefully arranged to conceal that she had recently sustained a fractured leg. Towards the end of her life, the social workers made more determined efforts to see Jasmine but her mother responded angrily and said that she would telephone to arrange a meeting. Eventually, the social worker hand-delivered a letter saying that she and her Senior would visit the following day to start their review procedure. However, Jasmine was fatally assaulted that same day.

These incidents at the end of Jasmine's life require us to explore an additional, critical facet of family–professional interaction during terminal closure. In a number of other cases as well as **Jasmine Beckford**, the professionals realised that violence to the children was increasing and that they were being denied access to the home. They therefore made more strenuous efforts to see and examine the children. Usually, such action could be expected to lead to successful protection of the children but, in these circumstances, it was followed soon after by their death.

For instance, as we have outlined above, one week before **Charlene Salt** was killed, her parents failed to attend a social services case review, although they had been informed how important their presence was deemed to be. The social worker followed up unsuccessful attempts to visit with a letter informing them of a further review date but Charlene was killed before that could take place. Similarly, there was closure for ten days leading up to **Claire Haddon**'s death, during which time both the health visitor and social worker increased significantly the frequency of their visits.

These events can be explained by a combination of controlling and caring crises. In Figure 4.4, we illustrated how parents who felt out of control of their lives resorted to punitive control of the children or sudden rages of frustration. It appears that they tried to regain control by closing off from professionals. When these workers increased their efforts to see the children, the parents may well have experienced it as an attempt to impose even greater control from outside which further exacerbated their sense of disequilibrium. An escalating vicious circle must have ensued, as shown in Figure 9.1. The more the professionals exerted control, the more the parents felt out of control, and so on.

Figure 9.1 also depicts withdrawal of care adding to the crisis. In the **Jasmine Beckford** and **Charlene Salt** cases, for example, professionals had been offering support to the parents as a means of improving their caretaking. By insisting on seeing the children they were refocussing their attention away from the parents and this probably reawakened the parents' sense of deprivation and compounded their frustration.

If our analysis is valid, professionals face a considerable dilemma when deciding how to respond to closure. They cannot ignore the abuse of the child, yet the risk is increased if they adopt a more controlling stance. We shall discusss the implications of this in Chapter 11.

FLIGHT

Flight was a variant of closure in which families closed their boundaries and retreated from contact with the external world by moving elsewhere. The families repeatedly withdrew to other temporary homes where they were not known or else said that they intended to do so. They usually moved 'anonymously', leaving no forwarding address and not registering with helping agents in the new area. The effect was the same as closure, since they created an emotional and physical distance between themselves and professionals, seemingly as a way to control the relationship. Indeed, some cases involved episodes of both flight and closure.

Before **Carly Taylor** was born, her parents had moved around to numerous different addresses: flats, houses, a homeless families' unit, relatives, a bedsit and drug squats. They were sometimes evicted for failure to pay rent or for holding noisy parties and Carly's mother was felt to be unpredictably violent. She received no ante-natal care with Carly's pregnancy and discharged herself from hospital, leaving Carly and her twin sister in the special care baby unit. Although subsequently the children were seen to be bruised from time to time, the main concern of professionals was the mother's lack of emotional contact and interest in them. However, from the time that the family were rehoused, the

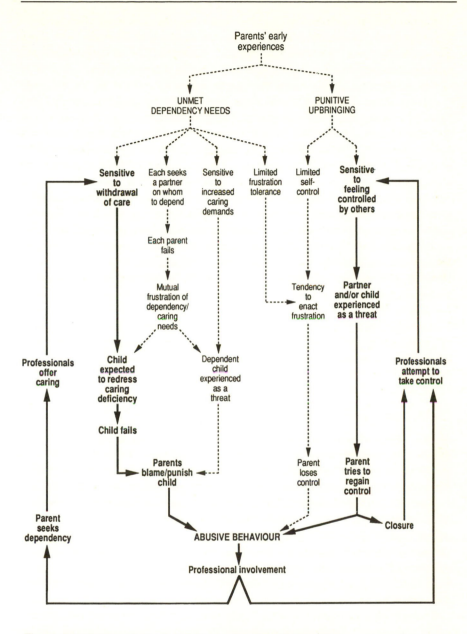

Figure 9.1 Vicious circles in family–professional interaction

family–professional relationship was more typical of closure rather than flight, with the health visitor, social worker and probation officer unable to gain access to the home on the majority of their visits.

Lester Chapman's mother, Linda, showed early signs of responding to stress with flight and in adolescence she was admitted to an adolescent unit from which she frequently absconded. After she married, she frequently left her husband and two children and when they were taken into care she disappeared and was located two months later at a gipsy camp. The children were returned to her after she had remarried, a decision taken by the judge because he was impressed by the new husband's employment and apparent stability. However, a year after Lester and his sister returned home, the family were evicted from their house and they moved to a mobile home. Nonetheless, they did allow the social worker regular access and eventually they were rehoused by the council. The social work file was closed when the family made plans to move to another county. During the year that they were living there, Wendy and Lester were admitted to hospital suffering from unexplained anxieties, Wendy was taken into care, both children's names were placed on the At Risk Register and a social worker visited the home regularly for three months. When the family returned to the original area, no referral was made to the local social services department, although the health authority did pass on information to the new health visiting service. The new health visitor found Lester's younger sister bruised and she contacted social services, only to learn that the case was not active and so her concern abated. Lester then began to show a flight pattern himself in response to stress, running away from home four times in two weeks after his parents severely assaulted him. His body was eventually found in sewage mud where he had died of exposure and drowning.

Flight, closure and fragmentation

As the **Lester Chapman** case illustrates, episodes of flight and closure often induce a fragmented response in the professional network. A family's flight from one home to another meant that they became known to a number of agencies. They often imparted selected information to each one and moved on again before a response could be planned. Discrete items of knowledge would then be held by different members of the professional network, who were largely unaware of others' involvement. No one agency obtained a coherent overview and assessments and interventions could not be co-ordinated. Thus, fragmentation amongst members of a professional network who were trying to monitor a family in flight must have been an additional factor preventing effective communication between them (see Chapter 7).

Darryn Clarke's parents were rarely seen by their extended family, who made ambiguous complaints to the police that they were worried about Darryn. At one time, the police misunderstood these expressions of concern to represent a family dispute. The police drew a blank in their search for Darryn when they contacted two hospitals and visited one possible address. They contacted social services but their referral was not believed to be urgent. However, the social worker and health visitor were also looking for Darryn but did not find him at various addresses. As concerns were passed around between the extended family, the NSPCC, social services and the health visitor, no one quite knew who was worried about what and the anxiety became diffused. Although information was often exchanged between the agencies, there was no agreement about who would pursue the investigation and each felt assured that the other was doing so. The health visitor visited the wrong address almost daily for a fortnight and although injuries to Darryn were reported to the authorities, these phone calls were either not recorded or were not followed up successfully.

Paul Brown's mother was unreliable in her contact with professionals, at times evasive or untruthful and changed address and partners many times. The inquiry report names at least twenty social workers who were directly or indirectly involved in the case over a four-year period, as well as four different health visitors and two general practitioners. There were many incidents of files, letters, transfer notices or records of phone calls getting lost and, at times, key workers did not even know where the children were staying.

The recruitment of new members to the professional network each time a family moved multiplied the complexities of inter-professional communication. **Stephen Menheniott**'s family showed episodes of closure and flight over many years. Stephen's father had run away from home to join the army and he and his wife had been imprisoned for ill-treatment of their two children. Afterwards, the father and his new partner began a nomadic existence and the next child was taken into care because they had no suitable accommodation. When Stephen was born, his parents were living in a caravan and soon he and his sister were taken into care because of the parents' homelessness. When Stephen was 1 year old, he was admitted to hospital for investigation of feeding difficulties but his father discharged him after two days. Later that year, Stephen was readmitted with weight loss but again his father discharged him. Stephen was taken into long-term care soon afterwards and remained there until he returned home aged 17. During that time, his mother had left the family and the others had moved to a remote part of the sparsely populated Isles of Scilly (off the Cornwall coast). Therefore, two different social services departments became concerned with Stephen: the one which had originally taken him into care; the other which had responsibility for the Isles of Scilly. While Stephen was in care, a planning conference offered some suggestions for his placement but they were not followed up and as he grew older his father made renewed requests for Stephen to return home. The local social services protested at the prospect that Stephen might return home but the other department disagreed and implemented the move. The assessment centre where Stephen had been staying believed that he was only going home for a holiday. The responsible social services department closed their file while Stephen was still 17 years old and officially in care to them but the local social services were unable to monitor the case effectively in such a remote area. Stephen's father killed him two years later.

DISGUISED COMPLIANCE

Sometimes, during cycles of intermittent closure, a professional worker would decide to adopt a more controlling stance. However, this was defused by apparent co-operation from the family. We have called this disguised compliance because its effect was to neutralise the professional's authority and return the relationship to closure and the previous status quo.

When **Kimberley Carlile**'s family moved to a new area, the local social services department was asked to monitor the children's care, although there was no statutory order empowering social workers to see them. A social worker wrote to the parents offering assistance which Kimberley's step-father aggressively rejected. However, her mother spontaneously called at the local health clinic and impressed the health visitor by her initiative. The health visitor was not to know that the mother had given selected information about the family, including the wrong address. A few months later, the children's schoolteachers became concerned about their welfare but again their mother managed to reinforce the health visitor's positive impression by taking one of her children to the health clinic. Then, social services received a complaint about a child being beaten in the house but, although two social workers were allowed into the home, they were refused sight of Kimberley and her younger sister, who were said to be asleep upstairs. Three days later, the social worker delivered a confronting letter saying that the two youngest children had to be medically examined or else the police would be informed. The next day the family telephoned social services, admitting that they had harmed Kimberley, and the duty social worker arranged an urgent meeting at the family's home the following afternoon with the social worker who knew them. However, in a move of apparent compliance which managed to undermine social services' more controlling stance, the family came instead to the department the next morning. Believing this indicated co-operation, the social worker agreed with them to seek a nursery school place for Kimberley and to have further meetings in a few weeks' time. The parents never took up the offer of the nursery place and they did not attend for health clinic appointments. Despite being concerned by what he had seen of Kimberley's appearance, the social worker still did not have any statutory powers and could only recommend medical examination for her. At a subsequent home visit, Kimberley's step-father allowed him into the house but only to glimpse her through a glass panel above a door and this pattern towards closure continued until Kimberley was killed.

After finding **Malcolm Page** severely neglected, the health visitor arranged a joint visit with a social worker and, at first, Malcolm's mother refused to open the door to them. Eventually, the workers confronted the parents with the state of the house and told them to clean up and to agree to regular health checks and social work visits. The next day, the social worker found the mother cleaning the house and this seems to have taken the sting out of her confronting stance, so that when she found that the children had not yet been medically examined she took them to the clinic herself. A home help was organised but was rarely allowed access to the house and, when she was, she described it as filthy. A case conference was called and the children were taken into care. The parents co-operated with the social worker, visiting their children and making strenuous efforts to clean the house and the children were returned. However, within a few days the social worker received no replies to her home visits and the home conditions deteriorated again. Although she spoke sternly to the mother and despite parental promises, the children were not taken to the next two health clinic appointments. At their next home visit, the social worker and home help realised that they had never been allowed upstairs, where they found sheets soaked with urine and encrusted with faeces. A case conference recommended that the social worker should put the position bluntly to the parents and that home help should be increased. The father agreed with the social worker that things had slipped a bit and he thought that his wife was depressed again. The case continued in this to and fro manner, with episodes of deterioration in the home and child care met with confrontation from the workers, followed by temporary periods of improvement and co-operation from the family. It ended in terminal closure, with the health visitor and social worker either unable to gain entry to the home or not shown Malcolm in his room upstairs.

THE 'NOT EXIST' DOUBLE BIND

Finally, we describe a process that requires explanation beyond the care/control framework used so far. At some time during the three cases involving what we have termed a 'not existing' pattern of abuse (see Chapter 4), the professionals realised that they had not seen the child and renewed their efforts to do so. The parents refused to allow them direct access to the child, yet the workers left the home satisfied that all was well and that the child was either safely asleep upstairs or staying with relatives. Our analysis of these three cases leads us to propose that the workers' mistaken satisfaction about the child's safety was because they were caught up in a double binding interaction with the parents. We shall first cite the examples and then describe the bind that we believe was operating.

The social worker visiting **Steven Meurs'** family was primarily concerned about the welfare of the two children his mother, Sandra Meurs, had informally fostered for a relative. The first alert about Steven came from an anonymous call to the police that Sandra was staying out all night and leaving the children alone. When the social worker saw Steven and found him to be 'pasty and dirty', Sandra became angry about the complaint and threatened to return the two fostered children to their mother. The social worker asked a health visitor to make an assessment but Sandra refused to let her see Steven. Despite receiving no reply on two subsequent visits, the health visitor reported back to the social worker that Steven seemed adequately cared for. She visited once more before his death, when Sandra again refused to let her see Steven and stood at the foot of the stairs saying he slept a lot. The health visitor left, apparently reassured about Steven's welfare.

The **Heidi Koseda** inquiry report records at least fifteen home visits by the health visitor over a period of a year to which she received no reply. During that year she was once allowed in but did not see Heidi because she was said to be asleep. Then, in response to a neighbour's alert, an NSPCC officer at first called to a wrong address and then falsified a report about a supposed second visit. A few days later, the health visitor was allowed into the home but was told that Heidi was asleep upstairs. However, when the health visitor spoke to the social worker she told her that she had seen both Heidi and her brother some months before and both seemed alright. Even after Heidi had died and her body lay in her room, the step-father told a visiting social worker and health visitor that Heidi was staying with friends. It was only after a telephone call many weeks later from Heidi's grandmother asking the social worker to ascertain her whereabouts, that the authorities realised that Heidi had not been seen.

During the final weeks of **Malcolm Page**'s life, the social worker made a number of home visits and found the downstairs of the house warm and clean. However, she did not see Malcolm upstairs, who was starving in a cold and filthy room, as though he had ceased to exist.

How might the workers' behaviour be explained? Although these incidents could be seen as attempts by the caretakers to exert control over the visiting professionals, we believe that the workers also were caught in a double bind which interfered with their monitoring role, as explained below.

The double bind

Double binds are communications which contain confusing contradictions and put people in 'no win' situations. A simple example is the person told to 'be spontaneous', who tries to comply but then, of course, is no longer acting spontaneously.

One of the best known double binds is enshrined in the title of Joseph Heller's novel *Catch-22* and concerned bomber pilots compelled to fly more and more missions:

> There was only one catch and that was Catch-22, which specified that a concern for one's safety in the face of dangers that were real and immediate was the process of a rational mind. Orr was crazy and could be grounded. All he had to do was ask; and as soon as he did, he would no longer be crazy and would have to fly more missions. Orr would be crazy to fly more missions and sane if he didn't, but if he was sane he had to fly them. If he flew them he was crazy and didn't have to; but if he didn't want to he was sane and had to.
>
> (Heller 1964: 54)

The double bind was originally described as a relationship dilemma leading to schizophrenia, in which one person repeatedly received two orders of message, one contradicting the other, but also covert prohibitions against escaping from the conflict (Bateson *et al.* 1956). The authors cited a psychiatric patient who was visited in hospital by his mother. He spontaneously tried to welcome her with a hug but she stiffened and so he withdrew, whereupon she asked: 'Don't you love me any more?' After he blushed, she added: 'You must not be so afraid of your feelings.' The dilemma for the young man was analysed as: in order to keep his tie to his mother, he must not show her that he loves her; but if he does not show her that he loves her, then he will lose her.

It has been shown that double binds operate in diverse situations, generating psychological distress or confusion but not necessarily insanity (Pearce and Cronen 1980; Cronen and Pearce 1985). Cronen and Pearce developed a means of illustrating the binds as figure of eight loops, which demonstrate how participants keep flipping between incompatible states of mind when caught up in a bind. The 'be spontaneous' bind is shown in Figure 9.2: anyone who is told to be spontaneous and obeys cannot be acting spontaneously and is therefore disobeying the instruction; however, refusing to obey the instruction reveals an inclination to behave spontaneously; and so on.

'Catch-22' is depicted in Figure 9.3: in the context of Orr being crazy, he did not need to fly; however, once he did not fly, this became the context for interpreting sanity, the incompatible opposite of craziness; further, not only was sanity the context for being able to fly but flying becomes the contextual definition of crazy behaviour; and so on. Orr could not win either way.

Cronen and Pearce's illustrations of the double bind helped us make further sense of the otherwise mystifying behaviour of caretakers and professionals in circumstances we have identified as the not existing pattern of abuse. The onset of this pattern coincided with family transitions (see Chapter 4): one couple came together to create a reconstituted family; one mother became pregnant again; and another mother took in additional children after her husband had gone to prison. Each of these transitions can be understood as escalating the dependency demands on the parent designated as the child's principal caretaker. Thus, from the time that Nicholas Price cohabited with **Heidi Koseda**'s mother, he made very controlling demands on her, as though believing that his needs took priority over everything else. We infer that his insistence that he was exclusively

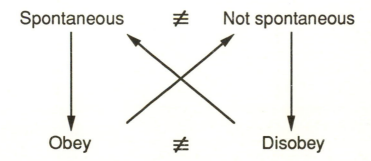

Figure 9.2 The 'be spontaneous' double bind

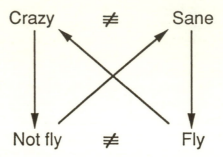

Figure 9.3 The 'Catch-22' double bind

dependent on her to fulfil all his needs, to which she accommodated, led to a shared belief that there was no room for Heidi's existence. Her physical needs could not be tolerated or thought about, even though this led to her physical existence ceasing. As shown in Figure 9.4, If Heidi were to assert her physical existence, she could not be thought about or her existence acknowledged psychologically; so she was shut away, as though not existing physically; only then could her caretakers tolerate thinking about her; but then they would be in danger of having to give priority to her physical needs and existence; and so on.

Although in these cases neighbours did alert statutory workers that they had not seen the child for some time, their concern was with the child's physical well-being and it must have been unimaginable to any of them that the child's very existence was in question. We believe that the professionals became caught up in double binding encounters with the families and confusing states of mind during the visits that followed. As represented in Figure 9.5, when no one worried that the child was in danger, there were no complaints to statutory authorities and no one thought of visiting to investigate problems of child abuse; however, the absence of external

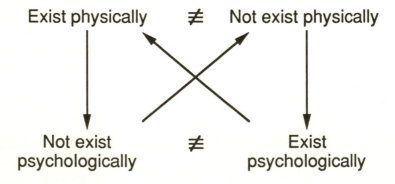

Figure 9.4 The 'not existing' pattern of abuse

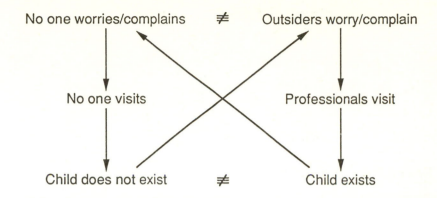

Figure 9.5 The 'not exist' double bind

scrutiny meant that the parents continued to behave as though the child did not exist; eventually, neighbours or professionals realised that they had not seen the child and someone visited to investigate; however, the very act of visiting transformed the child into 'existing', since the professionals were calling to see a real child, and so there no longer seemed a need to worry; and so on.

Even thinking about visiting the home in those circumstances must have lowered anxiety because the professional was entering the double bind loop and was led to the belief that there was no need to worry because the child existed. Furthermore, the professional's visit forced the parent to think about the child and therefore to claim, for that moment, that the child existed physically. Reassurances from that parent that the child was asleep upstairs or staying with friends appeared to be further confirmation to the professional that the child was well. The worker needed to be able to break free of the confusion about whether the child existed psychologically and into considering the child's physical well-being. We shall discuss the implications and resolutions of this bind in Chapter 11.

SUMMARY

Relationships within the families were dominated by marked conflicts about care and control, which were repeated in interactions with professional workers. The relationship between some parents and professionals was typified by requests for and provision of material resources and supportive input. We have referred to this as a dependency pattern. Relationships dominated by control conflicts led to patterns of closure, flight or disguised compliance. In some cases, a confronting approach by professionals exaggerated the parents' control conflicts and precipitated fatal abuse. Practitioners also became caught up in double binds in their contact with parents when a child had been shut away and forgotten about.

Chapter 10

The case as a whole

In order to present our ideas it has been necessary to break them down into specific topics, illustrated by relevant examples. We shall now bring the themes together and consider their mutual interaction during the evolution of individual cases. We shall present a single case study, that of **Doreen Aston,** which contains many examples of the patterns we have described. The events surrounding Doreen's life and death will be reviewed in some detail, as well as the working hypotheses that we generated about them.

THE DOREEN ASTON INQUIRY

This was the first inquiry to be set up under the new *Working Together* guidelines (Department of Health and Social Security and the Welsh Office 1988). Each of the local agencies concerned with Doreen's care had first conducted its own internal inquiry, following which the Area Review Committee established an independent review. The review panel was chaired by a solicitor conversant with child care law and practice and also comprised a senior health visitor and a senior probation officer. Their report was published in July 1989 by the Lambeth, Lewisham and Southwark Area Review Committee. In most newspaper accounts Doreen was referred to by her mother's maiden name of Mason but the inquiry report used the name Aston by which she was known when she died.

Synopsis of events

The family genogram is shown in Figure 10.1. Doreen's mother, Christine Mason, became pregnant with Karl at the age of 17, whilst she was still in care and placed at home with her father. She threatened that she would harm Karl unless he went into care and after he died, aged 10 weeks, Christine admitted to her social worker that she had smothered him. However, Karl was recorded as a cot death. Even so, following her birth, Doreen's name was placed on the At Risk Register because of Karl's 'suspicious death'. Christine then moved repeatedly between her mother's home in Lambeth and her home with Roy Aston in Southwark and consequently she had contact with two social services departments. Initially, Christine and Roy accepted visits from a health visitor but resisted contact with social services and so the monitoring of Doreen's care fell between social workers from Lambeth and from Southwark, a Lambeth social services day centre and health visitors in both areas. The health visitors believed their task was to monitor the risk of cot death to Doreen but over the months they became increasingly concerned about Christine's mothering. Christine twice said she wanted Doreen in care and once threatened her with a knife. However, in the last seven weeks of Doreen's life, no professional saw the family, despite efforts to do so. Doreen died aged 15 months from a blow to the head and Christine Mason and Roy Aston were convicted of her manslaughter. Each was sentenced to twelve years in prison, later quashed by the Appeal Court because the prosecution had not shown which of them was responsible for the fatal injuries.

The family

Many parents who fatally abuse their children have themselves experienced abuse and deprivation in their own childhood. This report contained little information about Roy Aston, except to say that his 'family background was as complex and disorganised as that of Christine' (p. 19) and that his mother's name was also Doreen. We do know that there was a *history of child abuse* in Christine Mason's family of origin. A case conference minute recorded that Christine had been subjected to child abuse herself and three of her seven siblings died in infancy, with the death of one child, whose name was Karl, reported as

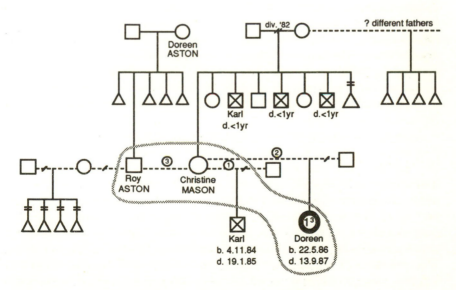

Figure 10.1 Doreen Aston's family genogram (see Figure A.1 in the Appendix for a key to the genogram)

'suspicious circumstances'. The youngest child of that family was placed for adoption and Christine was taken into care at the age of 14. Following her parents' divorce two years later, she was placed back with her father, still in care. Within two years, Christine was pregnant and she then left home to live with the man who was thought to be the baby's father.

Anticipating the child's birth, Christine said that if it were a boy she would strangle him. This raised for us the question of whether Christine's murderous feelings towards a male was because she had suffered sexual abuse as well as physical maltreatment and deprivation. The inquiry report itself gives us no further clues but newspaper accounts of the criminal trial report Christine's evidence that her father had sexually assaulted her when she returned home from care (*Guardian* 22 December 1988).

We hypothesised that Christine's *unmet dependency* resulted in ambivalent separation from her family of origin and cohabitation with a partner who had similar problems. Christine often went to a family day centre in Lambeth attended by her mother's family, where she seemed to present herself more as a daughter than a mother in her own right. Christine and Roy's relationship was characterised by cycles of separation and reunion, in which they often had violent rows, separated and returned to live with their respective parent. It is possible to track through the chronology of the case and see that, as the couple's relationship neared an episode of separation, one or both of them assaulted Doreen.

The meaning of the child

Parents sometimes identify their child with a figure in the family's history and attempt to resolve conflictual events from the past through that child. When this proves impossible, the burden is transferred onto a subsequent child. Therefore, in order to speculate on the meaning of Doreen to her mother we need also to consider the meaning of her brother, Karl. Christine seems to have had strongly ambivalent feelings to both her children: on the one hand, wanting them in order to fulfil a need; while on the other, violently punishing them for their failure to do so.

Baby Karl was given the same name as Christine's younger brother who had died in infancy in suspicious circumstances. We wondered whether unresolved conflicts about her brother's death which Christine carried from her childhood led her to name her own child after him, as though to replace him. Also, Christine might have hoped that Karl, her first baby conceived at the age of 17, would give her the love that she had missed previously, as well as provide a means of escape from sexual abuse by her father. However, because Karl was male, Christine could have associated him with her negative feelings towards her abusing father. This, together with his inability to meet her emotional needs, may have led her to kill him. After he died, Christine kept Karl's ashes in her flat and carried them around with her, as though trying to retain the idealised hopes and meaning invested in him.

Eight months after Karl's death, Christine became pregnant with Doreen and it seems likely that she hoped that this baby could be a replacement for Karl and the meaning she attributed to him. She openly stated that she had wanted another boy and bought things for a baby boy. However, Christine did not properly prepare for the baby's needs, receiving no ante-natal care during the pregnancy, and her investment appears to have been more in the anticipated role that the baby would play, rather than in the child as a person in its own right. There is much evidence that Doreen, like Karl, failed to satisfy her mother's hopes and that Christine was unable to tolerate Doreen's infantile needs and dependency. She fed the baby Doreen adult foods such as crisps, chips and hamburgers and failed to take her for immunisations and developmental checks. When Doreen was only 2 months old, Christine expressed disappointment that another pregnancy test had proved negative. Christine's tendency to give primacy to her own needs above those of Doreen was exemplified when she said that she would not let her go into care but would keep her just to spite everyone.

The professional network

As in so many other cases, the *work setting* was less than ideal. The allocated social worker was relatively inexperienced, having qualified and been appointed approximately eight months before the family was allocated to her. She had been extremely reluctant to take on such a complex case and had only accepted it when directed to by her Area Manager. There was a poor working atmosphere between social work managers and field workers and the social worker felt unsupported in her supervision. Social services was poorly resourced and everyone felt engulfed by the level of demand, while health visitors' workloads were also extremely high. Both social services and health visiting agencies suffered from high staff turnover, unfilled vacancies, inadequate clerical support and inexperienced managers, yet were dealing with the third most underprivileged area in the country. The health authority underwent a major reorganisation during Doreen's life.

This difficult work setting generated problems in *inter-professional communication*, for health visitors were aware of social services' workload and wondered whenever they telephoned: '"Who am I going to speak to today? or are they going to listen?"' (p. 91). Furthermore, the inquiry report comments that: 'as messages reached third parties, there was evidence of some events being described in an increasingly dramatic way, and at other times diminished, either through style of communication, or interpretation by the message giver' (p.105). For example, at one visit, the health visitor noted that Doreen was pale with jerky movements and stiff when her mother picked her up. Yet, when the social worker made notes of her conversation with the health visitor, she recorded the visit as 'baby alright'. A few days later, the day centre Project Leader telephoned the social worker to say that Christine had been seen hitting her child but the social worker only recorded from this conversation that Christine was planning to leave Roy. Then, the following day, the health visitor became very concerned about Christine's inappropriate handling of Doreen. She telephoned the social worker but the social services notes failed to reflect the health visitor's concerns. Within the space of six days, therefore, social services received three alerts about Doreen's welfare but each time the level of anxiety was not transmitted or appreciated.

A critical factor that influenced professionals' *assessments* was a *pervasive belief* that Karl had succumbed to the cot death syndrome. This was despite Christine's earlier threats to harm him, her admission that she had hit him six weeks prior to his death, post-mortem evidence of fractured ribs and a brain haemorrhage and Christine's disclosure to her social worker that she had smothered him. The belief may have been influenced by the police view that they had insufficient evidence for a criminal prosecution and the social worker's interpretion that Christine's confession was a grief reaction. Nonetheless, Doreen's name was entered on the At Risk Register because some considered her brother Karl's death to have been suspicious.

Lack of clarity about the real risk to Doreen, together with *partial closure* by the family, resulted in *role confusion* within the network. Even though Doreen's name was on the At Risk Register, it was health visitors who continued to monitor her welfare, based on the understanding that she was at risk from the cot death syndrome and also because the family tended to permit only health visitors and midwives access to the home while denying it to social workers. The health visitors carried no statutory powers and were primarily concerned with Doreen's development and prevention of another cot death, rather than protecting her from abuse.

The pervasive belief about the risk of cot death prevented workers from integrating contemporary observations with an accurate version of the history, so that *information was treated discretely* and out of context. The health visitors could only make sense of their observations in the light of the family's history as they understood it and, when Doreen was 6 months old, they decided to reduce the frequency of visits because the risk of cot death had receded. When the newly allocated social worker took over the case, she missed an opportunity to integrate current knowledge with the previous history of suspected child abuse as she did not read the duty team's records or previous case conference minutes. This failure to 'take on' the case in its entirety might well have been associated with the excessively stressful and insecure working context.

There were other examples of information being treated discretely. A case conference heard many concerns about Christine's parenting, including her emotional distance from Doreen, absence of eye contact between them, no physical contact during feeding, aggressive and neglectful handling, no maternal stimulation and Doreen being withdrawn and passive and tensing up when her mother approached. The conference decided that Doreen should be taken for a developmental check within a month. The examining doctor was unaware of the underlying concerns about the mother–child relationship and reported routinely on Doreen's normal physical development. Another opportunity to build up a fuller picture of Doreen's care arose three months later. During a crisis at the day centre, Christine threatened Doreen with a knife when she feared she would be taken away from her. Christine soon calmed down and so no further assessment was done and this incident was treated in isolation rather than integrated with the history.

On other occasions, information remained unintegrated and anxiety was allowed to dissipate because crises occurred when a *pivotal worker was absent* or at a *weekend*. Christine discharged herself and 1-day-old Doreen from hospital on the Friday before a bank holiday weekend. A Lambeth social work Team Leader, already concerned about Christine's mothering capacity, spoke to a Southwark emergency duty social worker that evening but it was left to a different duty social worker to visit the following day. Then, the Team Leader was away on two weeks' leave and, although the duty social worker who visited left a full report, decisions were left to a case conference two weeks after that. The following year, on the Thursday before the Easter weekend, Christine asked the day centre Project Leader to call the police so that Doreen could be taken away, while she herself could run away and not be found. When the Project Leader rang Lambeth social services, she was told to ring night duty in an hour. Christine soon calmed down and went home to her mother's but, when the emergency duty officer visited, no one was at home. On Good Friday, another duty social worker visited and was told that Christine had returned to Southwark. The matter was not followed up. In retrospect, this could be seen as a *warning signal*, since it coincided with escalation of abuse to Doreen five months before she died.

The family–professional system

Parents with unresolved conflicts about control are prone to react to emotional crises by assaulting their children and trying to distance statutory and other monitoring workers. In this case, the family–professional interaction was clearly one of *flight* from the time of Christine's pregnancy with Doreen. She left her mother's house, refusing to give her address to her mother, the social worker or health visitor. Her whereabouts was unknown for long periods and she received no ante-natal care. The day after Doreen's birth, Christine discharged herself and the baby from hospital against medical advice. Throughout Doreen's life, Christine kept moving to and fro between the homes of her own mother and of Roy Aston, and at one time she said she wanted to get rid of Doreen then go away herself so that no one could find her.

This flight was associated with *fragmentation* in the professional network. Three social services departments became involved for different reasons. Berkshire social services had carried a Care Order on Christine herself, Lambeth social services were visiting Christine's mother about her own family and Roy Aston's family were known to Southwark social services. Case conferences in Lambeth about Christine's mother's family only mentioned Christine and Doreen incidentally, even though they were living there at the time, and it is difficult to elicit from the report when Christine's care of Doreen became a primary concern of all professionals. We counted at least thirty different workers who became associated in some way with the case and, as Christine moved between boroughs, previous workers became reinvolved, sometimes more than once. Over the fifteen months of Doreen's life, the professionals worked very hard to keep their lines of communication open by discussing the case together, holding case conferences and transferring records in good time. However, they were inevitably at least one step behind the family. As soon as agreement was reached for one borough to hold responsibility, Christine moved again to the other borough. The number of health visitors increased through Christine registering with different general practitioners and, on one occasion early in Christine's and Roy's cohabitation together, she was being seen by one duty social worker at their home, while another duty social worker was seeing Roy in her office.

The family's flight was accompanied by *intermittent* and *terminal closure*. Within two weeks of Doreen's birth, social workers were being refused access, although health visitors were usually allowed to see Doreen, either at home or in the health clinic. Because the social worker had not gained access, her Team Leader decided that she should reduce the frequency of her visits and this led to the role confusion described above, with social services monitoring through third parties. When Doreen was 3 months old, the family closed off to all workers for several weeks and this coincided with increased tension between Christine and Roy, during which Roy hit Doreen, and a temporary separation between the couple.

Social services decided to adopt a more confronting stance on three occasions, each of which had a different outcome. During one episode of closure, the social worker wrote to the parents that either she or the health visitor had to see Christine and Doreen. The parents responded with *disguised compliance*, allowing the health visitor access the next time she called, but this was followed by a further twelve home visits to which she received no reply. Then, following a confronting letter from the social work Area Manager, the parents complied with demands for them to take Doreen for a developmental check. Finally, three weeks after Christine had threatened to stick a knife into Doreen at the day centre, the family closed off from all contact with professionals and this proved to be *terminal closure* lasting seven weeks. During that time, they did not attend the day centre, failed to keep appointments with the social worker, did not let her into the flat and only met the health visitor by chance. After weeks of failed contact, Roy answered the door to the social worker but Christine refused to let her see Doreen, despite the social worker's strong insistence. Doreen was killed four days later and it seems likely that this last incident of professionals adopting a more controlling stance fed into a *vicious circle* of abusive behaviour.

Integration

Our various hypotheses about this case can be integrated in the following way. Both Christine Mason and Roy Aston experienced depriving and abusive parenting when they were children and derivatives of this upbringing showed in their relationships in adult life. Christine oscillated between closeness and distance in her interactions with her parents, with adult partners, her children and professional workers. She seemed to have been struggling to resolve similar conflicts with most of these people, who were therefore not related to as individuals in their own right. In particular, Karl and Doreen appear to have been invested with idealised hopes which they were unable to fulfil and they were rejected and killed.

Professional concerns were not translated into effective child protection for various reasons. The parents tried to assert control over any contact that professionals attempted with them, by repeatedly changing addresses, denying them access to the home or temporarily complying with their instructions. Monitoring of Doreen's welfare was hampered not only by a misperception about the cause of her brother's death but also by inappropriate distribution of tasks between the workers and difficulties co-ordinating plans and responsibilities as Christine moved around. With so many workers involved, all of whom had heavy caseloads, their ability to share and integrate information fell short of the ideal. At intervals, the professionals made more determined efforts to see Doreen but the final occasion may have critically undermined Christine and Roy's precarious sense of self-control, for Doreen was killed a few days later.

A FRAMEWORK FOR THINKING

What further light does our study of **Doreen Aston** and the other cases shed on how the tragedies came about?

We have argued that psychological processes within the households, within and between professional agencies and between the families and their professional networks all influenced the evolution of events. These developments were themselves sensitive to factors in the wider social context prevalent at the time. Front-line workers were therefore operating within an intricate web of relationships and contexts and their decisions were dependent on information from diverse sources. It seems to us that professional behaviour in any one case can best be understood by considering each of these factors, as well as their combined interrelationship; in other words, the case as a whole. It is our view that no single phenomenon, nor one error of judgement, was 'to blame' for a tragedy. Instead, the many emotional and relational components of each case interacted and, as they came together, they progressively skewed the course of events.

Many of the processes we have described are known to intrude on professionals' considered thinking about their work. For example, Bion (1959) and Lewis (1979) discuss how professionals' emotional reactions to the problems presenting to them colour their responses and decisions. Britton (1981) describes workers' identifications with various family members which may unwittingly be enacted amongst the network and Menzies (1970) and Main (1975) identify the irrational qualities of large groups and institutions. We have argued that the combined effects of these processes have an even greater potential to dislodge workers from a consistent and coherent approach to the demands of child protection work.

An interactional approach can provide a valuable framework for thinking about complex cases. It offers workers in the field a structure within which to understand their observations, process information and review their own relationships and communications with others. An appreciation of the impact of these processes should empower practitioners and enable them to carry out their child protection tasks more effectively. We shall consider the practical implications of this in more detail in the final chapter.

If it is accepted that such a framework enhances professional practice, then it should also have relevance for the inquiry process itself. In many ways, the inquiry into **Doreen Aston**'s death was a transitional one. It was set up locally under new guidelines, took evidence in private and was conducted in a less adversarial manner in which questions were only asked by panel members. The panel emphasised that they were 'not seeking to allocate blame for Doreen's death' (p. 140) and no involved professional is named in their report. The panel's intentions were synonymous with ours in that they attempted to analyse the events impartially without attributing blame. Our review had the opportunity to develop this approach further because we applied it to thirty-five cases and have been able to compare features common to them. In the last chapter we shall consider the application of this framework to future inquiries.

SUMMARY

The **Doreen Aston** case illustrates many of the hypotheses we evolved and the phenomena that we noted during our review of all thirty-five tragedies. It also demonstrates the cumulative and interactional effect of these processes over time. Our hypotheses about intra- and inter-systemic functioning in the cases were developed within a 'beyond blame' framework, which offers a structure for thinking about professional practice and the conduct of future inquiries.

Chapter 11

Beyond blame

In this final chapter we shall consider some implications for practice which emanate from our review and shall argue that a 'beyond blame' approach also has implications for the conduct of future inquiries. As we have referred to inquiry reports from as far back as 1973, it is not surprising that some of our conclusions echo views already expressed and incorporated into everyday practice. We have tried as much as possible to confine our discussion to additional inferences that can be drawn using a beyond blame framework. The chapter was written just before the 1989 Children Act was implemented and we shall speculate about the impact of this new legislation on child protection work in the light of our review.

Many of the inquiry reports we reviewed have become renowned as a result of intense media and public interest. The **Jasmine Beckford** inquiry panel's conclusions that her death was 'predictable and preventable' (1985: 287) not only reflected public horror at such events but also widely held beliefs that professionals should prevent the deaths of all children known to them. This is an unrealistic expectation and it is important to acknowledge that deaths of children at the hands of their caretakers can neither be confidently predicted nor completely prevented (Dingwall 1989; Parton and Parton 1989), although this may be the ideal to which we aspire. As Horne argues:

> complete protection for children at risk in their own families is not possible unless society sanctions greater public/state scrutiny of the family. In the absence of this, an element of risk must inevitably exist in a large number of cases that come through the system. Whilst individual social workers may make mistakes in assessing degree of risk in a particular case, the existence of risk cannot be construed to be indicative of bad practice. In fact it could be argued that an acceptance of risk is necessary if the rights of parents, siblings, and 'potential' victims themselves are not to be denied.
>
> (Horne 1990: 101)

Recognising these limitations, we shall suggest how the inferences of our review could translate to everyday practice and might help reduce the number of future tragedies.

IMPLICATIONS FOR THE WORK SETTING

Professionals involved in child protection work operate in a complex, fluctuating, emotive and stressful context. As part of the public services, their resources and practices are prey to political initiatives and interests and neither society nor government demonstrably value their efforts, which are readily criticised but rarely praised. As a result, many workers tend to practice from a defensive posture. An example might be those who keep copious, but unprocessed, records because of an anxiety that their work might become the subject of intense public scrutiny.

It is well known in the business sphere that consideration given to the welfare of staff pays enormous dividends in their attitude to the work task (e.g. Sieff 1990). If the organisation supports its staff and shows concern for them as people, this investment translates into a more contented and efficient work force, a better 'end product' and greater 'customer satisfaction'. There is no rational reason why the same principles should not apply to the public services and it is remarkable that child protection practice takes place against a backdrop of appalling resources, severe underfunding, little social or political encouragement and ever-changing organisational structures.

Political as well as professional initiatives are necessary to redress this situation. All the agencies which comprise the child protection network require adequate funding to pay for appropriate numbers of staff but perhaps the most glaring inconsistency is between the prime responsibility placed upon social workers and the inadequate resources at their disposal. As an example, many social services departments are unable to allocate a named social worker to each child on their Child Protection Register. Some children at risk are thus left without a key professional thinking about their welfare and any problems that arise are dealt with on a duty basis. This seriously impedes assessments and communication with other professionals in the network because no one within social services has a coherent knowledge of individual cases and no forward planning is possible.

Increased attention needs to be paid within all agencies to supporting staff and legitimising structures that reduce stress. Dale *et al.* (1986) have articulated how essential it is for professionals involved with child protection to have built into their work setting adequate provision for their own welfare. This would include regular individual supervision from senior colleagues and continuing training for all practitioners. The agency's ethos should include permission handed down from the most senior managers that staff are entitled to look after themselves as well as their clients. There need to be planned and overt organisational structures that support workers at all levels of the agency, as well as informal measures to assist colleagues. It is easily forgotten that secretaries, clerks and receptionists are the least trained at handling stressful information, yet it is they who tend to be the first to receive messages about crises. Their capacity to register the distressing content and record it accurately can be enhanced by training and by consideration from other staff members. Senior staff, too, can benefit from support and training geared to their specific needs.

The ethos of the agency would need to include guidelines for good practice, such as allowing staff time to review the background of the case when taking it on. Adequate resources facilitate the maintenance of appropriate standards, including better-kept case files containing coherently processed and typed, or even computerised, records rather than copious hand-written notes. The organisational structures need to cater for staff absences and ensure that before weekends and public holidays there is a system for handing over worrying cases to covering colleagues and for providing easy access to records summarising the problems and plan.

Since child protection work is so demanding, it is particularly necessary for practitioners to have another person with whom to discuss their work and reflect on each case as a whole. In most instances, this other person will be a supervisor but the arrangement would not work well if they disagreed about the case or, conversely, shared a belief that rendered them a closed professional system. Occasionally, a managerial and hierarchical relationship inhibits the supervisee from being open about anxieties. In such circumstances, consultation with a professional from another agency can be beneficial. The options are for an outside consultant to attend staff meetings regularly in order to discuss a number of cases or for staff to seek an independent view on a particularly complex or worrying problem. The aim of such consultation is to help the worker review the history of the whole case and identify the relationship patterns within the professional network, in the family and between the family and professionals. In some instances, it may prove helpful for the consultant to name the undeclared dread that is paralysing the work and ask: 'What do you think your decisions would look like if they were being reported at a public inquiry?' The professional then feels freer to review information from that perspective and decide on an intervention.

Monitoring of staff morale and resolution of intra-team tensions are also achievable in regular meetings led by an outside consultant. Indeed, the provision of outside consultation is itself a demonstration that staff welfare is given a high priority by the agency. Consultation meetings can include reflection on such matters as staff attitudes to clients, agency belief systems and relationships with other members of the local professional network.

IMPLICATIONS FOR ASSESSMENT

In the course of our review, the systemic approach proved a useful set of ideas in its own right and a way of integrating other theories. Overall, these ideas provided us with a framework which furthered our understanding of the psychological and inter-personal components of the cases. Although other professionals might not directly apply these theories in face-to-face contact with clients, we suggest that they could be a valuable structure to guide their thinking. From this perspective, child abusing behaviour is seen not as an inherent characteristic of individual parents but as an interaction between parents with unresolved conflicts and vulnerable children, in the context of heightened tension in wider relationships and social stress. These ideas suggest a number of inter-related areas which must be included in assessments and which will guide future intervention strategies.

The importance of history cannot be overemphasised and much relevant information may usefully be summarised in a genogram. The personal history of the parents has relevance for their caretaking style and for the meaning they attribute to the child. Knowledge about previous episodes of child abuse or neglect can transform the significance of contemporary information about current child care problems. The history of a parent's use of professional interventions in the past is a preliminary guide to whether s/he can use help now. Reder and Duncan (1990) discuss this as 'the relationship to help'. In addition, information known by one worker needs to be integrated with that held elsewhere in the professional network to produce a coherent and comprehensive picture.

A repeated theme that emerged from this review was the way care and control conflicts dominated family relationships in the past and in the present. We shall refer to this theme as we describe the various contexts for assessment that need to be distinguished: assessment of immediate risk, assessment of overall parenting capacity and reassessment for rehabilitation.

Assessment of immediate risk

Greenland (1987) proposed that a high-risk checklist would be an aid to assessment, since it requires the worker to gather information from a variety of sources and provides a simple means of securing consensus among involved professionals. According to Greenland, an infant who has suffered a serious non-accidental injury is exposed to a high-risk situation when more than half of the items on the list are positive. These items are divided into those relating to parents and those concerning children – see Table 11.1.

There are arguments for and against checklists. In favour would be their ability to summarise factors that need to be assessed and highlight those which should be taken especially seriously. A list can help organise and guide the thinking of inexperienced workers. However, there are also a number of drawbacks to their use (e.g. Parton and Parton 1989). Workers can be lulled into a false sense of security, believing that generalisations automatically apply to specific cases and are reliably predictive. They may rely overmuch on the structure afforded by a checklist and focus their assessment only on the factors contained in it. As a result, workers' thinking is constrained and they may resort to a mechanical check down the attributes rather than processing their information and observations. We believe that factors on a checklist are only valid when considered within a wider and interrelational context. Furthermore, the nature of the risk indicated by such lists is not always clear, especially whether the criteria are meant to distinguish families more likely to abuse from others in the

Table 11.1 High-risk checklist, as proposed by Greenland (1987)

PARENT

Was previously abused/neglected as a child
Has a history of abusive/neglectful parenting
Has a history of criminal assaultive and/or suicidal behaviour
Is a single parent, separated or the partner is not the biological parent
Is socially isolated, including frequent moves and poor housing
Is poor, unemployed, an unskilled worker or received inadequate education
Abuses alcohol and/or drugs
Is pregnant or in the post-partum period or has a chronic illness

CHILD

Was previously abused or neglected, especially when under 5 years of age
Was premature or of low birth weight
Has a birth defect, a chronic illness or developmental lag
Had prolonged separation from the mother
Is adopted, fostered or a step-child
Is currently underweight
Cries frequently or is difficult to comfort
Shows difficulties in feeding or elimination

population or whether they point to increasing danger to a child who has pre-viously been harmed in a specific family. Checklists, then, have the advantage of helping organise workers' thinking but also have disadvantages when used routinely or thoughtlessly.

Instead, it would be more helpful for workers to base their assessments on an interactional model that indicates factors that must be considered within and between families and networks. Some situations will be highlighted as signifi-cantly more dangerous to the child's safety than others and such an approach helps the worker weigh up factors across many systems. For example, Greenland points out that 'failure to gain access to a previously abused child should be regarded as one of the most critical danger signals' (Greenland 1987: 167–8), a conclusion with which we would concur, yet this aspect of the family–professional relationship is not included in his checklist.

The histories of many of the *families* in this review indicated that crises in care/dependency relationships or in conflicts about control placed the child at greatly increased risk of abuse. Examples included intolerance of a child's immaturity or regression, the presence of a young infant in the household or the mother becoming pregnant again. A child was particularly at risk when the parents' relationship reached a crisis, including threats of, or actual, separation between them, escalating violence in their relationship or threats to their self-esteem.

The *meaning* attributed to children rendered them more at risk of abuse if they were failing to fulfil the role expected of them. The period immediately following children's return home after being in care was particularly dangerous. Similarly, children were at risk if their parents viewed them as property to be returned to them. The stress on caretakers and children following sudden changes of place-ment also pointed to such decisions being associated with risk. Our review casts doubt on whether step-children are more in danger than children living with natural parents.

Within the *professional networks*, practitioners were less able to monitor the child's safety when they had excessive case loads or inadequate supervision. Closed professional systems and polarisation between workers were indicators of risk, as were times of agency reorganisation, the absence of a pivotal worker or weekends and public holidays.

The most significant indicator of danger to the child was closure in the *family–professional* interaction. This was manifested as withdrawal from contact with outsiders, recurrent flight or disguised compliance. Furthermore, in the face of such closure, renewed efforts by professionals to take a controlling stance had the potential to escalate further the risk to the child.

The **Lucie Gates** case also serves as a reminder that a history of chronically neglectful parenting has a risk factor beyond that of undernourishment or psycho-logical harm, for Lucie died from an avoidable accident when all the children were left alone in the house.

Warning signals

This review revealed that some parents gave a warning signal of impending crisis and fatal assault on the child, although the association only became clear in retrospect. Greenland (1987) noted in his research that parents often sought help shortly before they severely assaulted their child, by taking the child to the general practitioner, complaining about the child's behaviour or asking for him/her to be removed. Korbin (1989) studied mothers imprisoned for fatally maltreating their children and found that they had provided similar warning signals to professionals and to members of their personal networks by alerting them to abusive incidents.

The inference must be that professionals should exercise a low threshold of suspicion when parents who have previously abused their child hint that abuse is recurring. It is not easy to anticipate how this will be disguised. However, the cases indicated that parents were prepared to reveal information about some injury to the child or about a deterioration in relationships within the family, either between a parent and child or between the parental couple. In our own practice, we have come across instances of parents revealing that they have already, or are likely to, harm their child, which professionals have interpreted as a sign of lessened risk. The practitioners have understood that, because the parents have verbalised their tensions, they are less likely to enact frustrations through abusive behaviour. There seems to be little substance in this belief and we infer that both covert and overt warnings of risk should be taken as a sign of danger to the child and not the reverse.

The 'not exist' double bind

Allied to professionals' need to be sensitive to warning signs of escalating abuse is their need to monitor whether they are caught up in a not exist double bind with parents. Realisation that this has occurred should be taken as an indicator of significant risk to the child.

As with other unwitting processes, the basis for resolving a double binding interaction is to be aware of its potential and to recognise when one is caught up in it. In a sense, the very realisation 'breaks the spell' and allows the relationship to change. In the specific instance of a bind being about whether or not a child exists in the parents' minds, professionals have to stop their state of mind flipping from concern for the child's welfare to a belief that the child is well. Their thinking must return to: 'I am here to see the child.' Workers can prevent themselves alternating from one belief to another by first realising that the child's psychological existence in his/her parent's mind is in question and then anchoring themselves in just one belief, namely that the child's actual well-being must be physically confirmed.

Assessment of parenting

Assessment of parenting is a planned procedure through which information about the adult's personal history, previous capacity to care adequately for children, current relationships and circumstances, attitudes to the child in question and readiness to be helped is integrated. Reder and Lucey (1991) have offered a structure to guide the assessment of parenting, which is summarised in Table 11.2. They emphasise interactional factors in the parent's relationship with the child, the parent's relationship to the role of parenting, influences from the family context and contacts with the external world.

In addition, this review has pointed to the need to assess care and control issues in all these areas. For example, absent ante-natal care, premature discharge from the post-natal ward, often following rages of frustration, failure to register the baby with a general practitioner, consistent failure to attend appointments with professionals, repeated violence to partners, children and/or professionals all indicate severe control problems. Unresolved dependency conflicts are suggested by the parent having left home as a young teenager in a crisis, such as when pregnant, excessive frustration at the demands of a young infant or regressed child, drug and alcohol abuse or excessive reliance on support from others. The assessment then needs to consider the degree to which these conflicts are enacted through maltreatment of a child and the degree of current risk.

The ability to parent adequately is not simply an attribute that someone does

Table 11.2 A framework for the assessment of parenting (after Reder and
Lucey 1991)

PARENT'S RELATIONSHIP WITH THE CHILD

Feelings towards the child
Shows concern for, and interest in, the child's well-being
Can empathise with the child's perspective on experiences
The child is viewed as a person in his/her own right
The child's needs are respected and given primacy over the parent's
Is able to anticipate the child's needs (e.g. for protection)

PARENT'S RELATIONSHIP TO THE ROLE OF PARENTING

Provides for the child's age-appropriate needs, viz:
    ante-natal preparation
    physical care (food, cleanliness, warmth, health, safety)
    socialisation
    opportunities to explore and learn
    self-esteem reinforcement
    availability
    continuity and consistency
Knowledge of, and views held on, parenting
Accepts responsibility for own behaviour
The child is not expected to be responsible for his/her own protection
Acknowledges if there are problems and that change is needed

INFLUENCES FROM THE FAMILY CONTEXT

Awareness of impact of own parenting on ability to parent
The meaning of the child to parent
Involvement of the child in dysfunctional family relationships (especially
    parental discord)
Family's sensitivity to relationship stresses and repertoire of responses
    available
The child's attitude to caretakers and figures of attachment and trust

CONTACT WITH THE EXTERNAL WORLD

Relationship between parent and professionals
Responses to previous attempts to help
Sensitivity to environmental stress and support networks available

or does not have. Instead, parenting is a relationship between parent and child
that responds to fluctuations in other relationships. This was particularly evident
in the families where children ceased to exist in their parents' minds. In each
case, we noted a transition in parenting which coincided with significant changes

in the family's structure or interactions. Hence, it seems important to include in assessments of parenting the ways in which the care of the child has varied in response to other critical events.

Reassessment with a view to rehabilitation

When children who have been abused are being considered for rehabilitation home, previous assessments need to be revised to incorporate information about the nature and effects of all changes since their departure (e.g. Hollander 1986). This should include appraisal of any new circumstances and especially whether the parent has a new partner. If so, that person's parenting capacity should be assessed in its own right, as well as the relationship between the couple. Indeed, Dale *et al.* (1986) stress that if the spouse relationship is not viable, then neither is the family and the child should not return home.

All changes are stressful and require adjustment and practitioners should consider how the change from one home to another is likely to affect the child and the family. In particular, they need to address how the meaning of the child in the past might influence the parental caretaking once the child is living back with the family. For example, is the child wanted back to resolve conflicts elsewhere in the family or because s/he is regarded as a piece of property?

IMPLICATIONS FOR WORKING TOGETHER

Coherent assessment and planning require that professionals communicate and liaise together. This review has indicated that the relationship aspects of these activities are as important as the organisational structures set up to facilitate them and both must be addressed by the child protection network. For example, updating the Area Child Protection Committee (ACPC) inter-agency guidelines on child abuse procedures involves more than the act of writing by each committee representative. One agency's guidelines have to be compatible with those of all other agencies and, therefore, the ability of professionals to work together and implement the procedures depends on resolution of any differences between agencies. It would seem valuable for ACPCs to set time aside to address this process while updates are being compiled.

Much has already been written about inter-professional co-operation (e.g. Hallett and Stevenson 1980; Cleveland Inquiry 1988; Department of Health and Social Security and the Welsh Office 1988; Home Office *et al.* 1991) and we shall focus our discussion on the case conference as a microcosm of the network and its functioning. It is evident from this review that the absence of case conferences is likely to be detrimental but also that their occurrence is not always beneficial because of the complex group processes within them. The conference's task of sharing information and planning interventions can be overtaken by its group dynamics and therefore everyone present must consciously strive to make the meeting effective.

The person chairing the conference needs to have the opportunity to see that all those relevant have been invited, especially if there is a danger of polarisation or closed professional systems developing within the network. The conference requires skilled chairing in order to allow all information and opinions to be heard and given appropriate significance. This must be facilitated regardless of perceived status of the speakers, the presence of the parents or any problematic relationships between network professionals. This review has particularly demonstrated how pervasive beliefs organise people's thinking and it is important to monitor whether they are influencing the discussion. In addition, tasks should not be allocated to those absent from the meeting on the assumption that they will carry them out as prescribed. For example, a newly appointed social worker may read in a recent case conference minute that s/he should refer the family to another agency. It is rarely possible for that social worker to communicate adequately the nature and degree of the concerns, the reason for referral or the intended focus for the new work.

Every participant needs to prepare for the conference by reviewing their information and anticipating how to present it. They can contribute more usefully if they have asked themselves beforehand: 'What additional information would I require to form a more definite opinion?' and 'What am I hoping to get out of the meeting?' During the conference, participants need to monitor their involvement in the group process and in what way it is a reflection of wider network relationships. Bruggen (personal communication) asks before any network meeting: 'Is there anything in our previous contacts which might interfere with our work today?' We shall consider below the relevance of these implications for training.

IMPLICATIONS FOR INTERVENTION

Assessments and case conference recommendations are the foundations on which interventions will be planned and this review has pointed to a number of implications concerning intervention strategies. At a general level, role confusion between professionals is avoided if tasks are undertaken by those who have the relevant skills and power and there is shared knowledge and agreement about who is doing what. It is also necessary in planning interventions to set the criteria for their success or failure and to arrange for them to be regularly monitored. This is particularly relevant when children are returned to their natural families from care or when parents are encouraged to clean up their home and to maintain those standards. In this way, professionals are making the family's response to their intervention a relevant part of the ongoing assessment.

The care/control issues suggest that support, material provisions or other concrete solutions, such as rehousing, should not be the only intervention offered to families. Although they have an important part to play, the overall strategy should also address relationship problems underlying the abusive behaviour. The aim should be to help parents internalise and own responsibility for the problems and their resolution. Without that, there is a danger that support and concrete provisions will reawaken the depth of the parents' unmet dependency needs rather than satisfy them. Crises during a pivotal worker's absence may be one signal of this problem, for which other members of the network need to be prepared.

Taking control

Professionals with statutory child protection responsibilities must, at times, introduce an authoritative and controlling posture into their relationship with parents. The 1989 Children Act makes provision for professionals to apply for Emergency Protection Orders and Child Assessment Orders in order to override parental resistance and arrange for the examination or removal of a child if deemed necessary.

This review suggests occasions in which these Orders are especially relevant. We found a striking association between escalating abuse of the child and parental withdrawal from contact with professionals and others in the outside world. The withdrawal usually took the form of closure but could also have been through flight. In addition, we saw how disguised compliance had a similar effect of keeping professionals at a distance, since it was followed immediately afterwards by further closure. We have concluded that workers should be particularly concerned that the risk to a child is increased when a family in which abuse has previously occurred shows any form of closure.

In a number of cases, a child was killed during an episode of closure. The problem, however, is one of prediction and we found no reliable clues which could help a worker anticipate the likelihood of closure being terminal. Hence, if there is a history of previous abuse within a household, professionals should assume that the child's life may be in danger once that family begins to close off from the network. If a worker is regularly denied access to the home or realises that the child has stopped attending the nursery or school or the family repeatedly fail to keep scheduled appointments, then closure should be suspected. The practitioner should contact other members of the network to check whether there is additional evidence of closure elsewhere. If so, the statutory agency should assume that the child is at increased risk and in need of immediate assessment and possible protection.

However, we found another perplexing theme running through the cases. Not only was it impossible to predict which episode of closure might end in the child's death but it was not possible to anticipate how the family would react to mounting control from outside. The **Doreen Aston** case illustrates that a family may show at least three different reactions. On one occasion, Doreen's parents complied with professional requests; on another, they showed disguised compliance, followed once again by closure; finally, there ensued a vicious circle ending in Doreen's death. It is impossible to predict, on present knowledge, what the parents' responses might be to a more confronting stance and whether it will increase the likelihood of the child being killed.

Such an analysis has two significant implications for practice. First, all episodes of closure should be considered as potentially fatal. Second, in such circumstances, the professionals' stance must not be half-hearted requests to see the child. Taking a little control may be more dangerous than taking none at all. The intervention needs to be authoritative and decisive so that the situation is assessed and the child protected before any vicious circle can spiral out of control. In other words, if professionals decide to take control, they should take a lot of it. Child Assessment Orders and Emergency Protection Orders of the 1989 Children Act allow for such action and we believe that they should be applied with determination when the situation demands it.

We wonder whether this need to take a confronting stance at times poses a dilemma for practitioners who have set out to work in partnership with parents? On one level it appears to do so, since the worker would be shifting from a relationship of relative equality to a situation of hierarchical imposition. However, it really depends how the notion of partnership is interpreted. Partnership could be seen as workers being more honest with parents about their views and openly confronting them with their concerns. Such clarity would have the potential to set out the aims of the partnership and facilitate the work to protect the child. Within this context, the need to adopt a more controlling stance would not necessarily disrupt the relationship of partnership.

Therapy

The aims of professional interventions are both to protect the child and to facilitate change so that the child's care might improve, whether within the natural family or with permanent alternative parents. While this review did not address therapy programmes as such, it is pertinent that the history of therapy for abusing families has swung from encouraging dependency (e.g. Kempe and Helfer 1972) to greater emphasis on control (e.g. Dale *et al.* 1986).

The importance of the Rochdale NSPCC Unit's work described by Dale and his colleagues is that it reminds workers to balance care and concern for clients with a clear and authoritative structure, such as agreed contracts with the family. Although this work is from a specialised unit, its principles have general application to work in the field. Another recent development is the NEWPIN programme (Pound 1991) which validates another of our inferences, that support and care for abusing parents are most effective when they are empowering and they do not need to imply dependency.

IMPLICATIONS FOR TRAINING AND RESEARCH

The need for close liaison and co-operation between professionals, together with the complex and emotional nature of child protection work and the high cost of errors of judgement, combine to make essential the regular training of all concerned professionals. In addition, changing legislation and procedural guidelines imply continued relearning. This has been recognised to some extent by the many inquiries and by the provision of increased resources for training. However, recommendations and money are only part of the solution. It is not widely appreciated that trying to organise multi-disciplinary training brings out the same inter-professional conflicts that it is hoped will be addressed in the training itself, such as who is in charge, who is invited, who declines to attend and so on. Many training events flounder because of this problem and valuable opportunities are lost for improving effective working together. On the other hand, once these processes are recognised, they become available for resolution by those responsible for organising the event, occasionally with the help of an outside facilitator. This should then allow the same issues to be addressed at a practitioner level during the course of the training. We believe that, for multi-agency events to be successful, they should allocate time to consider relevant inter-professional relationships, regardless of the topic that has brought everyone together.

Professional training should include awareness of relationship aspects of the work and, in particular, the need to recognise care and control balances being enacted with families. For example, the use of personal authority can be rehearsed, so that practitioners are able to introduce an appropriate level of controlling interventions when necessary. Field workers are helped by managers who themselves have acquired such a conceptual framework. The inter-personal skills necessary for a manager to listen to and guide the worker during supervision are often underestimated but can be learned from role models and in workshops. Again, the ability to help a supervisee organise information about a complex case depends on the supervisor being conversant with an appropriate model and having learned how to apply it and demonstrate its relevance.

Special training needs arise in relation to case conferences, since they bring together in one room the complex and often highly charged relationships between the parents and professionals and also within the professional network. Those chairing conferences must acquire and practice the art of guiding discussions so that they remain task-focused and allow all those present to contribute effectively. Conference members need guidance on organising their information beforehand and then presenting it. Video-recorded role play in workshops, for example, permits rehearsal of conference discussions and helps staff realise the importance of distinguishing fact from opinion, monitoring their own behaviour in the group, overcoming problems of perceived status and being honest in the presence of parents.

Ongoing training about the 1989 Children Act will need to focus on the meaning of partnership and whether workers experience conflict between this and their monitoring role. The Act also promotes the use of contracts with parents, which may lead to an overemphasis on concrete solutions. Training will need to provide guidance on how to set clear criteria for monitoring the success or failure of child protection plans and whether the relationship problems have been addressed.

Research should be integral to practice and an in-built means of monitoring the efficacy of interventions and the consequences of changes. The introduction of the 1989 Children Act, a major piece of legislation with far-reaching effects on practice, opens up many areas for investigation. Interactional studies, as opposed to attributional research, seems particularly necessary. It is desirable to accumulate more knowledge about which relationship factors heighten risk to a child. For example, investigation of family closure is needed, to find out whether there are any predictors to which episode of closure carries the highest risk. Again, measures of relationship factors impeding message-taking, transfer of information between workers or case conference decisons could be undertaken. It remains uncertain what helps families break out of an inter-generational cycle of abuse or what leads caretakers to commit a particular pattern of abuse. Research possibilities are clearly wide ranging.

IMPLICATIONS FOR THE INQUIRY PROCESS

We embarked on this review of child abuse inquiry reports because we shared a concern with other commentators (e.g. Dingwall 1986; Hallett 1989) at the nature and process of the original inquiries. Although there may have been a wish to learn constructively from the tragedies, the inquiry panels seem to have been set up primarily to dissipate social anxiety and, as a consequence, have reflected the compulsion in society to attribute blame. Despite all the disclaimers by inquiry panels that they were not conducting a trial, many witnesses have experienced the adversarial conduct of the proceedings and the judgemental tones of the final reports as exactly that.

The **Kimberley Carlile** panel commented on the adversarial process, suggesting that: 'it is based in part on the traditional dialectic approach that the truth will most likely emerge if each interested party is allowed to put his or her own case, from their own perspective' (**Kimberley Carlile** Inquiry Report 1987: 8). However, a courtroom-like atmosphere is likely to organise the panel into assuming that there is a truth to be found and that someone is guilty of wrong-doing. This probably contributed to the decision of some professionals not to present themselves to recent inquiries.

Some panel members were clearly sensitive to this problem and a number of reports debate the tension which they faced. For example, Stevenson felt com-pelled to write a minority report for the **Maria Colwell** inquiry because she did not 'wish to apportion degrees of blame', nor did she think that 'a hierarchy of censure is appropriate and therefore disassociate myself from it' (**Maria Colwell** Inquiry Report 1974: 115). Similar concerns divided the **Lucie Gates** inquiry panel and it is worth quoting from the introduction to the Chairman's report:

> Within a few days of the commencement of the Inquiry, however, some members of the panel raised strong objection to the court-like atmosphere produced by the adversarial system. As professional people, they felt able to highlight the relevant matters that needed to be explored. They reasoned that

their training in caring for others would allow for the adoption of a flexible approach to the witnesses which, whilst eliciting the truth, would still make it possible for those appearing before the Panel to live and work together subsequently. The convening authorities were consulted and the Chairman was requested to make such procedural changes as he considered necessary to retain the services of all his colleagues . . . Without these changes some members of the panel would have felt obliged to withdraw.

(**Lucie Gates** Inquiry Report, Vol. 1: 5–6)

Even so, the three other panel members finally wrote a separate report from the Chairman. Other reports have devoted whole sections to debate the nature and value of public inquiries and to speculate on their future (for example, the **Jasmine Beckford, Paul Brown, Kimberley Carlile, Tyra Henry, Heidi Koseda** and **Karen Spencer** inquiries).

It would therefore be wrong to suggest that inquiry panels have set out to scapegoat individuals, and they have tried to deal with painful, horrifying or complex material to the best of their ability. Yet, having read thirty-five reports and the experiences of some professionals who faced the panels (e.g. BASW 1982; Raymond 1987; Ruddock 1987; 'A social worker' 1982) there can be little doubt that discovering who was to blame dominated many of the panels' thinking. Hutchinson (1986) records that practitioners tend see such inquiries as expensive, legalistic, time-consuming and unsympathetic.

Furthermore, our review reinforces the impressions of BASW (1982) and Dingwall (1986) that inquiry panels often repeat the conclusions of previous ones. Whatever social or political pressure there were on inquiry panels to apportion blame, we believe that the panels' effectiveness has been hampered over the years by the unavailability of a coherent and sympathetic framework to facilitate understanding of the inter-personal factors contributing to the tragedy.

We appear to be moving towards a less blaming approach. **Darryn Clarke**'s death in 1978 was the last to be inquired into centrally, by the Department of Health and Social Security. The British Association of Social Workers went on to propose a local procedure for all case reviews, using an inquisitorial rather than adversarial setting (BASW 1982). In 1985, the Department of Health and Social Security published a consultation paper which proposed a primarily local framework for reviewing cases which had aroused concern. It suggested that there could be three types of inquiry: local case review by managers; review in private by a panel acting as a sub-committee of the Area Review Committee (now renamed the Area Child Protection Committee); or a Statutory Inquiry instigated by the Secretary of State. The first two types of review would be capable of considering the majority of cases.

In 1987, the **Kimberley Carlile** inquiry panel believed that their investigation and the concurrent Cleveland Inquiry (1988) would mark the end of an era of child abuse inquiries. The panel recommended that cases which had caused concern should be reviewed by the local ACPC or, if considered unsuitable, then the Local Ombudsman. But there was still considered a need for a full public inquiry set up by the Secretary of State if it was necessary to 'assuage public disquiet'. In 1988, the *Working Together* guidelines confirmed that sub-committees of ACPCs should be available to review cases when a child is seriously harmed or killed by his/her caretakers. However, the sub-committee would need to indicate whether there were: 'aspects of the case which seem to justify further inquiry. It will then be for the agencies individually or jointly to consider what form an inquiry will take' (Department of Health and Social Security and the Welsh Office 1988: 47–8). The update of this guidance confirmed the procedures and expected that ACPCs would indicate in their reports to the Department of Health whether: 'there were any aspects of the case which seem to justify further inquiry, either under the auspices of the ACPC or by an individual agency or agencies' (Home Office *et al.* 1991: 60).

The **Doreen Aston** inquiry was the first to be set up under the new procedure and its panel's intentions to avoid attributing blame resulted in a noticeably different and altogether more useful report. For example, sufficient information is included to allow a full genogram to be constructed. Furthermore, in recognition that workers need a framework for thinking, the panel proposed that case conferences could be called to consider the safety of as yet unborn children and that health visitors and social workers should prepare written case plans in readiness for case conferences or discussions with supervisors.

Clearly, then, central inquiries will still be held from time to time but the atmosphere may gradually be changing towards the need to review cases in a constructive light. One contribution to this would be for the adversarial, courtroom-like atmosphere to be replaced by an inquisitorial procedure. The panel could ask questions of the professionals about the case and in this way a picture about the psychological components is more likely to emerge. It would also be helpful for inquiry panels to review the history of agency relationships and to assess workers' interactions during the case by meeting with the multi-professional network, as well as with individual practitioners. Another possibility would be for ACPCs periodically to review all practice, the cases that go well as well as those that do not. Since these Committees send reports to the Department of Health it is feasible to build up a body of knowledge not only about problems but also about good practice.

We hope that this book will have demonstrated that analysis of the psychological components of a case is possible and that there is value in asking not only 'What happened?' but also 'How can those events be understood?' An appreciation of relationship influences on families and professional workers offered by systemic and other theories helps make sense of complex cases and aids any review of professionals' actions. It acknowledges the importance of professional accountability and, in addition, would help inquiry panels progress beyond the apportioning of blame. As a result, additional lessons could be learned from past tragedies which, if translated into professional practice, might help to protect children more effectively in the future.

We began by acknowledging the strong feelings aroused in us all when thinking about a child's death from maltreatment. We would like to close on such a note, by expressing our hope that this book will give a greater and lasting meaning to the lives of the children.

Appendix

Summaries of the cases

This appendix contains synopses of all thirty-five cases, arranged in alphabetical order. We have summarised the information in order to give an overview of each case, including the date of the child's death, the commissioning agent of the report and when it was published, the locus of events if not otherwise apparent, a genogram of the child's family, who was held responsible for the child's death and whether any statutory orders were in operation at the time.

The genogram is a diagrammatic representation of significant information about a family, such as sex, age, familial relationship, household composition, number and order of offspring, etc. We have used whatever information was available in each report to construct the genogram of the family as it was constituted at the time of the child's death, using the conventional symbols for genograms shown in Figure A.1.

ANONYMOUS (died 15.1.82)

Report: 'The report of an inquiry panel into the examination of the implications of the death of a child', published by Cheshire Central Review Committee for Child Abuse in July 1982.

Summary

This baby was born to parents who were of below average intelligence and who first lived in the maternal grandparents' home. After six months, they moved to their own accommodation and almost immediately their baby was found to have a fractured arm and was taken into care and placed with foster parents. All workers became pessimistic about the possibility of rehabilitation to the parents because they resisted attempts to improve their parenting skills. However, the court decided to return the baby home on a three-year Supervision Order and social services decided not to appeal because his parents were now co-operative. Four months later, an anonymous telephone caller alleged that the baby was being beaten by his mother but no signs of injury were found. Four days after this

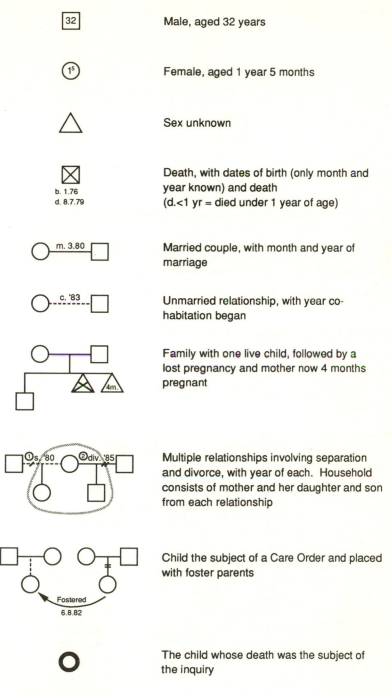

32	Male, aged 32 years
1⁵	Female, aged 1 year 5 months
△	Sex unknown
b. 1.76 / d. 8.7.79	Death, with dates of birth (only month and year known) and death (d.<1 yr = died under 1 year of age)
m. 3.80	Married couple, with month and year of marriage
c. '83	Unmarried relationship, with year co-habitation began
	Family with one live child, followed by a lost pregnancy and mother now 4 months pregnant
s. '80 ② div. '85	Multiple relationships involving separation and divorce, with year of each. Household consists of mother and her daughter and son from each relationship
Fostered 6.8.82	Child the subject of a Care Order and placed with foster parents
●	The child whose death was the subject of the inquiry

Figure A.1 Genogram symbols

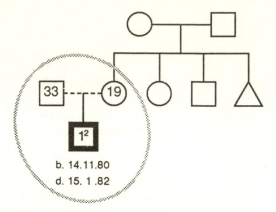

Figure A.2 Genogram of the anonymous baby's family

he was admitted to hospital with fatal injuries and his mother was eventually sentenced to Borstal training for his manslaughter.

Formal status at time of death: Supervision Order.

DOREEN ASTON (died 13.9.87)

Report: 'The Doreen Aston report', published by Lewisham Social Services Department, London in July 1989.
Commissioned by: Lambeth, Southwark and Lewisham Area Review Committee.

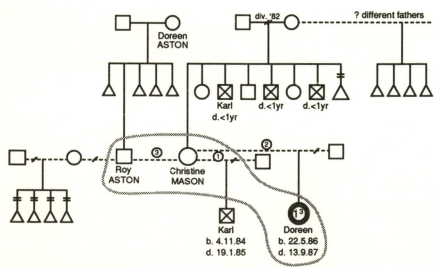

Figure A.3 Genogram of Doreen Aston's family

Summary

Doreen's mother, Christine Mason, became pregnant with Karl at the age of 17, whilst she was still in care and placed at home with her father. She threatened that she would harm Karl unless he went into care and after he died, aged 10 weeks, Christine admitted to her social worker that she had smothered him. However, Karl was recorded as a cot death. Even so, following her birth, Doreen was put on the At Risk Register because of Karl's 'suspicious death'. Christine then moved repeatedly between her mother's home in Lambeth and her home with Roy Aston in Southwark and consequently she had contact with two social services departments. Initially, Christine and Roy accepted visits from a health visitor but resisted contact with social services and so the monitoring of Doreen's care fell between social workers from Lambeth and from Southwark, a Lambeth social services day centre and health visitors in both areas. The health visitors believed their task was to monitor the risk of cot death to Doreen but over the months they became increasingly concerned about Christine's mothering. Christine twice said she wanted Doreen in care and once threatened her with a knife. However, in the last seven weeks of Doreen's life, no professional saw the family, despite efforts to do so. Doreen died from a blow to the head and Christine Mason and Roy Aston were convicted of her manslaughter and each was sentenced to twelve years in prison (later quashed by the Appeal Court because the prosecution had not shown which of them was responsible for the fatal injuries).

Formal status at time of death: At Risk Register.

SUSAN AUKLAND (died 11.7.74)

Report: 'Report of the committee of inquiry into the provision and co-ordination of services to the family of John George Aukland', published by HMSO, London in September 1975.
Commissioned by: The Department of Health and Social Security.
Locus: Shafton, Yorkshire.

Summary

John Aukland was chronically ill throughout his life, often off work, and described as having a nervous disposition. He was prone to drink excessively and be violent, whilst his wife, Barbara Aukland, was seen by others as incompetent. Their marriage was characterised by frequent arguments, separations and reconciliations. John killed their first child, Marianne, and was found guilty of manslaughter with diminished responsibility and imprisoned for eighteen months. Social services were first involved to help with John Roy who was a low-birth-weight baby but later because of family violence. When Barbara finally left John she took Susan with her but was persuaded to let Susan eventually return to

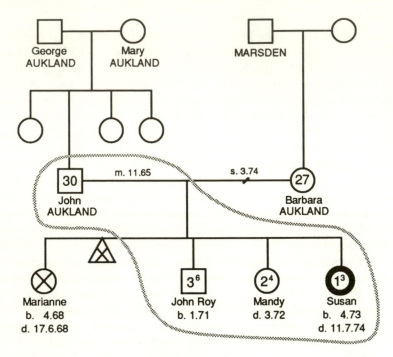

Figure A.4 Genogram of Susan Aukland's family

her father's care. Once settled in London, Barbara made efforts to get her children back but after a night of drinking John Aukland fatally assaulted Susan. He was sentenced to five years' imprisonment for her manslaughter.

GRAHAM BAGNALL (died 28.5.72)

Report: 'Report of inquiry into the circumstances surrounding the death of Graham Bagnall (D.O.B. 20/5/1970) and the role of the county council's social services', published by Shropshire County Council in September 1973.

Summary

When Graham was aged about 1 year, social services received a complaint that he was ill and his parents were refusing to take him to the doctor. Three months later Graham was admitted to hospital with non-accidental injuries and was discharged to foster parents in voluntary care. Concern was then focussed on Neil, who was admitted to hospital with non-accidental injuries and then returned home 'on trial'. After Lisa's birth, and when moves were made for Graham's foster parents to adopt him, Graham's mother and step-father successfully

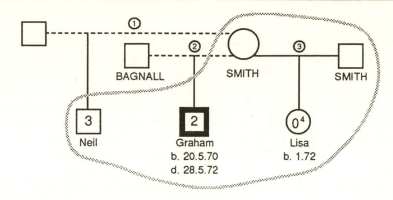

Figure A.5 Genogram of Graham Bagnall's family

requested his return home. Graham died five weeks later. His step-father, who had a history of violence and psychiatric hospital admissions, and mother were convicted of his manslaughter.

JASMINE BECKFORD (died 5.7.84)

Report: 'A child in trust: the report of the panel of inquiry into the circumstances surrounding the death of Jasmine Beckford', published by the London Borough of Brent in December 1985.

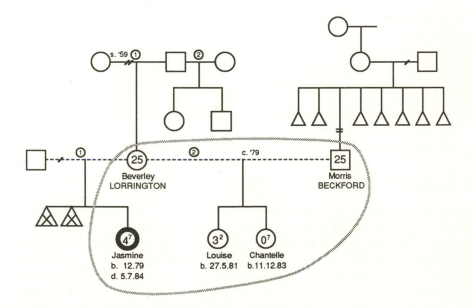

Figure A.6 Genogram of Jasmine Beckford's family

Summary

Both Morris Beckford and Beverley Lorrington had backgrounds of severe deprivation and they cohabited when Beverley was already pregnant by another partner. Jasmine's physical development and care was always a concern to health visitors and when her younger sister, Louise, was aged 3 months, both children were admitted to hospital with non-accidental injuries. They were subsequently placed in foster care under an Interim Care Order. Morris was convicted of actual bodily harm to Louise and given a six months' suspended sentence. When Full Care Orders were made the magistrate expressed the hope that the children would be reunited with their parents and Jasmine and Louise were later returned home. Social workers and health visitors monitored their care intermittently for the next two years. Jasmine was sporadically absent from her nursery and ten months before her death was totally withdrawn. She died from violence but had also been malnourished and abused over a long period. Morris Beckford was convicted of Jasmine's manslaughter and sentenced to ten years' imprisonment and Beverley Lorrington to nine months' imprisonment for child cruelty.

Formal status at time of death: Full Care Order

WAYNE BREWER (died 20.5.76)

Report: 'Wayne Brewer: report of the review panel', published by Somerset Area Review Committee in March 1977.

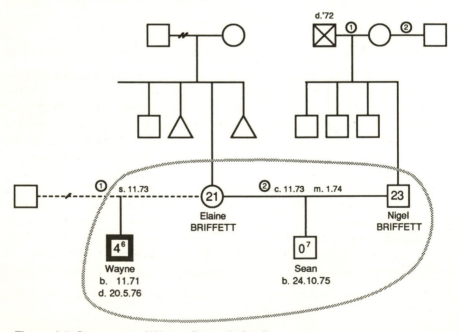

Figure A.7 Genogram of Wayne Brewer's family

Summary

Elaine Brewer became pregnant with Wayne at the age of 15 years after the break-up of her own parents' marriage. Nigel Briffett, who drank heavily and abused drugs, joined Wayne and his mother at the maternal grandmother's home when Wayne was 2 years old and the couple married soon after. Arguments with the grandmother about disciplining Wayne led the family to move to the paternal grandmother's home. Four months later, Wayne was admitted to hospital with non-accidental injuries and neglect. A Care Order was made and he was placed with foster parents. Elaine and Nigel successfully applied for revocation of the Care Order a year later and Wayne was returned home with a three-year Supervision Order, against social services' recommendation to the court. Over the next year there were intermittent reports that Wayne was being physically abused and, although injuries were noted, professionals felt that there was insufficient evidence to return to court. Wayne died after being severely shaken and Nigel Briffett was sentenced to five years' imprisonment for his manslaughter.

Formal status at time of death: Supervision Order.

PAUL BROWN (died 19.11.70)

Report: 'The report of the committe of inquiry into the case of Paul Steven Brown', published by HMSO, London in December 1980.
Commissioned by: The Department of Health and Social Security.
Locus: Wirral.

Summary

Pauline Brown formed a number of unstable partnerships, including a brief time together with her husband David Brown and with the fathers of Paul and Liam. Over the next three years, social services received occasional reports of poor child care, bruising and neglect and eventually Pauline asked for the children to be received into care because she was beating them and taking drugs. During the next year, Pauline had very little contact with the boys and was living at various addresses. When she reunited with David Brown the couple insisted on removing the boys from care and placed them with the paternal grandparents, who were registered disabled and had been suspected of maltreating their own children. Within six months, Paul was admitted to hospital with severe injuries from which he died six months later. Liam was found to be filthy and starving. Stanley and Sarah Brown were 'sentenced to a term of imprisonment' for ill-treating and neglecting the boys.

Formal status at time of death: At Risk Register and informal fostering arrangement.

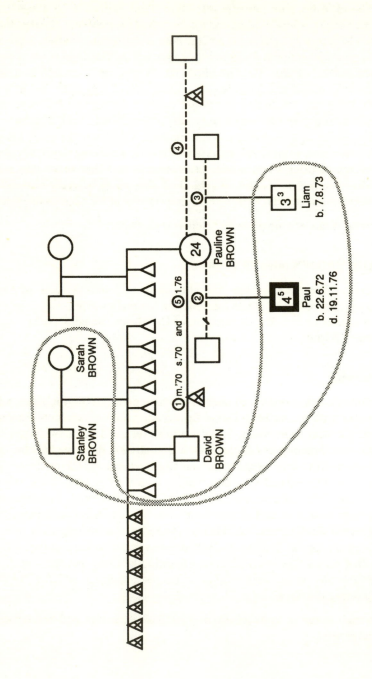

Figure A.8 Genogram of Paul Brown's family

JASON CAESAR (died 5.11.80)

Report: 'Report by the Social Services Committee on the involvement of the social services department in the events preceding the death of Jason Caesar', published by Cambridgeshire Social Services Committee in February 1982.

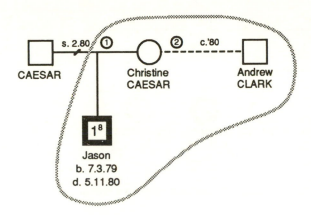

Figure A.9 Genogram of Jason Caesar's family

Summary

Both of Jason's parents had long-standing social work involvement prior to his birth, as a result of treatment for their drug dependency. When the couple separated, Christine Caesar began to cohabit with Andrew Clarke and Jason was soon noted to be bruised. The next month he was admitted to hospital with a fractured arm. Case conferences placed him on the At Risk Register and returned him home with support from his mother's social worker. Further minor injuries were noted during the next year and shortly before his death his mother asked for him to be removed from their home. Jason died from severe injuries and his mother and step-father were convicted of his manslaughter.

Formal status at time of death: At Risk Register.

KIMBERLEY CARLILE (died 8.6.86)

Report: 'A child in mind: protection of children in a responsible society. The report of the commission of inquiry into the circumstances surrounding the death of Kimberley Carlile', published by the London Borough of Greenwich in December 1987.
Commissioned by: The London Borough of Greenwich and Greenwich Health Authority.

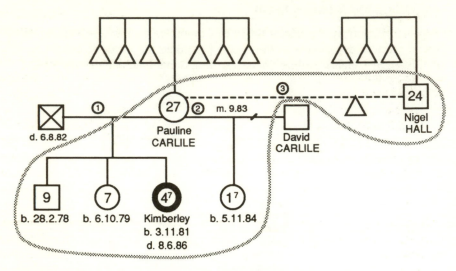

Figure A.10 Genogram of Kimberley Carlile's family

Summary

Pauline Carlile had marriages with two violent men before she lived with Nigel Hall. Whilst living in the Wirral, there were concerns for all three children from Pauline's first marriage and Kimberley, the youngest, was noted to be failing to thrive and bruised. Also, Pauline and David Carlile had several convictions for fraud and assault, during which time the children went into voluntary care. Following the birth of her fourth child, Pauline settled in Greenwich with Nigel Hall and withdrew her three older children from voluntary care to join them. In transferring the case, Wirral social services asked Greenwich to monitor the family but they rejected the offer of assistance. Over the next few months, concerns about possible child abuse arose but when social workers visited they were only allowed restricted sight of the children. The only other time the children were seen was when the family pre-empted the social worker's home visit by coming to the office. Kimberley's appearance on that occasion gave cause for concern but she was not seen alive again. Kimberley died from a blow to the head but she had clearly experienced physical abuse and starvation over a long period. Nigel Hall was sentenced to life imprisonment for Kimberley's murder and Pauline Carlile to twelve years for grievous bodily harm.

REUBEN CARTHY (died 4.2.85)

Report: 'Report of inquiry into the case of Reuben Carthy (d.o.b. 7.4.82)', published by Nottingham Area Review Committee in September 1985.

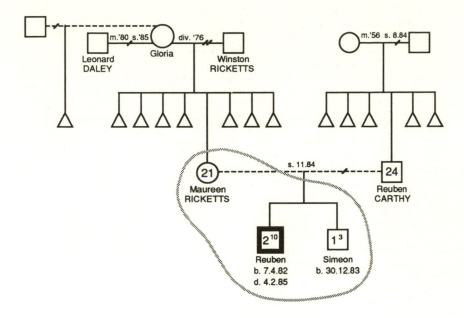

Figure A.11 Genogram of Reuben Carthy's family

Summary

Reuben's parents began to cohabit after Maureen Ricketts became pregnant with him. Reuben was seen a number of times in the local hospital casualty department with apparently accidental injuries, including a fractured arm. After his father left home, Maureen requested help from social services on a number of occasions, admitting that she felt like hitting Reuben and occasionally had done so. Reuben died from extensive injuries sustained over some time. Maureen Ricketts was charged with unlawful killing and Reuben Carthy Snr with previous wilful ill-treatment.

LESTER CHAPMAN (died January/February 1978)

Report: 'Lester Chapman: inquiry report', published in October 1979 (available from Berkshire Shire Hall).
Commissioned by: The County Councils and Area Health Authorities of Berkshire and Hampshire.

Summary

Linda Chapman married Lester Johnson when she was already pregnant with Wendy, two days after coming out of care at the age of 16 years. Lester was born

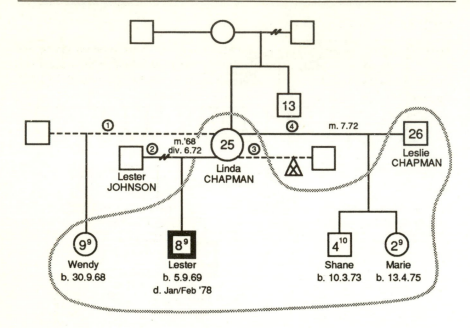

Figure A.12 Genogram of Lester Chapman's family

a year later. Over the next five months the couple repeatedly separated and came together, before Wendy and Lester were taken into care because of neglect, where they stayed for two and a half years. During that time, Linda began to live with Leslie Chapman and divorced her husband and the divorce court decided to return the children home on trial. The couple were eventually granted full custody and care of Wendy and Lester. Over the next four years, the NSPCC and social services were called in because of bruising to Lester and parental fights but when the family moved from Reading to Portsmouth their case was not transferred to the local social services. In Portsmouth, Wendy and Lester required hospital admissions because of signs of extreme anxiety and Wendy was taken into care for four weeks. Both children were placed on the At Risk Register for four months, before the family moved back to Reading. Anxiety about the children steadily mounted in their school and then Lester repeatedly ran away from home in response to physical abuse. On the fourth occasion he was not found until his body was discovered in sewage sludge.

Formal status at time of death: All the children's names were placed on the Provisional NAI Observation Register five days after Lester's final disappearance.

RICHARD CLARK (severe injury 2.5.74)

Report: 'Report of the committee of inquiry into the consideration given and steps taken towards securing the welfare of Richard Clark by Perth town council and other bodies or persons concerned', published by HMSO, Edinburgh in 1975. *Commissioned by*: The Secretary of State for Scotland.

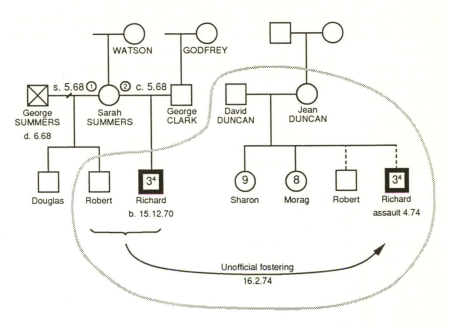

Figure A.13 Genogram of Richard Clark's families

Summary

For the first three years of his life Richard Clark lived with his parents, Sarah Summers and George Clark and his half-brother Robert Summers. Sarah Summers became friends and a drinking partner with Jean Duncan, shortly after Richard and Robert had been found neglected and the Duncans had been convicted of severe neglect of their children. When Sarah Summers was charged with attempted murder of George Clark, Jean Duncan agreed to care for Robert and Richard. Many workers, as well as the boys' father, became concerned at the steady deterioration in the condition of the Duncans' house and their poor care and punishment of the children. However, social services agreed to continue with the placement as an 'unofficial fostering' arrangement. Over the next three months, Richard was seen to be bruised and unwell by many workers, his father and his maternal grandmother, until he was admitted to hospital with a massive cerebral haemorrhage. He was never expected to recover from the effects of those injuries and Jean Duncan was sentenced to four years' imprisonment for assault and David Duncan to two years.

Formal status at time of severe injury: Unofficial fostering arrangement (and Supervision Order on Sharon and Morag Duncan).

DARRYN CLARKE (died 21.1.78)

Report: 'The report of the committee of inquiry into the actions of the authorities and agencies relating to Darryn James Clarke', published by HMSO, London in November 1979.
Commissioned by: The Department of Health and Social Security.
Locus: Liverpool.

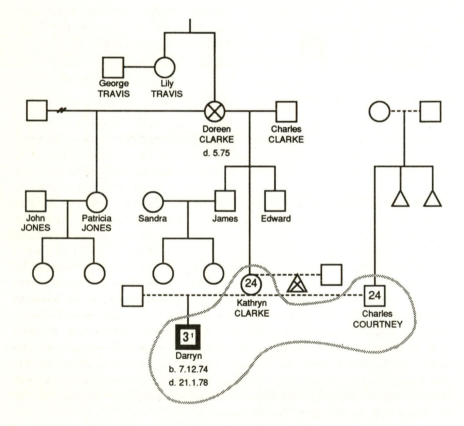

Figure A.14 Genogram of Darryn Clarke's family

Summary

Charles Courtney came from a severely deprived background and had a history of violence, Approved School and Borstal. Kathryn Clarke began a furtive relationship with him against the wishes of her closely-knit family. For the first three years of his life Darryn was well cared for but, as soon as his mother began cohabiting with Charles, he began to be beaten and mistreated. Over the next seven weeks Kathryn's extended family tried to discover their whereabouts because they were worried about Darryn's care and they contacted the police, the NSPCC and social services. However, no one was successful in locating them before Darryn died of extensive and severe injuries. Charles Courtney was sentenced to fifteen years' imprisonment for unlawfully killing Darryn and Kathryn Clarke to eighteen months for wilful neglect.

MARIA COLWELL (died 7.1.73)

Report: 'Report of the committee of inquiry into the care and supervision provided in relation to Maria Colwell', published by HMSO, London in 1974.
Commissioned by: The Department of Health and Social Security.
Locus: Brighton.

Summary

Maria's father left the family one month after she was born and he died three months later. Maria's mother, Pauline Colwell, 'went to pieces' and within a few weeks she took Maria to Mr and Mrs Cooper (Maria's uncle and aunt) to be looked after. Four months later, her other four children were taken into care because of neglect. Although Pauline removed Maria, she was soon returned to the Coopers on a Care Order, aged 1 year 7 months. Pauline lived with William Kepple, who had a 'wild reputation', and they eventually married and had four children. For the next four years, Maria thrived in her foster home and she showed distress when her mother made intermittent efforts for closer contact or for Maria to return to live with her. Pauline's wishes coincided with social services' intention that Maria would return to her mother at some stage and when she was 6 years old the social worker arranged for her gradual return home on trial, despite Maria's protests. Maria returned home permanently aged 7 years 6 months and her Care Order was changed to a Supervision Order. Over the next year, neighbours and her school reported evidence of her rejection and physical abuse, as well as neglect of all the Kepple children. Maria was seen less and less and progressively lost weight until she died from a severe assault. William Kepple's conviction was reduced from murder to manslaughter on appeal and he was sentenced to eight years' imprisonment.

Formal status at time of death: Supervision Order.

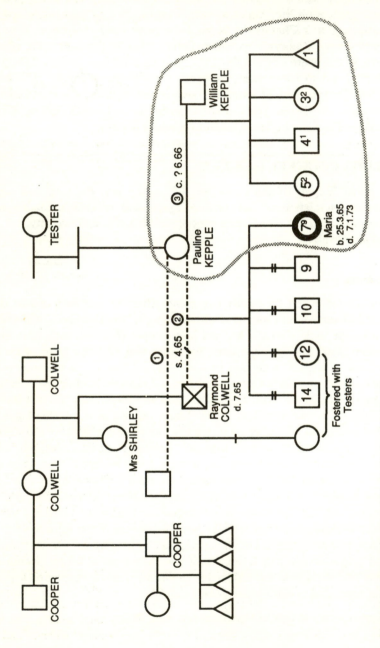

Figure A.15 Genogram of Maria Colwell's family

RICHARD FRASER (died 11.9.77)

Report: 'Richard Fraser: 1972–1977. The report of an independent inquiry', published by the London Borough of Lambeth in May 1982.
Commissioned by: The London Borough of Lambeth, the Inner London Education Authority and Lambeth, Southwark and Lewisham Area Health Authority (Teaching).

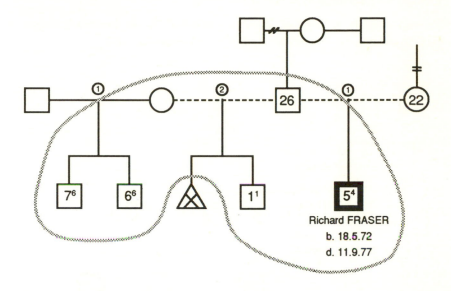

Figure A.16 Genogram of Richard Fraser's family

Summary

Richard's mother was of low intelligence and was in care at the time of his birth and his father had a history of violence. During Richard's first year, professionals were concerned about his development, the adequacy of his care and his father's violence to his mother. This concern intensified when his parents separated and Richard's care passed repeatedly from one to the other. Eventually, Richard's father took him to a reception centre, where they were joined by his cohabitee and her two children, just discharged from care. She looked after the children while Richard's father was twice imprisoned for violence but Richard needed to be removed from her care on a Place of Safety Order because of injuries. Social services obtained a Care Order but agreed that Richard could return home on trial provided that his father was present. When Richard's father was released from prison, the social worker maintained low-profile visits, fearing violence to herself, yet everyone believed that the risk to the children was from the step-mother. Over the next year, professional concern increased about the care of the couple's new baby, Richard's school non-attendance and the signs of deprivation and abuse shown by all the children. Finally, Richard was admitted unaccompanied to hospital with severe head injuries. Richard's father received a life sentence for his murder and his step-mother two years' imprisonment for wilful assault, ill-treatment and neglect.

Formal status at time of death: Full Care Order and At Risk Register.

LUCIE GATES (died 19.6.79)

Report: 'Report of panel of inquiry', published by the London Borough of Bexley and Bexley Area Health Authority in November 1982.

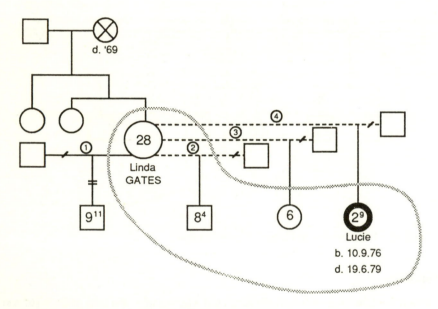

Figure A.17 Genogram of Lucie Gates' family

Summary

Linda Gates first became pregnant soon after her mother died and she subsequently had three more children, each from a different partner. The first child was adopted but there was continual professional concern about her severe neglect and abuse of the other children over many years. Although respite voluntary care was necessary on some occasions, the workers decided not to institute full care proceedings but to continue with support in the home. Lucie died from burns sustained when an electric fire fell on her, while all the children were left unattended. Linda Gates pleaded guilty to manslaughter and was sentenced to eighteen months' imprisonment, suspended for two years.

LISA GODFREY (died 23.10.73)

Report: 'Report of the joint committee of inquiry into non-accidental injury to children: with particular reference to the care of Lisa Godfrey', published by Lambeth, Southwark and Lewisham Area Health Authority (Teaching), the Inner London Probation and After Care Committee and the London Borough of Lambeth in 1975.

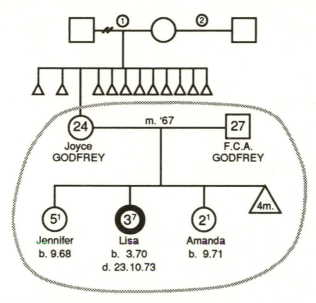

Figure A.18 Genogram of Lisa Godfrey's family

Summary

Mr and Mrs Godfrey separated and reunited repeatedly and when Mrs Godfrey was placed on probation for fraud the probation service began to work with 'the total family situation'. When concern arose about bruising to the children, the probation officer suggested that involvement of another worker would be unwise and social services agreed. Lisa regressed following surgery to her bladder and, over the next year, her mother admitted hitting her and many professionals saw that she was bruised and injured. In the final weeks, Mrs Godfrey's abuse of Lisa increased, culminating in her death.

CLAIRE HADDON (died 18.2.79)

Report: 'Report of the Director of Social Services to the social services committee' dated February 1980.
Locus: Birmingham.

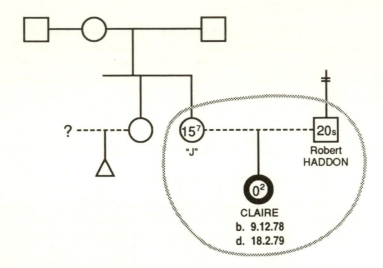

Figure A.19 Genogram of Claire Haddon's family

Summary

Claire's mother was a 15-year-old adolescent who had lost her own mother through parental separation. She ran away from home with an elder sister and was eventually located cohabiting with Robert Haddon and pregnant by him. The midwife referred her back to social services who decided to support this arrangement. Claire was born prematurely and her mother initially left her in hospital and gave a false address. One month later she took her home and received intensive professional help. When Claire's physical condition was stable the midwife withdrew but the couple refused to see the social worker and health visitor. Claire died when she was 10 weeks old, from extreme violence committed over about ten days. Robert Haddon was convicted of her murder and her mother of grievous bodily harm.

GEMMA HARTWELL (died 23.3.85)

Report: 'Report to the Social Services Committee', dated December 1985.
Locus: Birmingham.

Summary

Before Yvonne and Philip Hartwell met, social services had been concerned about Yvonne's care of her first baby and Philip had been imprisoned for violence to his 3-week-old daughter. One month after the couple began to cohabit, Philip was imprisoned for assaulting Yvonne's daughter of 2½ years,

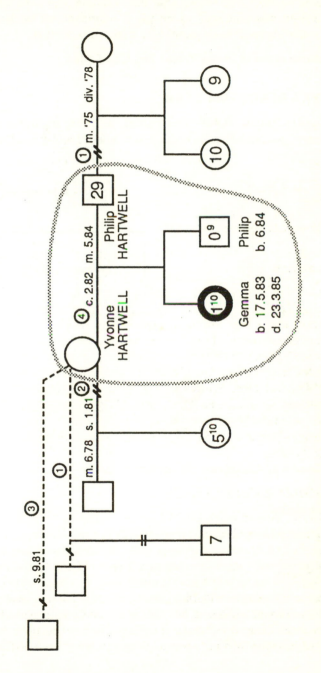

Figure A.20 Genogram of Gemma Hartwell's family

who was later removed from the family on a Care Order. Gemma was taken into care as soon as she was born and was placed with prospective adoptive parents. However, sixteen months later this couple separated and Gemma was returned home on trial. Two weeks after that, Gemma died from an assault and Philip Hartwell was sentenced to ten years' imprisonment for her manslaughter and Yvonne Hartwell to six months for wilful ill-treatment.

Formal status at time of death: Full Care Order.

TYRA HENRY (died 1.9.84)

Report: 'Whose child? The report of the public inquiry into the death of Tyra Henry', published by the London Borough of Lambeth in December 1987.

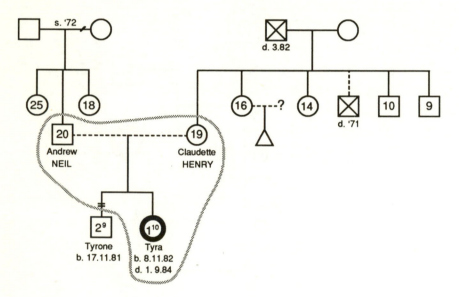

Figure A.21 Genogram of Tyra Henry's family

Summary

Claudette Henry became pregnant with Tyrone when aged 15. Andrew Neil, the baby's father, was a persistent offender who had a history of sudden rages, including one violent episode to a 2-year-old child. Andrew assaulted Tyrone severely when he was 4 months old, leaving him blind and mentally handicapped and he was removed into long-term care. Andrew was later convicted of cruelty to Tyrone and because of this history a Care Order was made on Tyra when she was born. However, it was left unclear whether Claudette or her mother was to be responsible for Tyra's care and the onus was placed on Claudette to withdraw from contact with Andrew to protect Tyra. Over the next twenty months, Claudette and Tyra moved between the maternal grandmother's flat, Claudette's council flat and finally the Neil family home, where Andrew was repeatedly violent to them both. Tyra died from multiple injuries and Andrew Neil received a life sentence for her murder.

Formal status at time of death: Full Care Order and At Risk Register.

NEIL HOWLETT (died 26.2.75)

Report: 'Joint enquiry arising from the death of Neil Howlett', published by the City of Birmingham District Council and Birmingham Area Health Authority in November 1976.

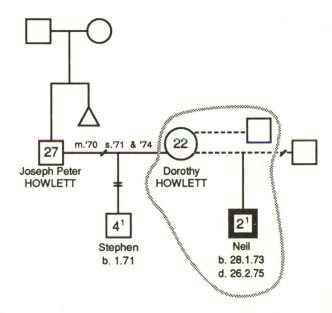

Figure A.22 Genogram of Neil Howlett's family

Summary

The relationship of Neil's parents was characterised by numerous separations and reconciliations. After their final separation, concern arose about Dorothy Howlett's neglect and abuse of her children. Neighbours made repeated complaints to the NSPCC and the police, especially saying that Neil was allowed to head-bang for hours. Stephen was taken into care when he was found locked in his room covered in fleas but Neil was left at home with his mother and her new boyfriend. Five months later, Neil died from injuries suffered over a few days. Dorothy Howlett was charged with manslaughter and cruelty and received a suspended sentence with a Supervision Order.

HEIDI KOSEDA (died November 1984)

Report: 'Report of the review panel of the London Borough of Hillingdon Area Review Committee on Child Abuse into the death of Heidi Koseda', published in March 1986.

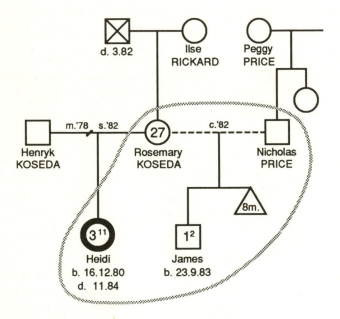

Figure A.23 Genogram of Heidi Koseda's family

Summary

Heidi was well looked after for the first two years of her life but she began to look scruffy when her parents separated and her mother started to cohabit with Nicholas Price. Little was seen of Heidi from this time on and the family actively resisted contact with outside agencies. Nicholas frightened hospital maternity department staff by his violent outbursts and during the next few months a neighbour telephoned the NSPCC to report that Heidi had not been seen and that James was bruised. However, an NSPCC officer fabricated a report claiming he had seen the family. Heidi remained locked away in her room and died of starvation but her body was not discovered for another two months. Nicholas Price was sentenced to life imprisonment for her murder and Rosemary Koseda pleaded guilty to manslaughter with diminished responsibility and a Hospital Order was made.

GAVIN MABEY (died 23.8.87)

Report: 'Report of the sub-committee set up to report into the circumstances surrounding the death of Gavin Mabey', published by Leeds Area Review Committee in 1988.

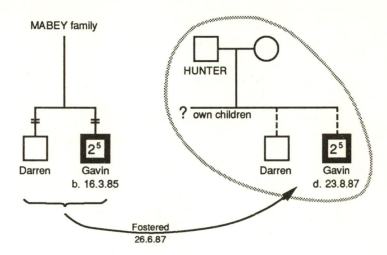

Figure A.24 Genogram of Gavin Mabey's families

Summary

Gavin and Darren were removed from their parents when sexual abuse of Darren was confirmed. Soon after the boys moved to their third foster placement, Social Services and the NSPCC received anonymous telephone calls alleging that their foster parents were ill-treating them. The foster parents suggested that Gavin had been injuring himself and sought medical attention, including for a fractured leg. Gavin died of a severe head injury two months after being placed in that foster home and the foster father was sentenced to life imprisonment for his murder.

Formal status at time of death: Full Care Order.

MARIA MEHMEDAGI (died 3.11.78)

Report: 'Maria Mehmedagi: report of an independent inquiry', published by the London Borough of Southwark, Lambeth, Southwark and Lewisham Area Health Authority (Teaching) and the Inner London Probation and After-Care Service in June 1981.

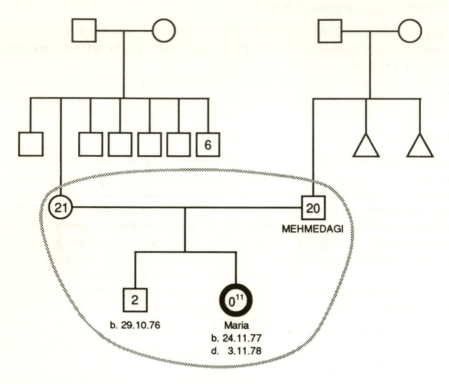

Figure A.25 Genogram of Maria Mehmedagi's family

Summary

Maria's parents became engaged and married against their own parents' wishes. Maria's birth was unplanned and during the first week of her life she underwent an operation for pyloric stenosis and was seen to be bruised. At 7 weeks of age she was readmitted to hospital with extensive injuries and her father was later convicted of causing her actual bodily harm and placed on probation. Maria spent six months in hospital before being placed with foster parents and then, six weeks later, began to spend part of each week home on trial. However, this coincided with a strike in social services and so the monitoring of Maria was taken over by a probation officer and health visitor. Maria returned home full time three months later, even though scratches and bruising had been noted after her visits home. Two weeks later, Maria received severe head injuries from which she died and her father was convicted of causing her actual bodily harm and was imprisoned for nine months.

Formal status at time of death: Full Care Order and At Risk Register.

STEPHEN MENHENIOTT (died January 1976)

Report: 'Report of the social work service of DHSS into certain aspects of the management of the case of Stephen Menheniott', published by HMSO, London in September 1978.
Commissioned by: The Department of Health and Social Security.
Locus: East Sussex and the Isles of Scilly.

Summary

Before Stephen was born, his father had twice been imprisoned for neglect or ill-treatment of his children. When Stephen was 19 months old, he was made the subject of a Care Order because his mother was considered unfit to look after him. Stephen remained in care until the age of 11, when he returned home to his parents, now living in a remote part of the Isles of Scilly. Within a year he was taken back into care because his father was charged with incest with Stephen's 13-year-old sister. Stephen stayed in care until he was 17 years of age and then returned to live with his father, his sister and three of her children. Two years later, Stephen's father killed him and a post-mortem examination showed multiple injuries sustained over a period of time.

Formal status at time of death: Stephen's Care Order had ended.

STEVEN MEURS (died 13.4.75)

Report: 'Report of the review body appointed to enquire into the case of Steven Meurs: 1975', published by Norfolk County Council in December 1975.
Commissioned by: Norfolk County Council and Norfolk Area Health Authority.

Summary

Denis Meurs, John and Barry Williams and Brian Skinner were together committed for trial for theft when Steven was a year old. Then, both Sandra Meurs and Carol Skinner began to live with other partners and Sandra took on the care of Carol's two eldest children because their mother had abandoned them. Sandra found these children difficult to manage and so the social worker focussed help on supporting this placement. Meanwhile, the NSPCC, the police and social services received complaints about Steven's care from his paternal grandfather and a neighbour. However, Sandra refused to let the social worker and health visitor see Steven and three months after Sandra took in Carol's children, Steven died from neglect and malnutrition. Sandra Meurs was imprisoned for manslaughter.

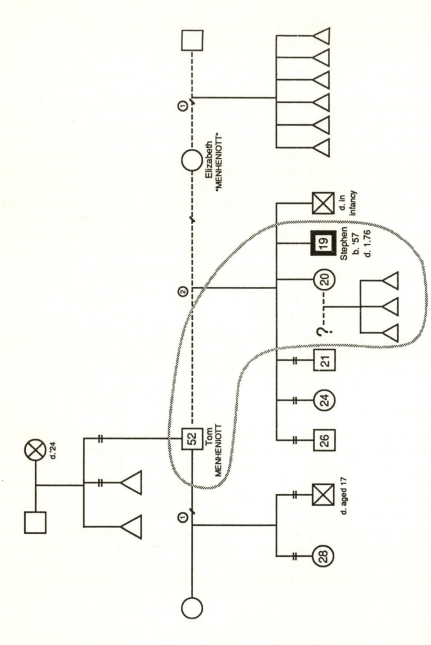

Figure A.26 Genogram of Stephen Menheniott's family

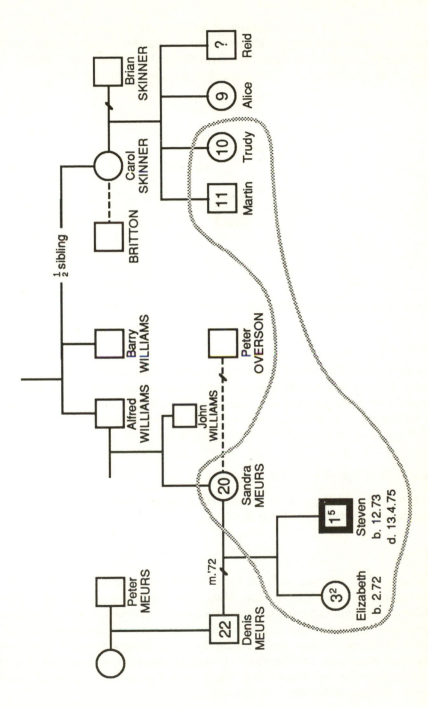

Figure A.27 Genogram of Steven Meurs' family

DAVID NASEBY (died 17.5.73)

Report: 'Report of the committee of enquiry set up to enquire into the circumstances surrounding the admission treatment and discharge of baby David Lee Naseby, deceased, at Burton-on-Trent General Hospital from February to May, 1973', published by Staffordshire Area Health Authority in 1974.

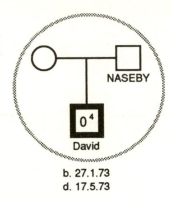

b. 27.1.73
d. 17.5.73

Figure A.28 Genogram of David Naseby's family

Summary

During his short life, David was taken to hospital three times: the first was with a scratch on his face, then he was admitted with pneumonia and a week after that discharge he was readmitted with a chest infection. Whilst in hospital he was seen to be bruised, cut, bleeding and neglected. He was killed the day after his discharge home and his father was convicted of his murder.

MALCOLM PAGE (died 7.2.79)

Report: 'Malcolm Page: report by the panel appointed by the Essex Area Review Committee', published in March 1981.

Summary

Professionals had contact with the Page family because of debts, violence and chronically poor standards of care. When Malcolm was 4 months old, all the children were removed on Care Orders for two months because of the appalling condition of the home. Over the next eight months, considerable home help was provided to try to maintain adequate hygiene. However, while standards improved downstairs, Malcolm was left in filthy conditions upstairs and he died from malnutrition and hypothermia. Both parents were found guilty of wilful neglect and imprisoned for twelve months.

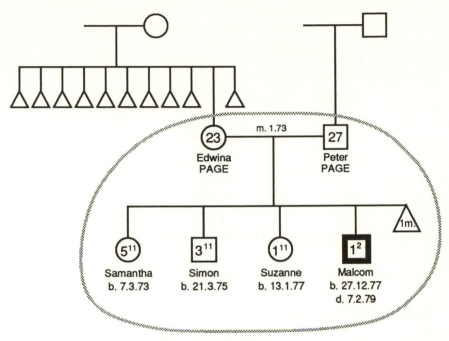

Figure A.29 Genogram of Malcolm Page's family

Formal status at time of death: Full Care Order and Non-Accidental Injury Register.

SIMON PEACOCK (died 8.12.76)

Report: 'Report of committee of enquiry concerning Simon Peacock', published by Cambridgeshire County Council, Suffolk County Council, Cambridgeshire Area Health Authority (Teaching) and Suffolk Area Health Authority in January 1978.

Summary

Christine and Colin Peacock married when she was seven months pregnant with Simon. Colin's aggressive behaviour on the post-natal ward led social services to apply for a Place of Safety Order to keep Simon in hospital. However, doctors discharged Simon and his mother home, after which the parents were reluctant to be visited by community professionals. Two months later, a case conference placed Simon's name on the Non-Accidental Injury Register because he was cut and bruised. Shortly after this, the family moved and professional contact was not fully re-established. Simon died of severe injuries but there was also evidence of previous abuse and both parents were found guilty of manslaughter and cruelty and were imprisoned for eight years.

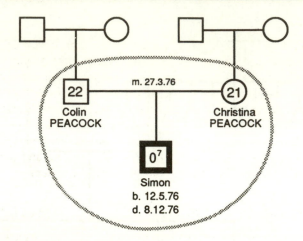

Figure A.30 Genogram of Simon Peacock's family

Formal status at time of death: Non-Accidental Injury Register

MAX PIAZZANI (died 4.8.73)

Report: 'Report of the joint committee set up to consider co-ordination of services concerned with non-accidental injury to children', published by Essex County Council Social Services Department in September 1974.
Commissioned by: Essex County Council and Essex Health Authority.

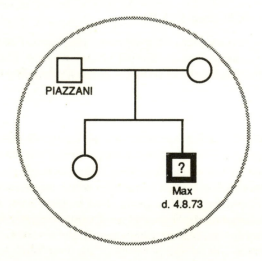

Figure A.31 Genogram of Max Piazzani's family

Summary

Max's parents were first challenged about their care of Max by a paediatrician who treated his injuries at the local hospital but the family withdrew from hospital and social services contact. Health visiting ceased three years later when the health visitor left her job and following her departure, Max's mother requested residential care for him. When the general practitioner visited he was sufficiently concerned about Max's emaciated state to negotiate hospital admission. However, the same night Max sustained a head injury from which he died. Both parents were found guilty of wilful neglect and sentenced to four years' imprisonment, reduced to eighteen months on appeal.

CHRISTOPHER PINDER/DANIEL FRANKLAND (died 8.7.80)

Report: 'Bradford Area Review Committee – Child Abuse Enquiry Sub-Committee. Report concerning Christopher Pinder/Daniel Frankland (born 19.12.79 – died 8.7.80)', published in July 1981.

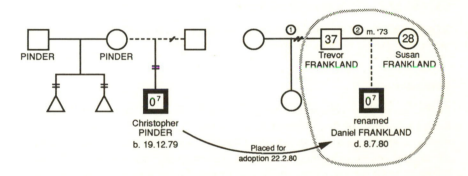

Figure A.32 Genogram of Christopher Pinder/Daniel Frankland's families

Summary

Christopher Pinder was placed with Susan and Trevor Frankland when he was 2 months old, four days after they had been approved as adoptive parents. They immediately changed his name to Daniel Frankland. Susan found problems coping with his needs and his feeding difficulties and received support from community and hospital professionals. Although Daniel was considered to be thriving, Susan became increasingly desperate about her ability to care for him. Daniel died after a severe assault, two days before the final adoption hearing. Susan Frankland's plea of manslaughter with diminished responsibility was accepted and she was detained without time limit under the Mental Health Act.

Formal status at time of death: Awaiting Adoption Order.

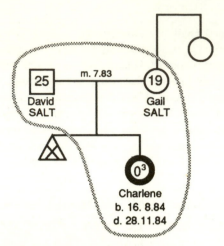

Figure A.33 Genogram of Charlene Salt's family

CHARLENE SALT (died 28.11.84)

Report: 'Oldham District Review Committee: review of child abuse procedures', published in October 1986.

Summary

Professionals were concerned about the Salt family from the time of Charlene's
birth because of the dirty state of their flat and David Salt's aggression towards
workers. When she was 2 weeks old, Charlene was admitted to hospital because
of neglect and bruising and a Place of Safety Order was taken out. Charlene
returned home ten days later and a Supervision Order was made but her parents
kept evading professional contact. Charlene died from a fractured skull aged 3
months and evidence was also found of old injuries dating from the time of her
discharge home.

Formal status at time of death: Supervision Order.

KAREN SPENCER (died 19.4.77)

Report: 'Report by Professor J.D. McClean concerning Karen Spencer to the
Derbyshire County Council and Derbyshire Area Health Authority', published in
1978.

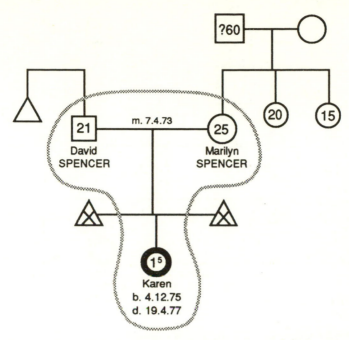

Figure A.34 Genogram of Karen Spencer's family

Summary

Both parents were considered to be of limited intelligence and they had a stormy and violent marriage, separating twice before Karen was born. Karen was taken into care when 2 months old after her mother admitted assaulting her and fracturing her skull. Karen was placed with short-term foster parents with weekend visits home, from which she sometimes returned with a severe nappy rash. A plan for Marilyn Spencer to receive psychiatric treatment before Karen could return home permanently was never realised and Karen went back home on trial a year later. One month after that, following an argument between her parents, Marilyn dropped and punched Karen and she died from the head injury. Marilyn Spencer pleaded guilty to manslaughter on the grounds of diminished responsibility and a two-year Probation Order was made with a condition of medical treatment.

Formal status at time of death: Full Care Order and Non-Accidental Injury Register.

CARLY TAYLOR (died 14.7.78)

Report: 'Carly Taylor: report of an independent inquiry', published by Leicestershire County Council and Leicestershire Area Health Authority (Teaching) in 1980.

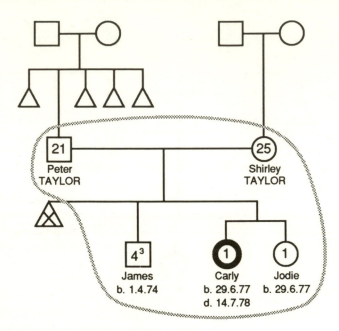

Figure A.35 Genogram of Carly Taylor's family

Summary

Peter and Shirley Taylor married when he was aged 17 and she 21 and James was born one month later. The family changed addresses frequently and Shirley's unpredictably violent behaviour and both parents' drug abuse raised professional concern about James' safety. Shirley received no ante-natal care before the twins, Carly and Jodie, were born and within a few weeks workers observed a lack of involvement with them by both parents. The twins spent seven of the first nine months of their lives living with either the maternal or paternal grandparents and were rarely visited by their natural parents. However, Shirley and Peter decided that they wanted the twins back because they felt that the grandmother's childminder was too attached to them. Almost immediately after the twins returned, now aged 10 months, professionals noted bruising, neglect, loss of weight and that they were unhappy. The paternal grandparents, neighbours and a lodger all reported mistreatment of the twins but, when professionals were able to gain access to the home, they were satisfied by the home circumstances and the state of the children. Carly died of a fractured skull two months after returning to live with her parents and Shirley Taylor was convicted of her manslaughter and ill-treatment and sentenced to five years imprisonment.

Formal status at time of death: All the children's names were placed on the At Risk Register the day that Carly died.

SHIRLEY WOODCOCK (died 4.4.82)

Report: 'Report on the death of Shirley Woodcock', published by the London Borough of Hammersmith and Fulham in August 1984.

Summary

Margaret and Adrian Woodcock came from broken homes and had experienced many placements while in care. Margaret had no ante-natal care during her pregnancies with Shirley or Shirley's elder brother. When Shirley was nearly 2 years old, she and her brother were taken into care because their mother had finally abandoned them, having threatened to do so on many previous occasions. Until that time they had experienced chronically poor care, neglect, many changes of address and caretakers and parental separations, including their father's imprisonment. In care, the first foster parents asked them to be removed because they were so difficult and only one other foster home was available at short notice, despite social services' reservations about that couple's suitability to look after young children. It remained unclear whether this would be a short-term or a long-term placement. Within a few weeks of it starting, Shirley was reported to be bruised and to be wetting and soiling, refusing food and making herself sick and her skin bleed. Four months later, Shirley was admitted to hospital with extensive injuries from which she died. Her brother was also found to be severely bruised. A coroner's jury returned a verdict of unlawful killing but the Director of Public Prosecutions decided that no further action should be taken.

Formal status at time of death: Full Care Order and foster placement.

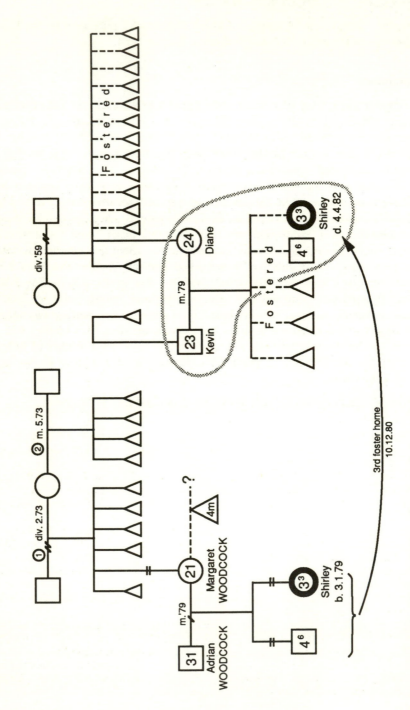

Figure A.36 Genogram of Shirley Woodcock's families

Bibliography

Adcock, M. (1989) Presentation to the Institute of Family Therapy's 'Child Care and the State' Conference, Middlesex Hospital, London, June.

Allen, D. (1983) 'Let us acknowledge our mistakes and try to learn from them', *Community Care*, 12 May: 14–16.

Anderson, H., Goolishian, H. and Winderman, L. (1986) 'Problem determined systems: towards transformation in family therapy', *Journal of Strategic and Systemic Therapies*, 5: 1–13.

Ariès, P. (1962) *Centuries of Childhood: A Social History of Family Life*, London: Jonathan Cape.

Asen, K., George, E., Piper, R. and Stevens, A. (1989) 'A systems approach to child abuse: management and treatment issues', *Child Abuse and Neglect*, 13: 45–57.

Baker, A.W. and Duncan, S.P. (1985) 'Child sexual abuse: a study of prevalence in Great Britain', *Child Abuse and Neglect*, 9: 457–67.

Baker, T. and Duncan, S. (1986) 'Child sexual abuse', in R. Meadow (ed.) *Recent Advances in Paediatrics*, No. 8, Edinburgh: Churchill Livingstone.

Barker, P. (1986) *Basic Family Therapy*, 2nd edn, London: Collins.

BASW (1982) *Child Abuse Inquiries*, London, British Association of Social Workers.

Bateson, G. (1972) *Steps to an Ecology of Mind*, New York: Ballantine.

Bateson, G. (1979) *Mind and Nature: A Necessary Unity*, New York: E.P. Dutton.

Bateson, G., Jackson, D.D., Haley, J. and Weakland, J.H. (1956) 'Toward a theory of schizophrenia', *Behavioural Science*, 1: 251–64.

Bentovim, A., Elton, A., Hildebrand, J., Tranter, M. and Vizard, E. (eds) (1988) *Child Sexual Abuse within the Family: Assessment and Treatment*, London: Wright.

Bion, W.R. (1959) 'Attacks on linking', *International Journal of Psycho-Analysis*, 40: 308–15.

Bion, W.R. (1961) *Experiences in Groups and Other Papers*, London: Tavistock.

Blom-Cooper, L. (1986) 'Caring for children', Sigmund Freud Birthday Lecture, Middle Temple Hall, London, May.

Boscolo, L., Cecchin, G., Hoffman, L. and Penn, P. (1987) *Milan Systemic Family Therapy: Conversations in Theory and Practice*, New York: Basic.

Bowlby, J. (1951) *Maternal Care and Mental Health*, Geneva: World Health Organization.

Britton, R. (1981) 'Re-enactment as an unwitting professional response to family dynamics', in S. Box, B. Copley, J. Magagna and E. Moustaki (eds) *Psychotherapy with Families: An Analytic Approach*, London: Routledge & Kegan Paul.

Broderick, C.B. and Schrader, S.S. (1981) 'The history of professional marriage and family therapy', in A.S. Gurman and D.P. Kniskern (eds) *Handbook of Family Therapy*, New York: Brunner/Mazel.

Burnham, J.B. (1986) *Family Therapy: First Steps Towards a Systemic Approach*, London: Tavistock.

Byng-Hall, J. (1979) 'Re-editing family mythology during family therapy', *Journal of Family Therapy*, 1: 103–16.

Byng-Hall, J. (1980) 'Symptom-bearer as marital-distance regulator: clinical implications', *Family Process*, 19: 355–66.

Byng-Hall, J. (1985) 'The family script: a useful bridge between theory and practice', *Journal of Family Therapy*, 7: 301–5.

Caffey, F. (1946) 'Multiple fractures in the long bones of children suffering from chronic subdural haematoma', *American Journal of Roentgenology and Radium Therapy*, 56: 163–73.

Campbell, D. and Draper, R. (eds) (1985) *Applications of Systemic Family Therapy: The Milan Approach*, London: Grune & Stratton.

Campbell, D., Draper, R. and Huffington, C. (1989) *Second Thoughts on the Theory and Practice of the Milan Approach to Family Therapy*, London: DC Associates.

Capra, F. (1982) *The Turning Point: Science, Society and the Rising Culture*, Aldershot: Wildwood House.

Cleveland Inquiry (1988) *Report of the Inquiry into Child Abuse in Cleveland 1987*, London: HMSO.

Creighton, S.J. and Gallagher, B. (1988) *Child Abuse Deaths*, Information Briefing No. 5, London: NSPCC.

Creighton, S.J. and Noyes, P. (1989) *Child Abuse Trends in England and Wales 1983–1987*, London: NSPCC.

Cronen, V.E. and Pearce, W.B. (1985) 'Toward an explanation of how the Milan method works: an invitation to a systemic epistemology and the evolution of family systems', in D. Campbell and R. Draper (eds) *Applications of Systemic Family Therapy: The Milan Approach*, London: Grune & Stratton.

Cronen, V.E., Johnson, K.M. and Lannaman, J. W. (1982) 'Paradoxes, double binds, and reflexive loops: an alternative theoretical perspective', *Family Process*, 21: 91–112.

Dale, P. and Davies, M. (1985) 'A model of intervention in child-abusing families: a wider systems view', *Child Abuse and Neglect*, 9: 449–55.

Dale, P., Davies, M., Morrison, T. and Waters, J. (1986) *Dangerous Families*, London: Tavistock.

Dell, P. (1989) 'Violence and the systemic view: the problem of power', *Family Process*, 28: 1–14.

de Mause, L. (1976) 'The evolution of childhood', in L. de Mause (ed.) *The History of Childhood: The Evolution of Parent–Child Relationships as a Factor in History*, London: Souvenir Press.

Department of Health (1988) *Protecting Children: A Guide to Social Workers Undertaking a Comprehensive Assessment*, London: HMSO.

Department of Health (1990) *Children and Young Persons on Child Protection Registers Year Ending 31 March 1989: England*. Personal Social Services Local Authority Statistics.

Department of Health (1991) *Child Abuse: A Study of Inquiry Reports 1980–1989*, London: HMSO.

Department of Health and Social Security (1974) 'Non-accidental injury to children', Letter, LASSL(74)13.

Department of Health and Social Security (1976) 'Non-accidental injury to children: Area Review Committees', Letter, LASSL(76)2.

Department of Health and Social Security (1982) *Child Abuse: A Study of Inquiry Reports 1973–1981*, London: HMSO.

Department of Health and Social Security and the Welsh Office (1970) *The Battered Baby*,

Prepared by the Standing Medical Advisory Committee of the Central Health Services Council, The Secretary of State for Social Services and the Secretary of State for Wales, London: HMSO.

Department of Health and Social Security and the Welsh Office (1988) *Working Together: A Guide to Arrangements for Inter-agency Co-operation for the Protection of Children from Abuse*, London: HMSO.

Dick, H.V. (1967) *Marital Tensions*, London: Routledge & Kegan Paul.

Dimmock, B. and Dungworth, D. (1985) 'Beyond the family: using network meetings with statutory child care cases', *Journal of Family Therapy*, 7: 45–68.

Dingwall, R. (1986) 'The Jasmine Beckford affair', *Modern Law Review*, 49: 489–507.

Dingwall, R. (1989) 'Some problems about predicting child abuse and neglect', in O. Stevenson (ed.) *Child Abuse: Public Policy and Professional Practice*, Hemel Hempstead: Harvester Wheatsheaf.

Dingwall, R., Eekelaar, J.M. and Murray, T. (1983) *The Protection of Children: State Intervention and Family Life*, Oxford: Blackwell.

Dingwall, R., Eekelaar, J.M. and Murray, T. (1984) 'Childhood as a social problem: a survey of the history of legal regulations', *Journal of Law and Society*, 11: 207–32.

Donzelot, J. (1980) *The Policing of Families: Welfare Versus the State*, London: Hutchinson.

Fairbairn, W.R.D. (1952) *Psychoanalytic Studies of the Personality*, London: Tavistock.

Ford, D. (1978) 'The emergence of the child as a legal entity', in S.M. Smith (ed.) *The Maltreatment of Children*, Lancaster: MTP Press.

Foulkes, S.H. and Anthony, E.J. (1957) *Group Psychotherapy: The Psychoanalytic Approach*, Harmondsworth: Penguin.

Freeman, M.D.A. (1983a) 'Freedom and the welfare state: child-rearing, parental autonomy and state intervention', *Journal of Social Welfare Law*, March: 70–91.

Freeman, M.D.A. (1983b) 'The concept of children's rights', in H. Geach and E. Szwed (eds) *Providing Civil Justice for Children*, London: Edward Arnold.

Freud, A. (1927/1982) 'Four lectures on child analysis', in *The Writings of Anna Freud: Volume 1 – Introduction to Psychoanalysis (1922–1935)*, London: Hogarth.

Freud, S. (1905) 'Three essays on the theory of sexuality', in *Standard Edition, Vol. VII*, London: Hogarth.

Furniss, T. (1983) 'Mutual influence and interlocking professional–family process in the treatment of child sexual abuse and incest', *Child Abuse and Neglect*, 7: 207–23.

Furniss, T. (1991) *The Multi-Professional Handbook of Child Sexual Abuse: Integrated Management, Therapy and Legal Interventions*, London: Routledge.

Garbarino, J. and Sherman, D. (1980) 'High risk neighbourhoods and high risk families: the human ecology of child maltreatment', *Child Development*, 51: 188–98.

Gelles, R.J. (1973) 'Child abuse as psychopathology: a sociological critique and reformulation', *American Journal of Orthopsychiatry*, 43: 611–21.

Gelles, R.J. (1975) 'The social construction of child abuse', *American Journal of Orthopsychiatry*, 45: 363–71.

Gil, D.G. (1970) *Violence Against Children: Physical Abuse in the United States*, Cambridge, MA: Harvard University Press.

Goffman, E. (1968) *Asylums: Essays on the Social Situation of Mental Patients and Other Inmates*, Harmondsworth: Penguin.

Goldstein, J., Freud, A. and Solnit, A.J. (1979) *Before the Best Interests of the Child*, New York: The Free Press.

Gorell Barnes, G. (1985) 'Systems theory and family theory', in M. Rutter and L. Hersov (eds) *Child and Adolescent Psychiatry: Modern Approaches*, 2nd edn, Oxford: Blackwell.

Greenland, C. (1987) *Preventing CAN Deaths: An International Study of Deaths due to Child Abuse and Neglect*, London: Tavistock.

Griffiths, D.L. and Moynihan, F.J. (1963) 'Multiple epiphysial injuries in babies ("battered baby" syndrome)', *British Medical Journal*, ii: 1558–61.

Guerin, P.J. (1976) 'Family therapy: the first twenty-five years', in P.J. Guerin (ed.) *Family Therapy: Theory and Practice*, New York: Gardner.

Haley, J. (1959) 'An interactional description of schizophrenia', *Psychiatry*, 22: 321–32.

Haley, J. (1980) *Leaving Home: The Therapy of Disturbed Young People*, New York: McGraw-Hill.

Hallett, C. (1989) 'Child abuse inquiries and public policy', in O. Stevenson (ed.) *Child Abuse: Public Policy and Professional Practice*, Hemel Hempstead: Harvester Wheatsheaf.

Hallett, C. and Stevenson, O. (1980) *Child Abuse: Aspects of Interprofessional Co-operation*, London: George Allen & Unwin.

Hardwick, P.J. (1991) 'Families and the professional network: an attempted classification of professional network actions which can hinder change', *Journal of Family Therapy*, 13: 187–205.

Heller, J. (1964) *Catch-22*, London: Corgi.

Hill, M. (1990) 'The manifest and latent lessons of child abuse inquiries', *British Journal of Social Work*, 20: 197–213.

Hoffman, L. (1981) *Foundations of Family Therapy: A Conceptual Framework for Systems Change*, New York: Basic.

Hoffman, L. (1982) 'A co-evolutionary framework for systemic family therapy', *Australian Journal of Family Therapy*, 4: 9–21.

Hollander, N. (1986) 'Homicides of abused children prematurely returned home', *Forensic Science International*, 30: 85–91.

Home Office (1945) *Report by Sir Walter Monkton KCMG, KCVO, MC, KC, on the Circumstances which Led to the Boarding Out of Denis and Terrance O'Neill at Bank Farm, Minsterley, and the Steps Taken to Supervise their Welfare*, London: HMSO.

Home Office, Department of Health, Department of Education and Science and Welsh Office (1991) *Working Together under the Children Act 1989: A Guide to Arrangements for Inter-agency Co-operation for the Protection of Children from Abuse*, London: HMSO.

Horne, M. (1990) 'Is it social work?', in The Violence against Children Study Group's *Taking Child Abuse Seriously: Contemporary Issues in Child Protection Theory and Practice*, London: Unwin Hyman.

Howells, J.G. (1974) *Remember Maria*, Woburn, MA: Butterworth.

Hutchinson, R. (1986) 'The effect of inquiries into cases of child abuse upon the social work profession', *British Journal of Social Work*, 26: 178–82.

Imber-Black, E. (1988) *Families and Larger Systems: A Family Therapist's Guide through the Labyrinth*, New York: Guilford.

Jay, M. and Doganis, S. (1987) *Battered: The Abuse of Children*, London: Weidenfeld & Nicholson.

Jones, M. (1962) *Social Psychiatry in the Community, in Hospitals and in Prisons*, Chicago: Thomas.

Joseph, K. (1972) Speech to the Preschool Playgroup Association, June.

Kelmer Pringle, M. (1978) 'The needs of children', in S.M. Smith (ed.) *The Maltreatment of Children*, Lancaster, MTP Press.

Kempe, C.H. (1979) 'Recent developments in the field of child abuse', *Child Abuse and Neglect*, 3: 9–15.

Kempe, C.H. and Helfer, R. (1972) *Helping the Battered Child and his Family*, Philadelphia: Lippincott.

Kempe, C.H., Silverman, F.N., Steele, B.F., Droegemueller, W. and Silver, H.K. (1962) 'The battered-child syndrome', *Journal of the American Medical Association*, 181: 17–24.

Klein, M. (1932) *The Psychoanalysis of Children*, London: Hogarth.
Korbin, J.E. (1989) 'Fatal maltreatment by mothers: a proposed framework', *Child Abuse and Neglect*, 13, 481–9.
Laing, R.D. and Esterson, A. (1964) *Sanity, Madness and the Family*, London: Tavistock.
Lewis, E. (1979) 'Counter-transference problems in hospital practice', *British Journal of Medical Psychology*, 52: 37–42.
Lewis, J. (1986) 'Anxieties about the family and the relationships between parents, children and the state in twentieth century England', in M. Richards and P. Light (eds) *Children of Social Worlds: Developments in a Social Context*, Cambridge, MA: Harvard University Press.
Lieberman, S. (1979) *Transgenerational Family Therapy*, London: Croom Helm.
McCarthy, I.C. and Byrne, N.O'R. (1988) 'Mis-taken love: conversations on the problem of incest in an Irish context', *Family Process*, 27: 181–99.
Main, T. (1957) 'The ailment', *British Journal of Medical Psychology*, 30: 129–45.
Main, T. (1975) 'Some psychodynamics of large groups', in L. Kreeger (ed.) *The Large Group: Dynamics and Therapy*, London: Constable.
Masson, J.M. (1985) *The Assault on Truth: Freud's Suppression of the Seduction Theory*, Harmondsworth: Penguin.
Mattinson, J. and Sinclair, I. (1979) *Mate and Stalemate: Working with Marital Problems in a Social Services Department*, Oxford: Blackwell.
Maturana, H.R. and Varela, F.J. (1987) *The Tree of Knowledge: The Biological Roots of Human Understanding*, Boston: New Science Library.
Mawby, R., Fisher, C. and Hale, J. (1979) 'The press and Karen Spencer', *Social Work Today*, 10, 22: 13–16.
Menzies, I.E.P. (1970) *The Functioning of Social Systems as a Defence Against Anxiety*, Tavistock Pamphlet No. 3, London: Tavistock Institute of Human Relations.
Minuchin, S. (1974) *Families and Family Therapy*, London: Tavistock.
Minuchin, S. (1984) 'Child murder: Maria Colwell', in *Family Kaleidoscope*, Cambridge, MA: Harvard University Press.
Morris, C.W. (1946) *Signs, Language and Behaviour*, New York: Prentice-Hall.
Office of Population Censuses and Surveys (1987) *Monitor: Deaths by Causes*, London: OPCS.
Parton, C. and Parton, N. (1989) 'Child protection, the law and dangerousness', in O. Stevenson (ed.) *Child Abuse: Public Policy and Professional Practice*, Hemel Hempstead: Harvester Wheatsheaf.
Parton, N. (1981) 'Child abuse, social anxiety and welfare', *British Journal of Social Work*, 11: 391–414.
Parton, N. (1985) *The Politics of Child Abuse*, Basingstoke: Macmillan.
Parton, N. (1986) 'The Beckford report: a critical appraisal', *British Journal of Social Work*, 16: 511–30.
Pearce, W.B. and Cronen, V.E. (1980) *Communication, Action, and Meaning: The Creation of Social Realities*, New York: Praeger.
Perelberg, R.J. (1990) 'Equality, asymmetry, and diversity: on conceptualizations of gender', in R.J. Perelberg and A.C. Miller (eds) *Gender and Power in Families*, London: Routledge.
Piaget, J. (1952) *The Origins of the Intelligence of Children*, New York: International Universities Press.
Pines, D. (1972) 'Pregnancy and motherhood: interaction between fantasy and reality', *British Journal of Medical Psychology*, 45: 333–43.
Poster, M. (1978) 'Models of family structure', in *Critical Theory of the Family*, New York: The Seabury Press.
Pound, A. (1991) 'NEWPIN and child abuse', *Child Abuse Review*, 5: 7–10.

Raymond, M. (1987) 'A child abuse inquiry – the lawyer's tale', *Social Work Today*, 7 December: 16–17.

Reder, P. (1983) 'Disorganized families and the helping professions: "Who's in charge of what?"' *Journal of Family Therapy*, 5: 23–36.

Reder, P. (1985) 'Milan in the East End: systemic therapy with lower-income and multi-agency families', in D. Campbell and R. Draper (eds) *Applications of Systemic Family Therapy – The Milan Approach*, London: Grune & Stratton.

Reder, P. (1986) 'Multi-agency family systems', *Journal of Family Therapy*, 8: 139–52.

Reder, P. (1989) 'Freud's family', *British Journal of Psychiatry*, 154: 93–8.

Reder, P. and Duncan, S. (1990) 'On meeting systems', *Human Systems*, 1: 153–62.

Reder, P. and Israelstam, K. (1988) 'A "consultation" workshop for child psychiatrists in training', *Bulletin of the Royal College of Psychiatrists*, 12: 216–19.

Reder, P. and Kraemer, S. (1980) 'Dynamic aspects of professional collaboration in child guidance referral', *Journal of Adolescence*, 3: 165–73.

Reder, P. and Lucey, C. (1991) 'The assessment of parenting: some interactional considerations', *Psychiatric Bulletin*, 15: 347–8.

Reusch, J. and Bateson, G. (1951) *Communication: The Social Matrix of Psychiatry*, New York: Basic.

Rosenfeld, A.A. and Newberger, E.H. (1979) 'Compassion vs control: conceptual and practical pitfalls in the broadening definition of child abuse', in R. Bourne and E.H. Newberger (eds) *Critical Perspectives on Child Abuse*, Lexington, MA: Lexington.

Ruddock, M. (1987) 'A child abuse inquiry – the social worker's tale', *Social Work Today*, 7 December: 14–15.

Schloesser, P., Pierpont, J., and Peortner, J. (1991) 'Active surveillance of child abuse fatalities', *Child Abuse and Neglect*, 16: 3–10.

Select Committee on Violence in the Family (1977) *First Report from the Select Committee on Violence in the Family: 1976–77. Violence to Children. Volume 1: Report (Together with the Proceedings of the Committee)*, London: HMSO.

Selvini Palazzoli, M., Boscolo, L., Cecchin, G. and Prata, G. (1978) *Paradox and Counterparadox: A New Model in the Therapy of the Family in Schizophrenic Transaction*, New York: Jason Aronson.

Selvini Palazzoli, M., Boscolo, L., Cecchin, G. and Prata, G. (1980a) 'Hypothesizing – circularity – neutrality: three guidelines for the conductor of the session', *Family Process*, 19: 3–12.

Selvini Palazzoli, M., Boscolo, L., Cecchin, G. and Prata, G. (1980b) 'The problem of the referring person', *Journal of Marital and Family Therapy*, 6: 3–9.

Shearer, A. (1979) 'Tragedies revisited. (1) The legacy of Maria Colwell', *Social Work Today*, 10(19): 12–19.

Sieff, M. (1990) *Management the Marks & Spencer Way*, London: Weidenfeld & Nicholson.

Simon, F.B., Stierlin, H. and Wynne, L.C. (1985) *The Language of Family Therapy: A Systemic Vocabulary and Sourcebook*, New York: Family Process Inc.

'A social worker' (1982) 'What did I do wrong?' *Community Care*, 18 November: 16–17.

Spock, B.Mc. (1946) *Common Sense Book of Baby and Child Care*, New York: Sloan & Pearce.

Stanton, A.M. and Schwartz, M.S. (1954) *The Mental Hospital: A Study of Institutional Participation in Psychiatric Illness and Treatment*, New York: Basic.

Steele, B.F. (1970) 'Parental abuse of infants and small children', in E.J. Anthony and T. Benedek (eds) *Parenthood: Its Psychology and Psychopathology*, Boston: Little, Brown & Co.

Stevenson, O. (1963) 'Co-ordination reviewed', *Case Conference*, 9: 208–12.

Stevenson, O. (1988) 'Multidisciplinary work – where next?', *Child Abuse Review*, 2: 5–9.

Stevenson, O. (ed.) (1989) *Child Abuse: Public Policy and Professional Practice*, Hemel Hempstead: Harvester Wheatsheaf.

Stratton, P., Preston-Shoot, M. and Hanks, H. (1990) *Family Therapy: Training and Practice*, Birmingham: Venture Press.

Taylor, S. (1989) 'How prevalent is it?', in W.S. Rogers, D. Hevey and A. Ash (eds) *Child Abuse and Neglect: Facing the Challenge*, London: Batsford and the Open University.

Tomm, K. (1984) 'One perspective on the Milan systemic approach: Part 1. Overview of development, theory and practice', *Journal of Marital and Family Therapy*, 10: 113–25.

von Bertalanffy, L. (1968) *General Systems Theory: Foundation, Development, Application*, New York: Braziller.

von Foerster, H. (1981) *Observing Systems*, Seaside, CA: Intersystems.

The Violence Against Children Study Group (1990) *Taking Child Abuse Seriously: Contemporary Themes in Child Protection Theory and Practice*, London: Unwin Hyman.

Watzlawick, P., Beavin, J.H. and Jackson, D.D. (1967) *Pragmatics of Human Communication: A Study of Interactional Patterns, Pathologies, and Paradoxes*, New York: Norton.

Winnicott, D.W. (1957) *The Child and the Family*, London: Tavistock.

Winnicott, D.W. (1965) *The Maturational Processes and the Facilitating Environment*, London: Hogarth.

Woolley, P.V. and Evans, W.A. (1955) 'Significance of skeletal lesions in infants resembling those of traumatic origin', *Journal of the American Medical Association*, 158: 539–43.

Young, M. and Willmott, P. (1957) *Family and Kinship in East London*, London: Routledge & Kegan Paul.

Name index

Subject index

adoption 58
age: of caretakers 31, 38; of children at time of death 27; of mothers at first child 40; of youngest child in household 41–2
alcohol *see* drugs and alcohol
anonymous baby 30, 138; case summary 138–40; exaggeration of hierarchy 75; fatal episode 82; feeding difficulty 41; intelligence of parents 39; mother's age at first child 40; parental dependency on drugs/alcohol 43; parental violence 44; special needs 41; weekend phenomenon 82
ante-natal care 48, 128; absent 40, 50, 99, 100, 102, 115, 117, 127
Area Review Committee *see* Child Protection Committee
assessment 83–94, 116, 122, 123–6, 130; of parenting 127–9; for rehabilitation 129; of risk 28, 83, 124–6
Aston, Doreen 30, 112–20, 136, 140; absent ante-natal care 115, 117; abuse of sibling 53, 114, 116; ambivalence to pregnancy 40; case as a whole 112–13; case summary 141; closure 131; disguised compliance 118, 131; early discharge from hospital 41, 117; family history 39, 113–14; family–professional interaction 117–18; fatal episode 118; flight 117; fragmentation 117; information treated discretely 116; intermittent closure 118; inter-professional communication 62, 115, 118; meaning of child 114; parental dependency 40, 114; parental violence 44; partial closure 116; pervasive belief 116; pivotal worker

absent 117; role confusion 116, 118; terminal closure 118; vicious circle 118, 131; warning sign 117; weekend phenomenon 117; work setting 115
At Risk Register *see* Child Protection Register
attachment 14, 21
Aukland, Susan 30, 141; abuse of sibling 53; case summary 141–2; family history 85; fatal episode 86; information treated discretely 85; meaning of child 54; parental dependency 85; parental dependency on drugs/alcohol 43, 85; parental mutual dependency 43, 54; parental violence 44; premature baby 41; special needs 41; work setting 70

Bagnall, Graham 17, 30, 142; case summary 142–3; child as property 41; family structure 35; intelligence of parents 39; meaning of child 54; role confusion 76; violent abuse 45
Beckford, Jasmine 2, 3, 9, 18, 30, 121, 135, 143; abuse of sibling 53; care/control conflicts 102; case summary 144; closed professional system 71, 73; concrete solution 94; exaggeration of hierarchy 75; failure to thrive 45, 91; family history 38; fatal episode 101; intelligence of parents 39; meaning of child 58; parental dependency 98; pervasive belief 71; polarisation 73; role confusion 77; selective interpretation 91; terminal closure 101; violent abuse 45; weekend phenomenon 80; work setting 70
behaviourism 14, 15